Nimble Believing

Nimble Believing

Dickinson and the Unknown

James McIntosh

Ann Arbor

THE UNIVERSITY OF MICHIGAN PRESS

Copyright © by the University of Michigan 2000
All rights reserved
Published in the United States of America by
The University of Michigan Press
Manufactured in the United States of America
∞ Printed on acid-free paper

2002 2001 2000 2003   4 3 2 1

*A CIP catalog record for this book is available
from the British Library.*

Library of Congress Cataloging-in-Publication Data

McIntosh, James, 1934–
    Nimble believing : Dickinson and the unknown / James McIntosh.
      p.   cm.
    Includes bibliographical references (p.   ) and index.
    ISBN 0-472-11080-2 (cloth : alk. paper)
    1. Dickinson, Emily, 1830–1886—Criticism and interpretation.   2. Women and
literature—United States—History—19th century   3. Religious poetry,
American—History and criticism.   4. Dickinson, Emily, 1830–1886—Religion.
5. Knowledge, Theory of, in literature.   6. Belief and doubt in literature.
I. Title.
PS1541.Z5 M22   2000
811'.4—dc21   99-054534

For Elaine

Acknowledgments

I am grateful to friends and colleagues who read this book at various stages in the course of its development as a manuscript, especially Michal Nahor Bond, Lawrence Buell, Cristanne Miller, and Robert Weisbuch. They were perceptive in their criticisms and generous with their encouragement.

Emily Dickinson's poems are reprinted by permission of the publishers and the Trustees of Amherst College from *The Poems of Emily Dickinson*, ed. Thomas H. Johnson (Cambridge, Mass.: Belknap Press of Harvard University Press). Copyright © 1951, 1955, 1979, 1983 by the President and Fellows of Harvard College. Emily Dickinson's letters are reprinted by permission of the publishers from *The Letters of Emily Dickinson*, ed. Thomas H. Johnson (Cambridge, Mass.: Belknap Press of Harvard University Press). Copyright © 1958, 1986 by the President and Fellows of Harvard College.

Contents

Note on Texts

The basic texts used in this study are *The Poems of Emily Dickinson,* 3 vols., ed. Thomas H. Johnson (Cambridge, Mass: Harvard University Press, 1955); and *The Letters of Emily Dickinson,* 3 vols., ed. Thomas H. Johnson and Theodora Ward (Cambridge, Mass: Harvard University Press, 1958). Ralph W. Franklin's new variorum edition of the poems was published too late for me to consult or use it. Johnson's numbers for the poems are preceded by P; the page numbers in Johnson's volumes of the letters are preceded by *L*. In most instances I use the text of the "earliest fair copy" of the poems as Johnson reproduces it, while taking variant readings and different versions of the poems into account when relevant. I give special weight to the texts of some poems as Dickinson transcribed them in letters.

As recent editorial scholarship has shown, Johnson's texts have their limitations. Contemporary scholars and critics such as Susan Howe, Martha Nell Smith, and Ellen Louise Hart argue persuasively that Johnson's editions were codifications of Dickinson's poetic designs and free irregularity.[1] Further, they show how Dickinson made each version of each poem and each letter she wrote an occasion in and for itself. They make the reader intensely aware of the value and excitement of reading as much of Dickinson as possible in facsimiles of original holographs, so that one can get as close as possible while reading to the scene of her writing.

At the same time, Howe, Hart, Smith, and others go further than I would in repudiating Johnson's work. Johnson certainly made mistakes of judgment or even careless errors in reproducing individual texts. He is open to the charge of wrongheadedness in seeking to establish a single definitive text for the poems and letters. He and Theodora Ward may well have been too eager in cobbling together Dickinson's supposed letters to Otis P. Lord so as to appease a reader's biographical curiosity concerning Dickinson's "love life."[2] Thus one needs to check his texts when a check is available. Nevertheless, in most cases he accomplished what he set out to do with remarkable fidelity, and the editions stand up pretty well under scrutiny. In my judgment they supply the appropriate texts available to me for a commentary concerned with Dickinson's thought and poetic sensibility.

I have followed Johnson by and large in the way he presents Dickinson's lines and stanzas except in a few instances, when a more precise representation of Dickinson's lineation in her holograph has seemed appropriate. Since the publication of *The Manuscript Books of Emily Dickinson,* ed. Ralph W. Franklin (Cambridge, Mass.: Harvard University Press, 1981), some commentators, such as Susan Howe and Paula Bennett, have tried to reproduce in print the appearance of the ways Dickinson wrapped around lines of verse in her manuscripts.[3] Yet, except in those rare instances where Dickinson seemed to want to call attention to the possible meanings that came with visual pauses in the middle of her lines, these reproductions seem to me counterproductive aesthetically. Johnson's judgment concerning lineation and stanza forms seems to me basically trustworthy.[4]

With some misgivings, I have also used Johnson's ordering and numbering of the poems and letters. His chronological ordering of the poems is at best approximate and has no sanction from Dickinson. Now that Franklin has largely clarified the order Dickinson herself gave some of her poems in her "fascicles" and "sets"—the packets of poems she sewed together in the 1860s and the sets of sheets she grouped without sewing somewhat later—we can read these poems in her ordering and her handwriting in Franklin's *Manuscript Books.* I think all serious students of Dickinson should study the fascicles and sets. Taken in themselves, the poems as ordered in fascicles are likely to be more suggestive of Dickinson's mind to a reader than the poems as printed in Johnson's massive chronological ordering. Moreover, it is easier to make sense of twenty-five poems at a time than it is of 1775. On the thematic or narrative meaning of the fascicles, however, I remain an agnostic. Given the ways we read, we are bound to make connections in the fascicles that we couldn't in the corpus of Dickinson's poems as a whole. At the same time, it is important to understand that we make these connections, not Dickinson. She says nothing, anywhere, about her intentions in the fascicles. Moreover, to find a single intention or design or story in them seems to me to misread her genius and violate her implied contract with her readers. As a good deal of recent commentary has emphasized, her texts are open-ended in that she refrains from giving them definitive form, and open to several readings rather than one singleminded reading. In addition, she writes so many different kinds of poems with different designs and implications—in the fascicles and outside of them—that it is entirely fitting that she has been interpreted as she has in so many different ways.

Dickinson's writings tell other stories, I believe, than any hinted at in the fascicles, taken in isolation. Though she once wrote facetiously, "Subjects hinder talk" (L, 2:512), she later expressed her fascination for "subjects of which we know nothing" (L, 3:728). The study that follows is in part the story of her lifelong concern with unknowable subjects.

1

Introduction: Nimble Believing

In the draft of a letter of Emily Dickinson's to Judge Otis Phillips Lord, the friend of her later years whom she almost mysteriously married but then didn't, appears an aphoristic sentence that gives us our title.

> On subjects of which we know nothing, or should I say *Beings* – is "Phil" [Judge Lord] a "Being" or a "Theme" we both believe and disbelieve a hundred times an Hour, which keeps Believing nimble – (*L*, 3:728)[1]

"Nimble believing," that is believing for intense moments in a spiritual life without permanently subscribing to any received system of belief, is a key experience, an obsessive subject, and a stimulus to expression for Dickinson. Like other major artists of nineteenth-century American introspection such as Emerson, Thoreau, and Melville, Dickinson makes poetic use of her vacillations between doubt and faith. Dickinson's Christian education affected her profoundly, and her desire for a humane intuitive faith motivates and enlivens her poetry. Yet what she has "faith" in tends to be left undefined because she assumes that it is unknowable. Nevertheless, her moments of illumination are real to her, and she seeks forms and styles to express these shifting inner conditions. Dickinson's sentence is itself an instance of appropriate form. Its assured tone, maintained amid its shifting thought, makes it a persuasive expression of the "volatile truth"[2] it embodies.

One of Dickinson's key principles is that "subjects of which we know nothing" are all around us. There are many unknown subjects in her mental universe, among them: Death and the afterlife, "God," "nature," artistic and poetic inspiration, one's own mind, and other human beings. Indeed, a related idea embedded in her sentence to Judge Lord is that "Phil," her beloved to whom she writes with intimate coyness and tenderness in this letter, is to her as mysterious a being (or theme) as Death or Immortality. For her as for Emerson, "souls never touch their objects,"[3] and other persons are ultimately unknowable. Yet that does not prevent her from reaching out lovingly to them. Toward her cherished correspondents generally, as well as her imagined readers, Dickinson takes the implicit stance of an intimate neighbor and stranger.

Another of Dickinson's key principles implied in the sentence to Judge Lord, one might even say her most far-reaching working assumption, is the idea that belief and thought and feeling are transient, that one's mental life is continually in flux. Mostly, Dickinson prefers it that way. We shall observe over and over how she cherishes evanescence and makes poetry out of "internal difference" (P 258), out of the dramatic changes she discerns in the inner weather of the mind. Even in this same letter to Lord she describes the spirit of love between them as "The Spirit never twice alike, but every time another – that other more divine." (The "prose" scans here as in a love scene from one of Shakespeare's late Romances.)[4] To her way of thinking this spirit needs to change and become "another" in order to grow; its mutability enhances its liveliness. One consequence of Dickinson's extreme sensitivity to the evanescence of thought and feeling is that in her world spiritual and emotional states such as love, despair, and imaginative enthrallment can be felt and represented poetically but not pinned down, analyzed, or known. Another is that her language repeatedly reflects her consciousness of flux. In "On subjects of which we know nothing," she manipulates abstractions elastically, moving from "subjects" to "*Beings*" to "theme" as if to exhibit thought in process. She seems here to enjoy not settling on any one of these categories. She presents herself as braced by the uncertainty of human belief and stimulated by the lability of her own language.

Yet this is not her only tone or style when she meditates on belief and unbelief. A literary career in which nimble believing is a key experience is predicated on an absence of constant certainties and entails its own times of blankness, times when she dreads ignorance and fears the utter annihilation of the spirit. What Dickinson calls "the abdication of Belief," the loss of traditional Christian certainty, might promote a mood more bleak than nimble. Intellectual resignation of all belief was at least an occasional temptation for her. In a poem Johnson dates "about 1882," the same year in which she apparently composed her letter to Judge

Lord, Dickinson reflects somberly on the spiritual emptiness of her skeptical age.

1551

Those – dying then,
Knew where they went –
They went to God's Right Hand –
That Hand is amputated now
And God cannot be found –

The abdication of Belief
Makes the Behavior small –
Better an ignis fatuus
Than no illume at all –

The poem works as a dialectical qualification to the confident assertion of "On subjects of which we know nothing." They are complementary evidences of her divided response to the question of how one believes and doubts at her point in history.[5] The undoing of Amherst orthodoxy in her mind, recalled in "Those – dying then," is a condition of her expositions of experimental faith in her poems and letters throughout her career. She found forms for nimble believing because a poetry based on settled beliefs was unavailable as well as undesirable. She might continue to draw on her Calvinist education for theological vocabulary, for patterns of inner drama, for a language with which to imagine her own salvation, for legend and history. She might—as we shall later see in detail—rework Bible stories as parables of her own. Yet her transcriptions of Christian ideas and her reworkings of Christian texts are not dogmatic but experimental, heuristic, and in their own way pastoral; she is trying to create a newly religious language and reach an audience, one that begins with herself and spreads to an imagined posterity. She uses the Bible as a source of metaphor as well as a means to solace. Her Protestant heritage provides her with figures for poetry and with textual strategies to "keep Believing nimble."[6]

Several partly connected historical circumstances help make Dickinson a poet of nimble believing. First, she was educated in a traditionally Protestant, provincial community and in religiously conservative schools and churches in Amherst and South Hadley. As is well known,

Amherst not only belonged to the sphere of "Connecticut Valley Puritanism,"[7] the Puritanism of Solomon Stoddard and Jonathan Edwards and later of Noah Webster, Edward Hitchcock, and Mary Lyon, but by the early 1820s it was also the seat of Amherst College, established by conservative Calvinists in part to resist the spread of Unitarianism from Harvard and Eastern Massachusetts. Dickinson's grandfather, Samuel Fowler Dickinson, was one of the founders of the college, and her father and brother were among its key sustainers in the community. Orthodox religion also played a significant if unremarkable role in the Dickinson household, where Emily Dickinson's mother was unquestioningly pious and her father read the Bible daily to the family. At Amherst Academy, an excellent school closely associated with Amherst College that Dickinson attended for seven years, religious and secular instruction were inextricably connected. When she went for a year to Mt. Holyoke Female Seminary in South Hadley she was subjected still more intensely to evangelical indoctrination. In addition, Dickinson went regularly to church during her childhood and young adulthood. She learned the Bible more or less by heart and kept it in mind as a possession throughout her career. More than any nineteenth-century American writer of comparable stature—even more, say, than Melville or Stowe—she knew it and had it at her command for her own idiosyncratic purposes.

This thorough education in Scripture and in orthodox Calvinism of course affected Dickinson as a poet of religious concern, stimulating her to opposition as well as reverence. The Calvinist God she was taught to worship was an arbitrary God of absolute sovereignty. She struggles prodigiously in her writing against such an image of God, as we shall see, but also invokes it normally. One of this God's attributes is that he is inscrutable, mysteriously beyond human conception, "a subject of which we know nothing." Sometimes, Dickinson extracts God's inhuman mysteriousness from a Calvinist context and celebrates it in and for itself. Her God on these occasions she called a God of "awe." Generally, however, a God of inscrutable sovereignty is a bugbear to her imagination. If he "causes all" (L, 2:376), he causes human and natural death. Still more outrageously, he also causes human sin and then requires human repentance for it.

Yet if in some moods Dickinson blames Amherst Calvinism and its God resoundingly for these misrepresentations of the human condition, in other moods she is less hostile to her Calvinist heritage. This heritage infiltrated her religious thinking in several ways as she searched for a God who would not "seem like bears" (*L*, 2:372). When disposed to faith she might find such a God in Calvinism itself, in a selective interpretation of what she learned in church and school. Though she was poetically drawn to a mysterious and distant God of power, she might focus alternatively on a God who works graciously through a loving Christ. Her schooling also gave her an indoctrination in the idea of God as creator, an idea in harmony both with traditional Protestantism and with her own intuitive faith. Her lifelong reading in the Bible profoundly informed her ethical and psychological sense of the workings of the human heart. In particular, she read the story of Christ's crucifixion as the central instance in history of human courage, love, and renunciation. Her quasi-Calvinistic sense of the power of divine grace informs her dramas of human transformation, and, as we have seen, her attraction to awe also has a basis in a Calvinist habit of feeling and thinking.

It may be useful to consider Dickinson's religious thinking in terms of the "Five Points of the Synod of Dort," a Calvinist set of doctrines still very familiar to those growing up in Congregational churches in Amherst in the 1830s and 1840s.[8] As I understand her, Dickinson had no use for the first point, "Total Depravity," the doctrine that as the result of Adam's sin all humankind is by nature "utterly indisposed, disabled, and made opposite to all good, and wholly inclined to all evil."[9] In her view life and the expectation of death were painful enough without adding Original Sin to the human burden. Likewise, she was impatient with "Limited Atonement," the doctrine that Christ died to atone for the sins of the elect but not for other human beings. Though she had friends and family members who at some point in their lives made a profession of faith and received assurances of salvation, throughout her career she distinguished herself intellectually from these "Saints" (saved persons), even if she remained intimate with orthodox believers such as her sister Lavinia and her sister-in-law Susan Gilbert Dickinson. Moreover, she shared with many educated persons in her New England culture the liberal view that such a doctrine encouraged believers to fail in charity toward their benighted fellow humans.

On the other hand, Dickinson made one of the core experiences of her poetry a version of "Irresistible Grace," the doctrine that when God calls a person the experience is so powerful that even sinful human beings cannot reject it. Repeatedly, she dramatizes an experience of dynamic illumination that makes her a poet with a sacred calling. In addition, that experience and that calling set her apart from those who have not known such a grace, "the Happy" who can be thankful like all of us for the gift of common life, but who unlike the spiritually inspired feel no "obligation / To Electricity" (P 1581). In that her calling as a poet distinguished her from others, it was a kind of "election." Yet her idea of election is idiosyncratic and poetic; it does not conform to the Synod of Dort's "Unconditional Election," the doctrine that God lays down no conditions nor requires good works of those he saves but elects them out of his free grace for his own pleasure.

Still, Dickinson, while never calling herself a "Saint," had her own version of the Synod of Dort's fifth point, "The Perseverance of the Saints." This is the doctrine that "they, whom God hath . . . sanctified by His Spirit, can neither totally nor finally fall away from the state of grace, but shall certainly persevere therein to the end, and be eternally saved."[10] Perseverance is a doctrine of comfort for the believer. Because an active God wills that one cannot be lost despite one's sufferings, uncertainties, and sinfulness, a believer can take hope and persist in a Christian life. In Dickinson's words, she will eventually reach "home" even after "decades of Agony" (P 207). Not only in poems like this that construct a myth of salvation but in her mission as a poet generally, Dickinson is sustained by a sort of martyred optimism that seems an offshoot of her Calvinist inheritance. Having accepted her calling, Dickinson persisted in it, sometimes dramatizing the hope or expectation that she might behold the faces of those she loved in "Heaven." She desires and discounts this unknown heaven by turns but perseveres in her mission to "seek in Art – the Art of peace – " (P 544) and share it with her readers. She perseveres also in a lifelong dialectic between doubt and faith, on the working assumption that this very dialectical process is a way to live in the spirit.

In my view Dickinson's orthodox and unorthodox "beliefs" are not in active contradiction with one another. Her system of believing has its own internal integrity. Nevertheless, her rudderless condition as a poet of intellect who resists Calvinism but still uses it gives her expression of religious ideas an experimental instability. She is willing to vacillate to get her whole truth down. By the same token, she is more open to an awareness of the flux of thought and belief and more prone to cultivate a rhetoric of nimble believing.

Dickinson's religious thinking is complex and sometimes apparently inconsistent partly because she responds to "liberal" influences abroad in New England in her period: Unitarianism, transcendentalism, and sentimentalism—all tendencies that in one way or another soften the rigor of strict Calvinism. In her lifelong argument with such Calvinist doctrines as Predestination, Total Depravity, and Limited Atonement, Dickinson articulates with idiosyncractic distinction views entertained by many educated persons in her culture, even in Amherst. Many of her contemporaries, including nominal Congregationalists, accepted William Ellery Channing's "moral argument against Calvinism."[11] Dickinson is hardly so unusual in her rejection of Calvinism except in her cheek-by-jowl familiarity with it. I will explore in more detail how both Calvinist and liberal religious influences live in Dickinson's writings in the next chapter. For now I will suggest only that there are many varieties of religion in Emily Dickinson's writing, that holding them all in her head puts her under a creative strain, and that she treats the popular dilution of Calvinism she found in "sentimentalism" as a means to her own experimental heresies. As Barton St. Armand has shown, sentimentalism offered her a group of potentially heretical religious ideas and images that she treated with her characteristic unconventionality and freedom of mind.[12]

A second historical circumstance that helps condition Dickinson's practice of nimble believing is her position as a woman writer, disposed to devise her own intellectual life but without a prescribed social or religious mission. Once Dickinson made the choice to write and not to marry and the additional choice to write for herself, her chosen friends, and posterity rather than for the *Springfield Republican,* a benefit that came with her construction of her vocation was her freedom—to do her work alone, interact with whom she wished, and write as she pleased, with scarcely a regard for standard generic or formal expectations. And she relished it. "It's just a turn – and freedom, Matty!" she is said to have exclaimed to her niece when the two of them were alone in her room.[13] In her freedom, however circumscribed, Dickinson entertains the unpredictability of experience as an enabling condition for the life of her mind. As she once wrote her closest confidante, her sister-in-law Susan Gilbert Dickinson, "In a Life that stopped guessing, you and I should not feel at home – ."[14]

Dickinson's freedom opens a space for the expression of a variety of attitudes toward the unknown. Much recent commentary, feminist

and otherwise, helps support my sense of her as a nimble poetic and in-
tellectual experimenter who makes the unpredictable vicissitudes of the
mind her subject and opportunity. Most fundamentally, we now under-
stand that the text of both her poems and her letters is less predictable
and more consciously experimental than was thought in the age of New
Criticism and old textual scholarship. While she was as attentive to her
choice of words as any great poet, she also fostered "a Hermeneutics of
Possibility"[15] in her compositions. She preferred not to settle defini-
tively on texts of the poems. Even in her own manuscript collections of
poems, the "fascicles" she sewed together from 1858 to 1864 or the "sets"
she assembled in the 1860s and early 1870s, she included "variants" for
possible substitution of individual words. When she enclosed poems in
letters, she did not stick to uniform texts but made subtle changes
among the versions she sent. She also apparently experimented with the
forms of letters in her transcription of poems, as well as with occasion-
ally underlined words, foreshortened lines, and "cartooning" cutouts of
poems or quotations.[16]

In her later writings, Dickinson seems less habitually concerned
with creating finished textual artifacts, even ones with built in alterna-
tive possibilities such as the poems in the fascicles. Her poems after 1875
are often briefer and sometimes less finished than her earlier poems,
more subject to the whims of process. Simultaneously, Dickinson's let-
ters in this later period become more unabashedly "poetic." Phrases or
whole sentences scan (we saw this in the "nimble believing" letter);
holographs of what purports to be prose look like free verse composi-
tions on the page; and in general distinctions blur between "verse" in-
serted in the letters and the "prose" that surrounds it.[17] In other words,
the writing of poetry is no longer confined to verse and becomes an on-
going, never-ending process of self-expression. Anticipating Derrida,
Dickinson savors the disappearing newness of every written thought,
while at the same time she composes shapes in this tide of mental
change, self-consciously producing one iconic aphorism or decisive
metaphor or metrical fragment or whole shaped poem after another.

Dickinson's awareness of the experimental and variable character
of her writing is of a piece with her interest in nimble believing. In her
life and practice as believer and writer she keeps guessing; she refuses
to be pinned down. At the same time, one should not infer that because
her writings are variable she means them to be irretrievably private and

peculiar to herself. She often chooses to speak for "human nature," to enrich the life of the imagination for her readers, and to formulate general truths as a means to human consolation. Nevertheless, her sense that one lives freely and transiently in the unknown was necessarily enhanced by her status as a private woman writer without the need to finish her work or make rules for her intellectual existence. As Paula Bennett suggests, since "nothing can be known for certain" in "the world which her poetry creates," "masculinist . . . ideals of order and perfection . . . give way to process and incompletion."[18]

If Dickinson accepts process and incompletion as givens of her mental and emotional experience, she also cultivates the dynamic, even erotic character of this experience. She seems to have responded disturbingly powerfully both to personal occasions and to art, and she makes use of her strength of response in her own fictions of "transport." One of her speakers recalls how "Existence – . . . some way back – / Stopped –" while she fixes her hair and does her household chores (P 443); another feels a Funeral in her Brain, which she survives ambiguously (P 280); another gets struck by the lightning of inspiration (P 1581); a fourth is deranged "For very Lunacy of Light" (P 593). But she often treats these dynamic disturbances as desirable, not merely as traumatic. "I would not exchange the Bolt / For all the rest of Life –" (P 1581). About 1878 she wrote with orphic whimsy to Susan Dickinson, "Cherish Power – dear – Remember that stands in the Bible between the Kingdom and the Glory, because it is wilder than either of them" (L, 2:631). In giving her own twist to these words from the Lord's Prayer, Dickinson both recalls the scriptural origins of her speculation and uses Scripture to construct a language for the unknowable and dynamic sublime. Her Bible is entangled in her Romanticism. As Garry Lee Stonum points out, Dickinson cultivated and celebrated "dread," "awe," "transport," and "exhilaration" – keywords from the lexicon of Romantic sublimity.[19]

Such a rhetoric of the sublime shades easily into the erotic in Dickinson.[20] In her poetry and letters she makes the erotic an attribute of her own dynamic responses. She keeps her erotic writing fleeting and labile, even when reaching out graphically to such correspondents as Susan Dickinson and Otis P. Lord.[21] She prefers "Rowing in Eden" (P 249) to "the honorable Work / Of Woman, and of Wife –" (P 732). She also practices an "erotics of reception" in a figurative language full of exaltations

and evanescence, rather than narrating stories of fulfillment and com-
mitment. In a number of poems she imagines reading as erotic listening
and the reader-poet's ear as open to erotic sumptuousness, as "Enam-
ored – impotent – content." Yet this speaker hardly stays content or im-
potent; in the next breath she asks to write and read with power, asks
for "the Art to stun myself / With Bolts of Melody!" (P 505)[22]

While some of Dickinson's speakers are devastated by the experi-
ence of power, as a writer Dickinson is able to dramatize such moments
because she stands apart from the dynamic melodramas of her inven-
tion and is capable of observing the quirks of power with bemused de-
tachment. Over and over in her writing the sublime gets whimsically or
humorously dispersed. For her the pleasure of the unpredictable and
the evanescent is partly a comic pleasure.[23] She uses her freedom as a
woman writer to stay loose. As the nimble believing letter illustrates,
Dickinson usually approaches problems of belief and doubt with more
casual indirection and less lasting anguish than her male counterparts
in the American Renaissance.

In Dickinson's sensibility her attraction to sublimity is balanced by
her awareness of the ridiculous in a world of dynamic change and
evanescence. Her humor makes itself felt as a woman's defence and ex-
pressive opportunity in a world of preaching and careers. She keeps
sane partly by observing her own grandiosity of speculation from a
comic distance. "Subjects of which we know nothing" can appear and
disappear with a comic turn, like her mushroom:

> The Mushroom
> is the Elf of
> Plants –
> At Evening, it
> is not –
> At Morning, in
> A Truffled Hut
> It stop upon
> a Spot
>
> As if it tarried
> always
> And yet it's
> whole Career

Is shorter than
a Snake's
Delay –
And fleeter than
a Tare –

(set 13; P 1298)[24]

The mushroom is a whimsical instance of evanescence, one of Dickinson's central, serious, and consuming themes. Themes, like doctrines, are occasions for playfulness as well as for consuming reflection.

The fleeting perceptions and dynamic transitions Dickinson cherishes, whether comically or seriously, also appear in her representations of religious experience. Dickinson is an untethered woman poet who makes it her business to live in the spirit and be swept away by it. If she adheres to no sect and has no prescribed religious role, at the same time she unmistakably has a religious calling. A poem that tells a story of her evolution as a poet will illustrate how she conceives her calling.

488

Myself was formed – a Carpenter –
An unpretending time
My Plane – and I, together wrought
Before a Builder came –

To measure our attainments –
Had we the Art of Boards
Sufficiently developed – He'd hire us
At Halves –

My Tools took Human – Faces –
The Bench, where we had toiled –
Against the Man – persuaded –
We – Temples build – I said –

The poem seems on one level a fable to defend the integrity of Dickinson's unpublished, private poetry. When asked by "Two Editors of Journals" for her "Mind," she refused (L, 2:404–5)[25] : she would not be hired "at Halves." Yet at the same time the poem summons its readers to pay attention to the Temples "We" build. When the "Builder" makes his proposition, the speaker is not only indignant in her response; she suddenly and uncannily realizes that hers is a human art with a sacred purpose. Its sacred character has been suggested from the start in that the speaker is "formed – a Carpenter," endowed with a form of work like Christ's. Poetry is a religious calling, not a mere craft. And it is "wrought" by the poet's "Tools" (her metaphorical inventiveness? her metrical strategies? her self-generating language? her unconscious inspiration?) as well as by the private, conscious self. More, those tools "took Human – Faces – ." In a splendidly Blakean transfiguration Dickinson acknowledges that a poet needs the support of the mysterious implements of the craft to do the work to which she is called, and endows them with the human capacity to support one another and her. Since the collective striving of her workshop is human, her art cannot be for sale to "the Man." Though this is intimated lightly rather than pronounced didactically, hers is a woman's art not bound by the publishing conventions that prevent women from building temples. And it is intended for readers prepared to respond to the summons of the final line and acknowledge a woman's full human power to shape the materials of the spirit.

If "Myself was formed – a Carpenter – " marks Dickinson as a woman writer determined to fulfill her calling, it also serves to set her apart from other women writers of the period in the United States. The speaker of the poem may resemble the familiar nineteenth-century "poetess"[26] in her pose of humility, but no newspaper poetess conscious of the limits of her role would write "We – Temples build." Indeed, I cannot think of any of Dickinson's female contemporaries who would make such a claim. Harriet Beecher Stowe might feel that she was transcribing a message from God in *Uncle Tom's Cabin* but to enforce moral truths, not to construct a sacred artifact. Dickinson's vaulting literary ambition brings her closer to the British women writers she revered—Elizabeth Barrett Browning, George Eliot, the Brontës—yet of these perhaps only Barrett Browning has her combination of religious seriousness and intellectual unpredictability, and none of them is so interested in unknowable transformations of the sort that take place in this poem, when Dickinson's speaker's recognizes with uncanny presumption that she is a builder of temples.

As a woman writer, Dickinson inevitably has interests and tastes in common with her contemporaries, but as a votary of nimble believing she stands apart from them. Her sense that she is inspired by sister poets, practices her craft in company with her "Tools," and fashions her

"Pang" (P 544) for the sake of others in need of encouragement, links her to women writers such as Stowe or Susan Warner who in one way or another practice an art of mutual consolation and depict a community of women supporting one another. Her feeling at home in a world permeated by "guessing" links her to women prose writers who experiment with unpredictable psychological changes such as Elizabeth Stoddard or who play with different genres in free-wheeling association such as Margaret Fuller or Caroline Kirkland.[27] When she avoids social issues in her writing and refrains from publishing her poems, she conforms to a common "American ideology of feminine reticence," as Joanne Dobson puts it.[28] Her taste for familiar natural details in garden and grove is in part a conventional woman's taste. It fits her social role as well as her literary purposes to write casually and reverently of familiar natural objects.[29] Still, even with respect to "nature," Dickinson is different. She recognizes it as "a stranger" (P 1400) as well as the ground of daily happiness.

None of Dickinson's contemporaries or precursors, then, evince her willingness to experiment with unbelief and ignorance for the sake of art and faith. None of them build "Temples," cherish "guessing," and cultivate "subjects of which we know nothing" all as part of a general effort to keep believing nimble. I at least come away from Joanne Dobson's fine study of Dickinson in the context of nineteenth-century women's literature with the confirmed suspicion that she stands alone among her (female) contemporaries as a practitioner of nimble believing.

Fortunately, Dickinson is difficult to categorize and impossible to stereotype, with respect to her sensibility, her ideology, and her literary achievement. She does not easily fit any prescribed fashion or position to which critics have assigned her. David Reynolds, for example, has performed a valuable service not only by projecting Dickinson against a background of popular women writings and ideologies of the period but also by suggesting how flexibly and variously she incorporated popular plots and stereotypes in the language of her poetry. Yet when he fits Dickinson into his category of "subversive" writers who set themselves against evangelical conformity and domesticity, he blanks out her religious sense of her calling and forgets the domestic scene she needed for her meditation.[30] Similarly, while Dickinson read sentimental fiction with pleasure in her early twenties and later may have invented her own narrative of love and deprivation based on a "sentimental love religion,"[31] hers is not sentimental literature set conventionally in a context of evangelical Protestantism and the cult of domesticity. Though Dickinson draws freely on sentimentalism, she cannot be locked into a sentimentalist grid, because her ambivalence concerning the Bible and Amherst Calvinism engages her too deeply, because she is never far away from her unsentimental obsession with the unknown, and because her mind is too volatile to adhere for long to any predictable, socially agreed on conventions of thought and feeling.

"Oh you man without a handle," wrote Henry James Sr. to Emerson.[32] Dickinson, it seems, is "a woman without a handle." However grounded in her culture, she is unique in her style of genius. Yet James's apostrophe when applied to Dickinson paradoxically suggests not only her uniqueness but also her affinity with other writers in the American Renaissance, especially Emerson, Thoreau, and Melville. To me Dickinson is a satisfactorily extreme case of tendencies within the "Renaissance," a culmination of her period's cultivation of fluid consciousness and uncertainty. If "to prefer the unknown or unknowable . . . was by [her] time a romantic commonplace,"[33] she made an obsession of it. If these mid-century American writers (and others like Whitman) prefer contradictions to fixed doctrines, Dickinson used her vacillations in a sustained way through her career as a means to thoughtful expression. If other writers in the New England orbit are troubled by doubt in an age of receding belief, no one other than Dickinson can write "Faith is *Doubt*" (*L*, 3:830). Yet, though Dickinson is the exemplary nimble believer, we can learn something about her by juxtaposing her with these other writers who manifest similar tendencies. In other words, in her practice of the poetics of the unknown she is less isolated from some of her peers than has been allowed and more pivotal to "canonical" American literature.

Another circumstance that helps make Dickinson a poet of nimble believing is that she comes after Emerson. Cautiously, I will link these two familiar ghosts again.[34] The link has some historical basis. We know from Dickinson's own testimony that Emerson was personally important to her. Her father's law student Benjamin Newton, who encouraged her in her late teens and early twenties to become a poet, gave her "a beautiful copy" of Emerson's *Poems* (1846) when the book was a new sensation in New England (*L*, 1:84). Clear echoes of Emerson's poems can be traced in hers, and she also refers to Emerson or his writings several times in her letters over the course of her career. Emerson was an example of enlightenment for Dickinson's intellectually minded friends—for Susan Dickinson "a revered hero," for Maria Whitney "the holiest of men," and for Thomas Wentworth Higginson the writer to whom he claimed to owe the greatest debt.[35] After Emerson's death Dickinson was deeply moved by her memory of his spirit. In a draft dated April 1882 to Judge Lord, perhaps a part of the nimble believing letter, she writes:

> it has been an April of meaning to me – I have been in your Bosom – My Philadelphia [Charles Wadsworth] has passed from Earth, and the Ralph Waldo Emerson – whose name my Father's Law Student taught me, has touched the secret Spring – . (L, 3:727)[36]

Emerson's death gets equal billing here with Wadsworth's death and Lord's affecting visit. His "name" evidently stayed powerfully with her ever since she first learned it.

Yet, though Dickinson enjoyed the intellectual climate Emerson helped create, she was not an Emersonian. It is difficult to tell how much she read him, borrowed his ideas, or indeed reacted against him. In an ideological sense he was but one religious liberal among many who helped her struggle with her Calvinist heritage. In her writings Dickinson betrays no infatuation with Emerson but, rather, a whimsical interest in his poetic language along with a vague respect for his public image. Both as a woman and as an immediate heir of Amherst Calvinist culture, she keeps her chosen distance from him. As a woman, her self-reliant freedom may be girdled about with dependent relations, but she also has a gift for imagining herself in communities that Emerson lacks. In addition, she wrestles with Calvinism much more intimately and extensively than Emerson. In her elaborate compromise with Amherst she keeps continually in touch with her religious heritage, both in her own writing and in her interaction with orthodox loved ones such as her sister Lavinia and her sister-in-law Susan Dickinson. As a builder of temples, Dickinson cultivates not only her heretical opinions but also her orthodox friends. They are part of the human community she would reach through her writing and her religious imagination. She hardly imagines Emerson or his followers as her primary audience but speaks to other women, "preceptors," and spiritual persons generally who are ready to partake of her Word.

Nevertheless, though she is too independent to acknowledge him as a poetic father or to belong to his school, Emerson stands behind

Dickinson's challenge to the unknown. In the general panorama of nineteenth-century intellectual history, Emerson (perhaps above all others) helped make poetically minded New Englanders aware that they faced an "abdication of Belief," while at the same time he claimed to give them the wherewithal to deal with it—the self-reliance, the intuitive faith in spirit. However different the particular Protestant background of the two writers, they take for granted a common Protestant heritage on the part of their readers, while at the same time they assume that this cultural and religious heritage is losing its currency. The Emerson of the Divinity School Address sees the absence of doctrinaire Christian belief as a problem and opportunity for himself and his audience of potential religious leaders. "The Puritans in England and America, found in the Christ of the Catholic Church, and in the dogmas inherited from Rome, scope for their austere piety and their longings for civil freedom. But their creed is passing away, and none arises in its room."[37] Emerson seems to offer to arise and fill the room himself, though even in 1838 he had doubts about his role as a public spokesman for a public cause.

The Emerson who effectively foreshadows Dickinson, in my view, is a more private writer and poet. This is the Emerson who shares with Dickinson a willingness to experiment with uncertainty and to rejoice in the flux of the mind. For her and for others who came after him Emerson opened up a way to live consciously with the instability of the inner life in a time of historical transition.[38] Indeed, as a woman poet, Dickinson has an interest in a literature of process, evanescence, and uncertainty even more thoroughgoing and radical than Emerson, while her conception of it is less programmatic. Yet it was Emerson who advertised the philosophical advantages of doing without order and perfection in the first place. Emerson used the opportunity of the unknown in a time of intellectual transition to create his own literature of nimble believing.

Emerson's sense of the divine is imbued with an evanescent unknown. While he employs the Calvinist idea of an arbitrary God far less readily than Dickinson (or Melville), like a good post-Calvinist he wants his God to be "mysterious and unexplorable."[39] For Emerson "power" inhabits the mysteriousness of things, waiting to be summoned and used. He has in his moments of powerful encounter no interest in issues that preoccupied his Harvard Unitarian teachers—in the harmony of God's attributes, in the central function of the rational conscience among the faculties of the soul, or in empiricist arguments for historical miracles—but an obsessive interest in the surprise of God's immediate presence. As he writes characteristically, "the sense of being which in calm hours rises, we know not how, in the soul, is not diverse from things, from space, from light, from time, from man, but one with them, and proceeds obviously from the same source whence their life and being also proceed."[40] Such a being is always latent in Emerson's transcription of experience but apprehended in some hours while not in others. It makes its presence known mysteriously and evanescently, in the ebb and flow of time.

Like Dickinson, Emerson puts his poetic faith in transforming or disturbing moments of illumination. Only "the transcendental and extraordinary" counted for him, in his reading, his private meditation, and his writing. Similarly, a key thing she wanted from literature was to be carried away by sudden spiritual experience. As she once wrote of a book she disdained, "Transport is not urged" (L, 2:491). For Dickinson more directly than for Emerson, "transport" was erotic as well as spiritual, a "Word made Flesh" she could taste "with ecstasies of stealth" (P 1651). Yet for both illumination came and went in time, bringing and erasing belief in a yoga of apprehension. Emerson, like Dickinson, was fascinated with the momentary and unsettled character of any grace he finds ways to represent. Both writers prefer not to fixate or codify their experiences of ecstasy and doubt. Yet their introspective experiments in writing are not less religious for being unsettled. They seek appropriate styles and forms for representing an untethered inner life.

"People wish to be settled. Only as far as they are unsettled, is there any hope for them."[41] Emerson's appeal to New England rested on his ability to project a private religion marked by inner activity that did not depend on fixed forms and that "made the Behavior large" by reasserting the centrality of humankind reconceived as the active soul, as consciousness in action. Perhaps also he is congenial to Dickinson because he shows an awareness of the fluctuations of his own believing. Intrinsic to Emerson's record of the mind's workings is his repeated demonstration of the destabilizing exhilaration his faith-in-transit brings. If "Nature is not fixed but fluid,"[42] human nature cannot afford fixations and fixed ideas, lest it go dead or permanently inert. "There are no fixtures to men, if we appeal to consciousness," he writes in "Circles." But an unsettled consciousness is not one that always trusts itself. A person may see "a dreary vacuity" one day where earlier he or she has seen "much." As he summons his reader to higher and higher aspiration,

Emerson's speaker admits to his own moments of blankness. "Alas for this infirm faith, this will not strenuous, this vast ebb of a vast flow! I am God in nature; I am a weed by the wall."[43] To ebb and flow vastly like a natural tide is more comfortable than to shrink from God to a weed. Truer to the transformations of consciousness, the second analogy corrects the first to express with drastic precision the drama of human instability, the more than natural changes that beset persons of untethered faith. The alteration from belief to disbelief may entail a temporary change from exhilaration to emptiness.

If, as Emerson says, "there are no fixtures . . . to consciousness," the static abstractions of conventional philosophical language will not properly convey our thought. In keeping with this awareness, Emerson's own abstractions are imbued with a sense of passage, as if invented to stimulate a reader to enter his stream of thought.[44] He translates the moral ideas he gets from Unitarianism into his own fluid idiom, construing them as ideas in flux. For example, the key Unitarian conception of an innate "moral sense" that governs our behavior becomes for Emerson equivalent to "rapid intrinsic energy,"[45] the energy of the active soul. Similarly, when Emerson writes in "Circles" that "every man believes that he has a greater possibility,"[46] he assumes the truth of the Unitarian doctrine that man can improve himself through the education of the moral sense. But by "possibility" Emerson does not mean just ethical opportunity that comes with reform of conscience but also an expansion of individual consciousness. He reconceives and reimagines the desire for moral improvement as private inner activity, as a living belief in a flexible abstraction.

Especially good examples of this manner of thought and style are the abstractions Emerson calls "the Lords of Life" in the essay "Experience": "Illusion, Temperament, Succession, Surface, Surprise, Reality, Subjectiveness." Each of these words conveys in context the speaker's awareness that we live in time, not in a realm of thought abstracted from it. Illusions besiege us in time, as "Dream delivers us to dream." Temperament blocks our vision in the morning after the fancies of the night. Then we are surprised out of ourselves by an influx of power from "the subterranean and invisible tunnels and channels of life." For through the vicissitudes of experience Reality does not change, but a door within us opens to it over and over while "we dress our garden [and] discuss the household with our wives."[47] His use of temporally conscious abstractions distinguishes Emerson's language from that of other Romantic and Victorian "sages" and contributes to his originality as a stylist and thinker.

It also brings him close to Dickinson. What Emerson and Dickinson have perhaps most profoundly in common as writers is their use of abstractions. As in Emerson's "Experience," conceptions in Dickinson's writing appear in process of formation, not as fixed or conventional entities or doctrines. For a quick instance, let us look at her use of "Conjecture," along with "terror" and "merriment," in some lines from one of her comic poems, "These are the Nights that Beetles love –" (P 1128). Dickinson's beetle is both portentous and amusing.

> The terror of the Children
> The merriment of men
> Depositing his Thunder
> He hoists abroad again –
> A Bomb upon the Ceiling
> Is an improving thing –
> It keeps the nerves progressive
> Conjecture flourishing –
>
> terror] transport
> merriment] jeopardy

"Conjecture" is one of Dickinson's nimble abstractions, which she conceives differently on different occasions. In this poem it is "an improving" activity of mind that "keeps the nerves progressive." Reveling in not knowing stimulates the spirit. Conjecture flourishes not only in situ on this "Summer evening" but also in the verbal possibilities contemplated in the text. The variants in the first two lines suggest that Dickinson considered calling the beetle "The transport of the Children / The Jeopardy of men," hence making children exhilarated and putting men in peril instead of the reverse. Transport, jeopardy, terror, and merriment all come into play in a complex of possibilities for responding to the grotesque intervention of a beetle. Such alternatives not only allow for different readings but exemplify the workings of conjecture in the poem.

Yet elsewhere "Conjecture" can be an invitation to a speaker's terror.

> The possibility – to pass
> Without a Moment's Bell –
> Into Conjecture's presence –

Is like a Face of Steel –
That suddenly looks into our's
With a metallic grin –
The Cordiality of Death –
Who drills his Welcome in –

(P 286)

Here conjecture means not knowing what happens when we die, giving
the unknown "a Face of Steel" one is thankful to turn away from. The
other side of Dickinson's celebration of uncertainty is her obsession with
the uncertainty of death, "whose if is everlasting" (*PF,* 49; *L,* 3:919).
Dickinson's focus on the dread of death here reminds us of her differ-
ences from Emerson, while her willingness to face the disturbing logi-
cal obverse of her own thought is consistently Emersonian.

When Dickinson writes "I dwell in Possibility – / A fairer House
than Prose –" (P 657) she may or may not remember Emerson's "Cir-
cles." In any case, she uses another flexible abstraction to invoke her call-
ing. "Possibility" in the poem is a religious state of mind happening
temporally in the speaker's experience and the House of Possibility a
residence for a poet with a vocation for nimble believing. She constructs
her house knowingly as a fiction, an invented fabric of words not things,
a house not made with hands but one that calls attention to its own ten-
uousness. It has numerous windows (for lovelier visions), superior
doors (to keep out prosy intruders), impregnable chambers (likewise),
and the sky for a roof. Open to the fairest visitors and to the infinite, it
is paradoxically tightly enclosed and sealed from the outside world.
When with her sky-roof Dickinson stretches her analogy of possibility
to a house beyond plausibility, she advertises the fictionality of her par-
adoxical construction. Yet her tone asks that we believe experimentally
for the space of the poem in the words of which the house is made,
words that point to "subjects of which we know nothing." A fairer
House than Prose, the House of Possibility is a figure for poetry, but po-
etry conceived as the spiritual capacity "to gather Paradise" and believe
in it—nimbly.

Dickinson is not Emerson's only follower in the New England orbit who
cultivates the mysteries of the spirit and engages in the expression of
"fluid consciousness." Thoreau and Melville are as prone as Emerson
and Dickinson to court the chance to be unsettled and share with Dick-

inson a prehensile memory of Calvinism and a consequent interest in the poetics of the unknown. For a host of reasons Dickinson stands apart from these publishing male writers as a private woman writer. Yet when she is seen in connection with them, she becomes a bearer of a common nineteenth-century consciousness. As she shares the cultural dilemmas of feminine repectability with other women writers, so she shares a con-sciousness of metaphysical uncertainty with Emerson and his succes-sors, however uniquely she remains herself.

A key feature of the work of Emerson, Thoreau, Melville, and Dick-inson is the search for belief in a world in which one accepts the insta-bility of thought. All four focus on temporal fluctuation in their thought and reflect the makings and unmakings of time in their styles. All four are acutely aware that the mind lacks fixtures, and they look for ways to express belief or disbelief that will be true to the unfixed temporal flow of consciousness. Within their volatile writing, however, they evoke epiphanies of belief or conversion or inner disturbance in vital passing moments. Their interest in sudden inner transformation amounts to a common project recurring in different contexts. How can one express one's anxiety to improve the nick of time, or convey one's unexpected delight in a bosom friendship with a South Sea idolator who reminds you of the ungraspable phantom of life, or convey the heavenly hurt in a certain slant of light? How can one express one's faith in these sudden internal experiences so as to allow for one's own intruding skep-ticism?—this is a recurrent task for all these volatile thinkers.

The Thoreau I have in mind in connection with Dickinson is not the polemicist who excoriates his neighbors in the first pages of *Walden* but the consciously elusive writer who hints a bit later "at some of the en-terprises I have cherished":

> In any weather, at any hour of the day or night, I have been anxious to improve the nick of time, and notch it on my stick too . . . You will par-don some obscurities, for there are more secrets in my trade than in most men's, and yet not voluntarily kept, but inseparable from its very nature.

One of these enterprises—a rite of preparation that has given his life meaning—is "waiting at evening on the hill-tops for the sky to fall, that I might catch something, though I never caught much, and that, manna-wise, would dissolve again in the sun." Another is "trying to hear what was in the wind, to hear and carry it express!" Like Dickinson's, this

Thoreau's "trade" requires "obscurities" because it depends on sudden, unpredictable illuminations of consciousness, on intimate hearing of "what was in the wind." His "business" (Dickinson's word too) is a quest for the manna of heaven. He too builds temples to a God he prefers not to name traditionally, to "the workman whose work we are," to "the old settler" who dug Walden Pond. He will "improve the nick of time" because his mind is knowingly changing in time. He knows himself as "the scene . . . of thoughts and affections," with a "spectator" inside his mind observing his inner transitions.[48] This more elusive Thoreau is the inner face of a Thoreau Dickinson seems also to have enjoyed, the exemplary rebel who heard church bells and fire bells as equally significant of harm.[49]

Melville and Dickinson are the two writers of these four most obviously tied to Calvinism and most clearly concerned with "the abdication of Belief." If he is not a source for Dickinson, he is her closest contemporary analogue in his willingness to experience the conflicts and test the assumptions of nineteenth-century Protestant theology. As we shall observe, their quarrels with an imagined arbitrary God have an edge missing in Emerson and Thoreau, and their attraction to a humane, loving Christ is correspondingly more poignant. They put their knowledge of the Bible fully to use, as if to make it an instrument of their own dialectical struggles with belief. At times they confront the prospect of unbelief with greater anxiety. Indeed, in the course of his career Melville goes underground partly because of the ravages of his own skepticism. We recall Hawthorne's famous journal entry on Melville's state of mind in November 1856, when Melville confided to him that

> he had "pretty much made up his mind to be annihilated"; but still he
> does not seem to rest in that anticipation; and, I think, will never rest
> until he gets hold of a definite belief . . . He can neither believe, nor be
> comfortable in his unbelief; and he is too honest and courageous not to
> try to do one or the other.[50]

Melville wrestles with this irresolution to the end, exuberantly in *Moby-Dick,* with melancholy earnestness in *Clarel,* with passion spent in *Billy Budd, Sailor.*

The Melville of *Moby-Dick* glories in his irresolution and uses it expressively. He is as open to transport and as aware of the transience of thought as a Dickinson. Soon after Sophia Hawthorne met him, she wrote of him with qualified admiration: "Melville's fresh, sincere, glowing mind . . . is in a state of 'fluid consciousness,' & to Mr. Hawthorne speaks his innermost about GOD, the Devil, & Life if so he can get at the Truth for he is a boy in opinion—having settled nothing yet."[51] *Moby-Dick* makes this volatility expressive both in its drama and in its expository discourse. Dramatically, it turns on incidents of uncanny transformation, or transport, that not only advance the plot but also accumulate in a spiritual record of hope and dread. Ishmael experiences Queequeg's hug as the grasp of a friendly phantom that frees the soul from its terrors. More frighteningly, Pip sees God's foot on the treadle of the loom and is henceforth mad, though bound for heaven. Discursively Ishmael makes use of speculative vacillations to develop a form of self-acceptance and, ultimately, to survive as a credible voice of Melville's uncertainty. For example, in "The Fountain" Ishmael facetiously contemplates the spout of a whale and decides it is "nothing but mist." Yet he rejoices quasi-reverently in the rainbow that irradiates it. He concludes with a provisional speculation:

> And so, through all the thick mists of the dim doubts in my mind, divine intuitions now and then shoot, enkindling my fog with a heavenly ray. And for this I thank God; for all have doubts; many deny; but doubts or denials, few along with them, have intuitions. Doubts of all things earthly, and intuitions of some things heavenly; this combination makes neither believer nor infidel, but makes a man who regards them both with equal eye.[52]

At least in *Moby-Dick* such a never-ending dialectic of doubt and intuition allows Ishmael to face the unknown and survive with his jaundiced cheerfulness intact.

Why should these writers have a common propensity for highlighting unpredictable illuminations and moments of temporary belief? A judicious answer, I think, cannot be an exhaustive one. A literary phenomenon like nimble believing is in part a human miracle, however distinctly it may arise within a specific human culture. As Emerson, exasperated by all materialisms, insists, "the definition of *spiritual* should be, *that which is its own evidence.*"[53] We can but guess at a global historical context for this literature. I will offer some brief hypotheses concerning context that seem to me relevant to Dickinson. The first, clearly, is that Thoreau, Melville, and Dickinson come after Emerson. As we have seen, Emerson made legitimate a volatile style that exhibits its own processes, whether in meditative prose, verse, or prose fiction.

Second, these four writers were strongly rooted in their Protestant culture while also practically disaffected from it. Through the 1830s in New England at least, the educated population began their learning with the Bible and the Shorter Catechism and shared something of a common training in social and moral attitudes. The lawyers, college teachers, ministers, and women in academies who administered this training and spoke for these attitudes were guardians and preservers of what Terence Martin calls the "social orthodoxy" of early-nineteenth-century America, an orthodoxy that lingers powerfully in a place like Amherst through most of the century.[54] These guardians joined in reinforcing a set of conservative social values and habits of mind: the value of the Christian home and family, the importance of "competence" and "industry" in "the flourishing village,"[55] the encouragement of benevolent social affections and the discouragement of individual rebellion or moral experiment, and finally a nervous skepticism concerning theoretical speculation or any "metaphysics" not compatible with one's practical duties as a Christian American. This common set of values existed despite local peculiarities. Different religious groups had different educational centers with their own theological orientations but a common social mission. Harvard might be more cosmopolitan and patrician than other colleges, but its professors were well aware of their moral responsibility to safeguard the character of the nation bequeathed by the founders. Amherst might encourage science and sanction revivals, but it was no hotbed of revivalist democracy; rather its leaders saw themselves as sources of moral authority for the Connecticut Valley Christian community.

A common program was possible in this federated group of religious and educational centers partly because nearly every college and academy in the northeast adopted the writings of Scottish common-sense philosophers as their basic texts in moral and educational philosophy.[56] However strident their exchanges on theological questions, Unitarians and Trinitarians shared a similar approach to knowledge based on similar readings in the Scots. The teaching of the common-sense school were of enormous help in ensuring the cohesion of the nation. They seemed the very basis of enlightenment for some of the shrewdest guardians of the social order, from Thomas Jefferson to Harriet Beecher Stowe. They provided underlying assumptions for the Fireside poets, for the Romantic historians, for Dana and Cooper. Yet almost inevitably, common-sense principles operated to smother literary individuality; Dickinson, like Emerson, Thoreau, and Melville before her, rebelled against them. The young Dickinson was perfectly aware of common-sense teachings, as represented in the attitudes of her Yale-educated father, and she quietly set herself to oppose them. At the age of twenty-one she wrote her brother, "we do not have much poetry, father having made up his mind that its pretty much all *real life*. Fathers real life and *mine* sometimes come into collision, but as yet, escape unhurt!" (*L*, 1:161). What was "real" to her might be unintelligible to her father. Nimble believing has no place in common-sense thinking—it is by nature speculative, unpredictable, and individualistic—it deals with "subjects of which we know nothing" and is centered in an interior life independent of self-evident moral truths and employing sense perception not as the only source of cognition but as an initial source and stimulus for free mental activity.

Throughout their careers our four writers are deeply versed from childhood in Protestant texts and rituals as well as in common-sense teaching. They come to maturity thoroughly knowing the Bible and the Shorter Catechism. Yet for them the older Protestant "creed is passing away, and none arises in its room." Given this awareness, they have a double-minded relation to their religious heritage as well as their Yankee common-sense culture. This is one reason they are "unsettled." For example, their double-minded attraction to and estrangement from the Bible and the Catechism may exacerbate their sense that spiritual phenomena are both real and mutable. These texts are at times welcome to them as familiar means of understanding the human mind and heart, while at other times they are disposed to play with them critically or turn against them with informed disdain. Emerson remembers with distaste "the injurious impositions of our early catechistical instruction,"[57] but especially Thoreau, Melville, and Dickinson use the Bible as a great resource of language and lore that only needs to be jostled to come alive.

Moreover, their religious heritage is complicated by the interaction of Calvinism, with its emphasis on sudden grace followed by the soul's difficult struggle for renewal, and Unitarianism, with its emphasis on rational choice and human possibility. All four in different ways are influenced by these two strains in the religious life in New England. Emerson drew self-consciously on both strains. He prided himself on his difference from most Unitarian ministers in that he owed his theological education to his Aunt Mary and to "influences of ancestral religion" as well as to Harvard.[58] Thoreau has less sectarian consciousness, yet he was made to attend both Unitarian and Calvinist churches in his youth, and the religious authority he projects and opposes in his writings is an amalgam of the two.[59] Melville had a Unitarian father and later a Unitarian wife and in-laws, a Calvinist (Dutch Reformed) mother and childhood nest. As T. Walter Herbert has shown, a Calvinist minister was a powerful influence on him during his early years.[60] Dickinson, we know already, was grounded in latter-day Calvinism but sought out liberal religious influences throughout her intellectual life. What do they share from this mixed heritage?

All four writers take advantage of liberal currents in religion to liberalize their own sensibilities. Yet I would argue that they are perhaps influenced even more profoundly in their imagination by "ancestral religion." Indeed, what Unitarianism, New England's alternative religion, seems most to have given the writers is a chance to use their Calvinist heritage, perhaps partly unconsciously, while at the same time they reject Calvinism as a body of dogma. Without subscribing to Puritan doctrines, they inherit Puritan imaginations.

Several Puritan imaginative tendencies in these writers help generate a literature of nimble believing. As I have intimated, they all have a specific fascination for sudden influxes of spiritual gladness or fear, for moments of grace when one is aware without warning of the power of the divine, or for moments of dread before the unknowable. When Dickinson, Emerson, or Thoreau hint or state what motivates them as writers, they recreate a memory of transport, of sudden illumination or personal vastation. So Dickinson in a late poem tells a representative anecdote of the origins of her inspiration.

> The farthest Thunder that I heard
> Was nearer than the Sky
> And rumbles still, though torrid Noons
> Have lain their missiles by –
> The Lightning that preceded it
> Struck no one but myself –
> But I would not exchange the Bolt
> For all the rest of Life –

                                                              (P 1581)

This common interest of our writers in attesting to experiences of grace or dread or the soul's undoing is not an interest that was encouraged by American critics intent on fixing literary or social norms. Such socially orthodox critics called for moral fiction that would reinforce social bonds, not for *Moby-Dick;* for a poetry of standard meters and conventional sentiments, not for the work of Dickinson; and for logically argued essays on public issues, not for the essays of Emerson.[61] Instead of fulfilling the generic expectations prompted by common-sense teaching, our writers gravitated toward critically unsponsored imitations of Puritan patterns of thought, toward the representation of influx in fragments and journals.

More abstractly, Dickinson and Melville patently, and Emerson and Thoreau more distantly, share an imagination of God that seems an adaptation of Puritan metaphysics. This God is in Melville's word "ungraspable." As Perry Miller writes;

> Puritan thinking on the subject of the Deity always confronted the intital difficulty that in one sense thinking about Him was impossible. The Puritan God is entirely incomprehensible to man . . . God can never be delineated even momentarily in any shape, contour, or feature recognizable to human discourse, nor may His activities be subjected to the laws of reason or of plausibility. He is a realm of mystery. . . . Though individual Puritans might forget its implications, to Puritanism itself the idea was fundamental that God, the force, the power, the life of the universe, must remain to men hidden, unknowable, and unpredictable . . . The soul of Puritan theology is the hidden God, who is not fully revealed even in His own revelation. The Bible is His declared will; behind it always lies His secret will.[62]

Miller works out these dramatic formulations with due caution. If "in one sense" God was incomprehensible even to the regenerate, it is clear already from the opening chapter of *The New England Mind* that Puritans thought about him incessantly and assiduously—by conceptualizing his "attributes" and constructing possible relations between them, by using the Bible as a fount of evidence for his designs, by reflecting legalistically on the ramifications of his rule, by describing his created order as clearly and plainly as possible. Their paradoxical insistence on clarity in the order of nature and on the necessary obscurity of one's relation with divinity is one of the most interesting features of the Puritan enterprise and is a source of tension and variety in Puritan writing.[63] Moreover, Miller slights the importance of Christ in the pietistic thinking of the Puritans. Calvinists as well as other Protestants gave their deepest hopes to the belief that Christ not only atones for the sin of those whom God has chosen but also transforms the hearts of the Elect and brings them miraculously close to God. Conrad Cherry writes as if in answer to Miller that in Calvin's system "The God who concerns the believer is not the hidden God but the God who reveals himself in all his mystery in the Christ."[64] To the Elect, God in Christ makes himself known as an intimate presence, however mysterious. Both the Puritans' hope for Christ's saving love and their acknowledgment of God's incomprehensible distance from man were crucial to their imaginations of divinity. These complementary conceptions appear juxtaposed in the work of some of the best New England colonial writers. If often in his Preparatory Meditations Edward Taylor can delight in the sweetness of Christ's intimacy, when he considers "the force, the power, the life of the universe" he stresses the incommensurable distance between God and man and the unknowableness of God's activities.

As I read them, our nineteenth-century writers are also caught up with these interrelated issues: the obscurity of divinity, the temporary workings of gracious apprehension, and the tenuousness of language when one is "part or particle of God."[65] Though the God of each writer is different, all four tend to present him as hidden, impersonal, and incalculable. Their attraction to inexplicable moments of influx is of a piece with such a sense of God, in whom one believes and disbelieves a hundred times an hour. They part company with Unitarian rationalist writers such as Channing, Ripley, Longfellow, and Norton in their fascination with God's mysteriousness and in their tendency to abstract God from human social order. Their sense of God is equally different from that of the New Haven theology emanating from Yale, the theology of Timothy Dwight, Nathaniel Taylor, and Lyman Beecher. Though these influential writers espouse the tradition of Calvin and Edwards, they play down God's mysteriousness, make him congenial to common-sense principles of understanding, and seek to clarify and codify God's moral government so that it will operate as a model for American society.[66] For both the Channings and the Beechers God is the guarantor of American social good, whereas for our writers he is "a Force illegible" or "the sense of being which . . . rises, we know not how, in the soul" or "Indra in the sky looking down on" the driftwood in the stream or a "Shekinah, intolerably bright."[67]

Like her Puritan forebears, Dickinson also makes a division be-

tween an awesome God and a kindly Christ, a division latent but re-
solvable in Puritan writers such as Edward Taylor but evident and of-
ten troubling in nineteenth-century American Protestantism. She shares
this closely felt sense of Christ's separate human power and pathos with
Melville, hardly at all with Emerson or Thoreau.[68] In the Melville of *The
Confidence-Man* and *Clarel* as well as in Dickinson's poems on the life
and afterlife of Christ, the possible division (or connection) between
Christ and the Father brings both energy and a yearning uncertainty
into their writing. In her more renegade frame of mind, however, Dick-
inson is closer to the Ahabian Melville of *Moby-Dick* and *Pierre.* In such
moods and fictional recreations God tends to be not only incomprehen-
sible in his being but also arbitrary in his rule. This Dickinson and this
Melville share a willingness to imagine such a God as distant and terri-
fying. God's arbitrary character is an obsessive figure of their imagina-
tions. More than any of their literary contemporaries, they represent
"the force, the power, the life of the universe" as arbitrary in its work-
ings. In some late poems Dickinson achieves a distance from this con-
cept of God and satirizes Amherst Calvinism with whimsical ferocity,
yet in earlier dramatic poems she represents fears prompted by her
local religion with the distinctness of remembered experience.

Dickinson's narrators are not only impressed by God's power but
deeply baffled by God's "illegibility." No one writes as well as she of
victimized awe before the unknowable power at the heart of things. In
one poem the speaker hopes for comfort from her God, but he seems to
her so vast and baffling that his presence in the poem decimates the
meter. At the end the speaker's voice trails off in properly uncertain
prayer. At first she thought she might turn to him in her affliction. She

> Could dimly recollect a Grace –
> I think, they call it "God" –
> Renowned to ease Extremity –
> When Formula, had failed –
>
> And shape my Hands –
> Petition's way,
> Tho' ignorant of a word
> That Ordination – utters –
>
> My Business, with the Cloud,
> If any Power behind it, be,

Not subject to Despair –
It care, in some remoter way,
For so minute affair
As Misery –
Itself, too vast, for interrupting – more –

Grace] Force   vast] great

(P 293)[69]

Is the Cloud all that one can do business with, or is there a God behind
it? Whatever this "Power" may be, is it free from despair? Can it care
even remotely for misery? How much can it care if it is too vast to be in-
terrupted? All these uncertainties underscore the sufferer's minuteness
in the face of "Its" vastness. The hypothetical "Power behind the Cloud"
reminds us of the principle of power Ahab would confront behind the
pasteboard mask of visible things, or the "joyous, heartless, ever-juvenile
eternities" Pip sees beneath the surface of the sea, or Ishmael's weaver-
god deafened by the humming of his own loom and unable to hear the
voice of human supplication.[70] In the work of both writers such experi-
ences of divine power are occasional and unpredictable and all the more
dynamic because the power cannot be rationally known or described.

Neither Dickinson nor Melville represents only dread before God.
Dickinson plays repeatedly with different images of divinity, loves Je-
sus Christ in many poems, seems honestly pious when writing to cer-
tain correspondents, and is just as apt to commend "Our Old Neighbor
– God" (P 623) as to dramatize God's unreachableness. Melville devel-
ops unceasingly in his career; thus no single paradigm will exhaust his
religious thinking even in *Moby-Dick,* much less beyond it. Neverthe-
less, the two writers represent at times the distress of those bred to
Calvinism while also attracted to liberal religious ideas. At such times
they work from the premises of two contradictory convictions—that
man suffers horribly in his alienation from God and that man is a crea-
ture of abounding life who merits the favor of divine benevolence. Ed-
ward Beecher, Lyman's son and Harriet's brother, considers such dis-
tress sympathetically. As he explains, "God's glory is eclipsed" when
one is troubled by these divisive thoughts, and the contradictions be-
tween one's fallen condition and one's liberal hopes "present to the
mind a malevolent God."[71] Or, for Dickinson and Melville, a cruelly

capricious, arbitrary God. Both writers make full artistic use of the condition Beecher describes.

Dickinson's religious heritage, then, enabled her both to dramatize anger at an arbitrary God and to express gratitude for an unknowable but real "waylaying Light" that she claims informs all poetic endeavor (P 1581). Both her anger and her attraction to epiphany are signs of a kinship she has with other key American writers of her period and before it, of their common religious and poetic sensibility. If she shares a vivid imagination of an unresponsive God with Melville, an acute apprehension of the manna of a New England heaven with Thoreau, and a readiness to employ temporally conscious abstractions with Emerson, these are connections to contemplate gratefully, not scorn. Collectively, the fragmentary and changeable expression of religious hope and uncertainty in the work of these writers is a singular feature of nineteenth-century American literature worth celebrating. I at least have not found it elsewhere, neither in Victorian literature in England and Scotland nor in later American literature as it emerges in the aftermath of the Civil War. True, this mode of expression helps make Emerson, Thoreau, Melville, and Dickinson hard to read, teach, and categorize. These seekers after "volatile truth" cannot be packaged or labeled so easily as writers who follow more stable conventions. They are all writers without handles. They do not as a rule follow set literary forms but use available forms to distort them, thereby in effect inventing their own. Yet their unpredictable elusiveness and willful originality are part of their appeal.

One reason for Dickinson's elusiveness (and originality) is that she is unusually conscious of the element of time in the expression of thought, conscious that one believes and disbelieves by turns as one faces the unknown. Abstracting categories will not by themselves do justice to this lability of belief. Vacillation can even be a structural principle, a means to her own coherence, in some of her most interesting poems. Under these circumstances the critic should seek a mode of commentary that gives adequate specific attention to how her texts make the reader aware of the element of time, how her expression of thought changes within the forms she produces, and how she evades single-mindedness and strives for a complex balance in her representations of belief and doubt.

Dickinson of course creates poetic forms on models other than that of the nimble believing sentence to Judge Lord. She can develop single

conceits in the manner of the metaphysical poets, as in "I dwell in Pos-
sibility – ," in which her thought is framed within an extended metaphor
or analogy. In such a poem she does not seek to reflect changes in think-
ing but creates the illusion of a stable consciousness. The speaker
"gather[s] Paradise" as a steady occupation, not changeably. Dickinson
can also compose self-enclosed fictional narratives like "Myself was
formed – a Carpenter – " in which an event has its own narrative direc-
tion and unity undisturbed by vacillation. She can observe a scene and
reflect logically on it, as in "These are the Nights that Beetles love – ," or
construct poetic definitions sufficient unto themselves, as in (e.g.) "Pre-
sentiment – is that long Shadow – on the Lawn – " (P 764). In none of
these cases are we especially aware of a consciousness working ideas
out in time, however stamped the poems may be with the vitality of the
poet's thinking.

Nevertheless, Dickinson allows for believing and disbelieving even
within the form of her texts. Simply on a verbal level her practice of not
choosing definitively among alternatives for the words of her poems is
itself a form of knowing vacillation. Spun out diachronically, her will-
ingness to experiment with changes of thought creates structures of
meaning in individual poems. To take a familiar and vivid example:

501

This World is not Conclusion.
A Species stands beyond –
Invisible, as Music –
But positive, as Sound –
It beckons, and it baffles
Philosophy – dont know –
And through a Riddle, at the last –
Sagacity, must go –
To guess it, puzzles scholars –
To gain it, Men have borne
Contempt of Generations
And Crucifixion, shown –
Faith slips – and laughs, and rallies –
Blushes, if any see –
Plucks at a twig of Evidence –

And asks a Vane, the way –
Much Gesture, from the Pulpit –
Strong Hallelujahs roll –
Narcotics cannot still the Tooth
That nibbles at the soul

Species] A sequel – Strong] Sure –
guess] prove it –   Tooth] Mouse –

This poem has what one might call a structure of nimble believing. It begins with positive assertion but ends in conclusive irresolution. The speaker in the first four lines sounds like a more or less conventional preacher proclaiming a belief in another world beyond the one we know. Even here, however, Dickinson's variants "Species" and "sequel" induce the reader to wonder what such an afterlife might be rather than take its conventional contours for granted. In lines 5 and 6, "It beckons, and it baffles – / Philosophy – dont know – ," the tone changes subtly and decisively. From now on, and despite later modulations of thought, the poem sustains a pose of uncertainty about the "it" that "beckons." "Philosophy" is like a baffled schoolboy who cannot even claim the authority of adult grammar in his search for knowledge. Yet in the third quatrain the tone and import change again: the speaker shifts into a mode of reverence. She expresses, I think, a grand if distanced respect for the "Men" – the Christian martyrs and others like them – who have "shown Crucifixion" to gain their heaven. This speaker allows herself first to believe, then doubt, then compensate for doubt by showing respect for religion.

The brilliant fourth quatrain, however, is less respectful and returns the reader to a bemused skepticism. Dickinson invents an allegorical figure of "Faith" as "a silly young girl meandering blithely toward an uncertain destination."[72] The "Strong Hallelujahs" of the evangelical preacher in the final quatrain are no help to this Faith, only a narcotic that obscures the soul's needs. Yet the end of the poem is not simply skeptical. I read the "Tooth" (or "Mouse") that "nibbles at the soul" as the possibility of an afterlife that beckons and baffles earlier. It is not so much the tooth of "doubt"[73] as of Dickinson's doubt-that-is-also-faith that keeps nibbling comically beyond the borders of the poem. The soul, after all, is not erased but persists (however nibbled at) in the poem's understanding. The speaker's stance is that of "neither believer nor infidel"; she regards "both with equal eye."[74] Though Dickinson adopts no fixed position toward received belief in the poem, she displays the opposite of "a finless mind."[75] She manages the poem's vacillations expertly, with the effect of leading her readers toward wondering habits of thought.

Dickinson's control is often but not always so assured in poems in which she displays her shifting thought. Sometimes her changes in perspective are more interestingly self-revealing than artful or logically plausible. Occasionally, Dickinson writes a poem that shifts its subject in such a way as to lose touch with its own beginnings. A poem cited earlier that ends with an appeal to a God "too vast, for interrupting – more – " begins with the recollection of a loss of human love: "I got so I could take his name – / Without – Tremendous gain – / That Stop-sensation – on my Soul – / And Thunder – in the Room – " (P 293). Yet though this poem makes the reader strain to give it coherence I am still partial to it. I would defend it for what it reveals about the range of Dickinson's imagination. I like moving from "Thunder – in the Room" to "My Business, with the Cloud, / If any Power behind it, be," as from the shock of deprivation to the terror of meaninglessness. Such a poem that seems to forget its beginnings is not only an instance of Dickinson's daring but the sort of chance she takes as a poet of constant transformation. Yet she gets away with it, and with her whole enterprise in my view, because she is here as so often a mistress of tonal modulation. She shows this mastery in many of her poems that expose her variety, her uncertainty, and her questioning spirit. Thought and tone change and keep pace with one another in her lifelong effort to keep believing nimble.

2

Varieties of Religion in
Emily Dickinson

Affirming Variety

In this chapter I will explore Emily Dickinson's religious imagination in
its dynamic diversity, as it emerges from its personal and historical con-
text. Her imagination is dynamic partly because she thinks of her men-
tal world as always in flux and prefers not to adhere for long to any pre-
conceived religious or philosophical doctrine. At different times she
advances opposed positions on such central questions as the goodness
of God, the reality of heaven, or the presence of the divine in nature. She
applies her imagination to these unknowable subjects by meditating on
them dialectically, repeatedly, and intensively. As a child of her culture,
the fixed positions of her local Calvinism are inscribed in her mind and
heart, while at the same time she distrusts them and seeks an alterna-
tive faith that will be truer to her moral conceptions.

Dickinson's thinking is consciously in historical transition between
the Calvinism of her teachers and whatever might later replace it, and
her historical self-consciousness contributes to the volatility of her
imagination. Since she takes different positions on religious questions,
it has proved hard for commentators to summarize her religious per-
spective. Some who think of her as essentially a traditional believer tend
to treat her skepticism as the expression of an occasional passing mood.[1]
Some who think of her as essentially a rebel tend to treat her quasi-or-
thodox poems and pronouncements as aberrations.[2] Still others treat
her religious concerns as transformations of her psychological struggles
and her religious language as the particular language she had available

to address her personal needs as a nineteenth-century woman.[3] In my view her spiritual longings are genuine (not just a front for something else), and her expressions of them central to her achievement as a poet. Yet she "keeps Believing nimble" and does not allow herself to be assigned summarily to any ideological camp. One needs a strategy that allows for her variety in order to present her range as a speculative artist and thinker.

The various attitudes Dickinson adopts do not radically change over the course of her career. Already by 1858–59, when she begins to copy her poems into the fascicles, she has begun to articulate her differences from the Connecticut Valley Calvinist tradition in which she was raised. Already, as well, she is busy reimagining that tradition, so that when she chooses she can dramatize her own temporary faith in a divinity or a paradise. Her ideas and themes repeat themselves in the course of her career; her development is circular as well as linear. Her self-delighting process of speculation is to a large extent self-enclosed and self-referential. She lives in her own intellectual frame of reference and comes back over and over to the same introspective preoccupations. Like Whitman she "contains multitudes," in 1859 as well as in 1886, but they remain more or less the same multitudes. Since she is committed to her frame of reference, she chooses not to be distracted from it and prefers not to respond overtly to changes or catastrophes in the political and social realms surrounding her privacy.

> If nothing larger than a World's
> Departure from a Hinge
> Or Sun's extinction, be observed
> 'Twas not so large that I
> Could lift my Forehead from my work
> For Curiosity.

> (P 985)

Viewed in this light, her repetitions and circlings back to earlier themes are intrinsic to her cultivation of a poetry of introspective process.

Yet in its own ways Dickinson's work develops over the course of her career. The view that her poetry remains aesthetically and spiritually unchanged from its earliest to its latest period seems to me mistaken, or at least oversimplified.[4] Certainly, the form and appearance of

her texts develop significantly. We have seen how at the start of her ca-
reer she assembles her poems in fascicles and sets, thus giving them a
separate existence as poems, while later she experiments increasingly
with a style of letter-writing in which the border between verse and
prose tends to disappear, and she writes poetically wherever she wants
to. More and more she seems to conceive of poetic writing as an all-
engaging process with only temporary closure. In addition, Dickinson's
poetry changes with the vicissitudes of her personal experience. In spite
of her withdrawal from society and the persistence of her themes and
preoccupations, her work not only circles back on itself but also reflects
her intense response to personal changes that encroach on her world.

Her very early poems (1858–60) are generally smoother in form,
more sprightly and less troubled in spirit than the prodigious group of
poems assigned to her most productive years (1861–65). These are years
of apparent crisis and of profound poetic inventiveness, when Dickin-
son composes many poems with dramatized speakers who anxiously
explore religious questions as these affect their own happiness. After the
trauma of her eye operations and enforced convalescence, Dickinson's
poems from 1866 on focus less on dramas of love and more on repre-
sentations of nature, frequently imagined at a distance. Her speakers are
apt to be confessionally meditative rather than dramatically afflicted. In
Dickinson's last years (ca. 1875–86) her poetry reflects her awareness of
the deaths of many closest to her and her contemplation of her own
death. She turns often in this last period to general speculations con-
cerning God, nature as God's creation, the relation between flesh and
spirit, and the afterlife, often expressed in condensed and elliptical
verse. Indeed, at the end of this chapter I will examine a set of late po-
ems that represent this final phase, in which Dickinson contemplates the
abyss of God's unknown with unterrified agnosticism. The shape of her
career, then, is paradoxical. Dickinson both abides and develops as a
poet. Hence as I evoke Dickinson's religious attitudes I will allow her
both to repeat herself and to embark in new directions.

Dickinson's penchant for believing and disbelieving alternatively
appears not only in her career as a whole but also within the confines of
particular poems and letters. One of her less familiar poems about her
experience of religion will illustrate this key principle. Johnson assigns
the poem to 1873, relatively late in her career. It is among other things a
retrospective summation of her religious education.

1258

Who were "the Father and the Son"
We pondered when a child,
And what had they to do with us
And when portentous told

With inference appalling
By Childhood fortified
We thought, at least they are no worse
Than they have been described.

Who are "the Father and the Son"
Did we demand Today
"The Father and the Son" himself
Would doubtless specify –

But had they the felicity
When we desired to know,
We better Friends had been, perhaps,
Than time ensue to be –

We start – to learn that we believe
But once – entirely –
Belief, it does not fit so well
When altered frequently –

We blush, that Heaven if we achieve –
Event ineffable –
We shall have shunned until ashamed
To own the Miracle –

The first two stanzas of the poem tell the beginnings of a familiar story.
The Calvinist doctrine that she heard as a child concerning the charac-
ter of the Father and the Son was to her both "portentous" (forbiddingly
impressive) and "appalling." Indeed, the speaker indicates she decided
even in childhood that "they" could not be "worse / Than they have
been described"—she rejected the description of such a Father and Son
and partly ceased to believe in them. Moreover, by making the speaker
a plural "we," Dickinson suggests that she can speak with authority for
others who have undergone a similar experience. She uses a represen-
tative voice, the voice of the doubter who has emerged from her culture.

Many of her poems and letters reiterate the point: the God her culture offered her was appalling, and she was ready to employ any verbal strategy she could muster to exorcise his spell.

Yet in this poem Dickinson hedges as well as pronounces. This appalling story of God may not truthfully represent who he is. Who indeed are the Father and the Son? The poem gives no definitive answer to the question. And by putting "the Father and the Son" within quotation marks she intimates that there is more than one way of construing their meaning (or "his" meaning—she suggests that "they" may be aspects of a single deity when she quirkily refers to "'The Father and the Son' *himself*"). The possibility of a different meaning for the idea of God is tentatively explored in the last four stanzas. Yet even if the speaker momentarily entertains the notion of a kinder God, she has been too damaged by early experience to believe in it unselfconsciously. As Dickinson writes in an earlier poem, "faith," if lost, cannot be "replenished."

> Inherited with Life –
> Belief – but once – can be –
> Annihilate a single clause –
> And Being's – Beggary –

                                                                    (P 377)

The speaker of Poem 1258 has become something of a wandering beggar for faith. Unable to approach "the Father and the Son" openheartedly, still she cannot get them out of her head. Likewise, "Heaven" remains a reality for her. Yet if she is finally to "behold" or "achieve" heaven,[5] it will have been as a habitual doubter.

In this poem, then, the speaker leaves uncertain who the Father and the Son are as well as what Heaven is. Yet at the same time she entertains the fantasy of achieving heaven and acknowleges that she has a latent interest in construing God as a "better Friend." Though this speaker now professes a diffidence with respect to this "Friend," in fact the larger story of Dickinson's practice as a religious poet involves not only a rejection of the Calvinist God but a search for something to put in its place. Like the poem, however, this larger story comes to no conclusion. The poem is characteristic of Dickinson in that it exhibits a search rather than finding a definitive answer.

Poem 1258 is a concise, if partial, illustration of the varieties of religious thinking in Dickinson's writing. It also gives us the beginnings of a scheme for displaying that variety. In the poem the speaker suggests that she has experienced a phase of rebellious skepticism, followed by a phase in which she searches for belief. In this chapter I will present a series of tendencies that her work repeatedly illustrates over the course of her career. I will treat her first more or less exclusively as a rebel infected with doubt and at war with her heritage. Then I will explore the ways she searches for alternatives to unbelief. I will sketch what seem to me the fundamental tenets of her own intuitive faith, a faith that uses her Calvinist inheritance without being hamstrung by it, and will also suggest how her faith was influenced and her skepticism sometimes reinforced by currents of liberalism that made their way into her culture. This order seems suited to the way her mind got its basic orientation. A crucial decision she makes as a young writer is not to conform to her local Calvinism and to expose its cruelties and illogicalities to herself and her imagined readers. With part of her mind she never gives up her anger at a doctrine of God that terrorized her. Even in her very last writings she is still intermittently engaged in mocking at or wrestling with "the Father." As a fundamentally religious poet, however, she is never merely a rebel for long and must cope with the difficulty of how to express her religious impulses authentically. She wants both to struggle against Calvinism and to use what it has given her. One of the peculiar strengths of her imagination is that she does not willfully resolve this quandary and has the ingenuity to reinitiate it over and over throughout her career.

A key transformation of residual Calvinism that survives in Dickinson's thinking is her idea of God as impersonal and unknowable. When she sought an alternative to the Father, she sometimes imagined such a God, daunting as Jehovah but flexibly abstract and inscrutable rather than anthropomorphic.[6] She was attracted like her ancestors to an image of God that highlighted his power and inscrutability. Her posture of reverence toward such a divinity she called awe, and it was fundamental to the integrity of her philosophical position that she be in awe of what she could not know.

Dickinson's openness to variety, her willingness to change her attitudes to suit given occasions, and her insistence that one needs the unknown to be true to one's spiritual experience are all of a piece with her aversion to received abstract systems of thought, especially to systematic Calvinism. "I do not respect 'doctrines,'" Dickinson once wrote, with specific reference to "predestination" (L, 2:346). Her mind, once liberated from her early dogmatic instruction, tended to become centrifu-gal. In moderation I can accept David Porter's emphasis on her bewil-derment at the chaos she observed and generated.[7] I see her cultural sit-uation in somewhat the same terms as Porter does. She is unmoored from authority, dubiously freed to try out a variety of conflicting atti-tudes. Nevertheless, I will contest Porter's assertion that Dickinson's work lacks "a project,"[8] meaning that she had no underlying ideologi-cal aim or "artistic goal" in her poetry and that she wrote on to express her uncontrollable verbal energy and to exorcise the chaos in her con-sciousness. I would argue, instead, that she has a cluster of interrelated aims, each of which she pursues occasionally and fragmentarily because her genius was suited to condensed imaginative expression. Some of these aims relevant to my own project are: to reimagine God as a better friend or, alternatively, as a God of awe; to undermine the orthodox imagination of God and construe religion without a sense of sin; to cel-ebrate the human apprehension of the natural world and the mysteri-ous workings of that world that God has created; to discover a paradise within at the heart of human nature, since properly understood it is the only nature we experience; to exalt poetry, fiction, painting, ballet, and music as forms of art by means of which we "see God face to face" and yet are "not consumed" (P 1733); to teach "the Art of Peace" (P 544), an art that consoles even for the pang of remembered death; and to face the unknown in all its power and even terror and yet draw spiritual nour-ishment from it. Finally, an artistic goal she pursues generally is to cel-ebrate the spirit that "bloweth where it listeth" (John 3.8). Except per-haps in moments of extreme self-doubt, she believes in the permanence of spirit, and relishes the spontaneity of its workings. By extension, she represents and justifies the lability of her own mind, as well as of the hu-man mind as she conceives it.

The Rebel

Let us begin, then, with Emily Dickinson's quarrel with God. What fun-damentally sets off the quarrel is the doctrine of God's sovereign om-nipotence. This, one presumes, she absorbed with her catechism and in adversarial moods never got over believing and disliking. God, in such a view, plans and determines all things. Occasionally, the early Dickin-son manifests gratitude to a God who relieves suffering rather than inflicting it. In a letter of 1854 to Abiah Root she reports that Sue Gilbert is recovering from "a Nervous Fever" not only with the help of "an excellent Nurse" and "a faithful Physician," but also because "*God* has been loving and kind" (*L,* 1:298). Later, however, she is more apt to blame a sovereign God for human misfortune. The world this God has made is full of misery and cruelty; he has placed humankind in a desperately skewed condition in an unfair world. In Dickinson's view one can find dramatic illustrations of the workings of such a God not only in the sermons of Connecticut Valley preachers but also in the Bible itself, in God's Draconian annihilation of Ananias (P 1201) or his toying like a bully with Moses (P 597), to use two of her examples.

If God determines all things, he is responsible for human pain and death. For this Dickinson cannot forgive him, especially since in a soberly rebellious frame of mind she dismisses orthodox ideas concerning salvation and election - she finds nothing in the Calvinist doctrine of God that compensates for what seems his indifference to human life and human suffering. Dickinson has a streak of stubborn this-worldliness. The life she cares about is usually the one we are living every precious moment of our earthly existence, and orthodox hopes of a life beyond are vain. "The meek members of the Resurrection" (P 216) simply molder in their alabaster chambers. Over and over in her poems and letters Dickinson expresses sorrow at death and rage at God for causing it. "Oh God / Why give if Thou must take away / The Loved?" her speaker cries with heart-felt simplicity in Poem 882.

Sometimes Dickinson is more ferocious and ironic in her response to the loss of those dear to her. It is worth putting some passages in her letters from widely separated periods together to dispose of the idea that she ever reconciled herself to a God who was the author of pain and death. In 1861 she writes the Norcross sisters: "The seeing pain one can't relieve makes a demon of one. If angels have the heart beneath their silver jackets, I think such things could make them weep, but Heaven is so cold! It will never look kind to me that God, who causes all, denies such little wishes" (*L,* 2:376). In 1865 she explains to Mrs. Holland that her sister-in-law Susan is trying to comfort her own sister Martha Gilbert Smith who has just lost a second infant child. Susan "is still with the sister who put her child in an ice nest last Monday forenoon. The redoubtable God!" (*L,* 2:444). In 1881, after President Garfield dies of a gunshot wound, Dickinson is fiercely scornful of Christian attempts to palliate the facts with conventional sentiment. "I go to read to mother about the President. When we think of the lone effort to live, and its bleak reward, the mind turns to the myth 'for His mercy endureth forever,' with confiding revulsion" (*L*, 3:711).[9] Finally, and perhaps most emphatically, Dickinson writes eighteen months before her own death to her Aunt Katie Sweetser to express her sympathy with her after an illness: "It is very wrong that you were ill, and whom shall I accuse? The enemy, 'eternal, invisible, and full of glory' – but He declares himself a friend!" (*L*, 3:851).

Such an idea of God, omnipotent but heartless, she held onto throughout her career in one compartment of her mind at least, though the particular voice she adopts to dramatize him might vary in her poems. Perhaps a good summary illustration of her resentment is this poem:

724

It's easy to invent a Life –
God does it – every Day –
Creation – but the Gambol
Of His Authority –

It's easy to efface it –
The thrifty Deity
Could scarce afford Eternity
To Spontaneity –

The Perished Patterns murmur –
But His Perturbless Plan
Proceed – inserting Here – a Sun –
There – leaving out a Man –

God here gambols playfully like Ishmael's "unseen and unaccountable old joker,"[10] and the speaker plays back. The alliteration in the last stanza, and the management of sound and form generally, ingeniously convey her voice of independent intelligence. Dickinson's art lightly exposes the lack of love in this necessitarian conception of divinity.[11] "His Perturbless Plan" leaves no place for the murmurs of human feeling.

Very early poems tend to treat such a monstrous conception of the world and its creator with bemusement rather than outrage.

61

Papa above!
Regard a Mouse
O'erpowered by the Cat!
Reserve within thy kingdom
A "Mansion" for the Rat!

Snug in seraphic Cupboards
To nibble all the day,
While unsuspecting Cycles
Wheel solemnly away!

(ca. 1859)

In "Papa's" world animals devour one another to fulfill their roles in the
everyday economy of living and dying. Why not, to mitigate these cir-
cumstances, imagine a heaven for a mouse (or rat) where it can nibble
in its cupboard all day? The tone of the poem is hardly anxious. Yet even
the early Dickinson can react in her poems more critically to what she
views as God's responsibility for death. Perhaps in the same year she
also wrote a smoothly phrased elegy for "fragile" children buried in
"the thoughtful grave" in which the last stanza reads:

This covert have all the children
Early aged, and often cold,
Sparrows, unnoticed by the Father –
Lambs for whom time had not a fold.

(P 141)

The sentiment of regret for the children may be conventional but not the
attack on the unnoticing "Father." Even before her years of crisis Dick-
inson has laid out the terms of her argument with such a God.

In the prolific years 1862–65 the victims of God's indifference are
sometimes Dickinson's speakers themselves. In such poems she dram-
atizes her own suffering and anger more immediately than she has ven-
tured to do earlier. For example, in the marvelous "'Twas like a Mael-
strom, with a notch" (P 414), God takes his own sweet time to provide
a pittance of relief for the speaker's "Agony":

And not a Sinew – stirred – could help,
And sense was setting numb –

When God – remembered – and the Fiend
Let go, then, Overcome –

The dashes around "remembered" deftly mimic God's delay; he is too loftily distant from human suffering to remember it sooner. In another poem dated 1862, perhaps written as a commentary (it would bely the tone to call it an elegy) on the battle death of Frazar Stearns, Dickinson returns derisively to Jesus' claim in Luke 12 that God is mindful of sparrows and thus how much more of humankind.

690

Victory comes late –
And is held low to freezing lips –
Too rapt with frost
To take it –
How sweet it would have tasted –
Just a Drop –
Was God so economical?
His Table's spread too high for Us –
Unless We dine on tiptoe –
Crumbs – fit such little mouths –
Cherries – suit Robins –
The Eagle's Golden Breakfast strangles – Them –
God keep His Oath to Sparrows –
Who of little Love – know how to starve – [12]

God's bounty is "spread too high for *Us*," not just for the dying warrior but also for the rest of us, for whom the warrior's deprivation is emblematic. As Ahab puts it, "there can be no hearts above the snowline."[13] For a moment the speaker decides to think small—perhaps God will provide crumbs for little mouths. By the end of the poem, however, that strategy of limitation seems makeshift and useless. Though the Bible promises sparrows "little Love," even if they keep their appetites modest they starve anyway on what they get.

A poem like "Victory comes late" ought to remind us that the psychological tack Dickinson takes in "Success is counted sweetest" represents only one way she deals poetically with deprivation.[14]

Success is counted sweetest
By those who ne'er succeed.

> To comprehend a nectar
> Requires sorest need.
>
> (P 67, st. 1)

Sometimes comprehending leads to the bitterness of the sorely afflicted. Especially the orthodox justification of the way God's economy works, that our suffering in this life will enhance our enjoyment of the next, she treats with outraged contempt.

> Defeat whets Victory – they say –
> The Reefs – in old Gethsemane –
> Endear the Coast – beyond!
> 'Tis Beggars – Banquets can define –
> 'Tis Parching – vitalizes Wine –
> "Faith" bleats to understand!
>
> (P 313; version sent to Sue)

The "Faith" that relies on maxims such as these is a faith of wishful sheep. "The Reefs – in old Gethsemane – / Endear the coast – beyond!" recalls in its cadence the sentimental longing for a heavenly home often voiced in popular visionary hymns, but the sentiment has been turned into ridicule. The stanza reminds us to be cautious in crediting what "*they* say" anywhere in Dickinson.

> 'Tis Kingdoms – afterward – they say –
> In perfect – pauseless Monarchy –
> Whose Prince – is Son of None –
>
> (P 721)

"They" are the repressive guardians of childhood and society who forbid the poet her search for a "new circumference" (P 313) and offer as an alternative a heaven after death presided over by a Nobodaddy God.

Dickinson continues to be dismayed at God's heartless omnipotence into her last years. A well-known poem Johnson dates "about 1884" illustrates the staying power of her preoccupation.

1624

> Apparently with no surprise
> To any happy Flower

The Frost beheads it at it's play –
In accidental power –
The blonde Assassin passes on –
The Sun proceeds unmoved
To measure off another Day
For an Approving God.

The satire is terse and finished, but its range is far-reaching. The speaker chronicles not only the Frost's assassination of the happy Flower but also the Flower's lack of surprise. The poem acknowledges that natural things that attract us show no capacity for suffering or sympathy. Only humans can be shocked at the injustice of a world of death. We are lonely as well as bereft in the created universe.

If an omnipotent God is the author of pain and death, then to accuse humankind of sin is a stupendous impertinence. On other religious questions Dickinson may be glad to entertain inconsistencies; in her disdain for the doctrines of Original Sin and Total Depravity she hardly ever wavers. "'Sown in corruption'! / Not so fast! / Apostle is askew!" (P 62) she exclaims breathlessly in a poem of 1859, as if she were writing marginal comments in verse on Corinthians 1.15, a chapter of Paul's that deeply engaged her. Her late, finished satires on the received view that humankind is "the supreme iniquity" (P 1461) are more clever and less direct. I would single out a poem in which she not only ridicules this doctrine but attempts gnomically to imagine how human beings ever thought of it. Like "Who were 'the Father and the Son'" this poem seems retrospective. It seeks to fathom not so much her own experience as the ethical imagination of her culture. It is also another instance of the way the form of some of her most interesting poems follows the procedures of her consciousness. The poem begins as satire but ends as meditation.

1601

Of God we ask one favor,
That we may be forgiven –
For what, he is presumed to know –
The Crime, from us, is hidden –
Immured the whole of Life
Within a magic Prison
We reprimand the Happiness
That too competes with Heaven.

A key to reading the poem is understanding what Dickinson means by "we." Her use of the first-person plural is always interesting, for the reader must then ask in turn what community her speaker means to join. Here "we" seems to mean those persons brought up like Dickinson in a religion such as Trinitarian Protestant Christianity, both true believers and questioners like herself. The poem appears in a draft of a letter written in 1885 to Helen Hunt Jackson. Jackson was convalescing from a serious injury to her leg, and Dickinson prefaces the poem with the words, "Knew I how to pray, to intercede for your Foot were intuitive, but I am but a Pagan" (L, 3:867). Thus she insists on her difference from her culture as playfully and emphatically as she did in her second letter to Higginson in 1862, when she informed him concerning the other members of her family: "They are religious – except me – and address an Eclipse, every morning – whom they call their 'Father'" (L, 2:404). Jackson is an appropriate reader for the poem, since she was the daughter of an Amherst minister who was a figure of religious authority for Dickinson as a child. In this culture "we" ritually ask forgiveness, but there is no evidence for the general "Crime" we have supposedly committed.

The message in the first four lines is familiar in Dickinson's writings, and in conveying it her syntax is brisk, her treatment of meter predictable. In the second half of the poem, however, tone and style change. An obscurity that engages the reader to solve its riddles is created through indirect syntax (the reader must await an explanation of the initial phrase, "Immured the whole of life . . .") and through outlandish usage. By "reprimand the Happiness" Dickinson means that we condemn our happiness and reprimand ourselves in fear that we may prefer earthly life to glorifying God and enjoying him forever in heaven, as the catechism instructs.[15] More, we feel impelled to self-condemnation because we are "Immured . . . Within a magic Prison." Not only, as Emerson would say, are we ignorantly caught inside our own "temperament . . . a prison of glass which we cannot see,"[16] but this prison is magical—delightful as well as mysterious—and we cannot abide the mystery. The spirit of self-denial embedded in her culture coexisted with a retreat from the magic of inner mystery. Perhaps such self-denial permeates the social culture of human beings generally; we readers too may be afraid of the joys of our magic prisons and avoid the happiness that belongs to our natures. Emily Dickinson, however, grounded her authentic religious sense, even her vocation, on not retreating from mystery.

The Child of Faith

If Dickinson reacted so vigorously against her inherited Calvinism, how did she continue to find expression as a religious poet? For a religious poet she surely is and one who draws her imaginative strength and intensity both from a Calvinist tradition and from other contemporary religious currents available to her.

Though Dickinson testifies often to the "portentous" and "appalling" character of her education, she seems from other testimony to have learned belief as well as unbelief as a child. A concise indication of her memory of early faith as well as of the grounds of her continuing hope appears in one of the letters she wrote in 1883 to her sister-in-law Susan Dickinson after the shocking death of Susan's late-born and beloved son Gilbert.

> Awe is the first Hand that is held to us –
> Hopelessness in it's first Film has not leave
> to last – That would close the Spirit, and no
> intercession could do that –
> Intimacy with Mystery, after great Space, will
> usurp it's place –

(L, 3:800)

Dickinson here condenses key elements of the faith she seems to have wanted to have for herself and express to her friends. She claims that "the Spirit" cannot be "closed" or destroyed even by the most painful experience—though elsewhere she may worry about this possibility more than she acknowledges here. Nevertheless, her confidence that "intimacy with Mystery" will eventually reestablish itself helps to give direction to her poetry of pain. To assert such a faith as a means to consolation is part of her project. Moreover, if "Awe is the first Hand that is held to us," we are given an "intimacy with Mystery" early in our lives. Awe, the context suggests, is here the experience of the divine. Gilbert had that intimacy, Dickinson clearly implies in the letters she wrote Susan after his death,[17] and we who survive him can recover it.

In an 1881 letter to the Norcross sisters, occasioned by the death of George Eliot, Dickinson reiterates the conviction that "Belief" is "Inherited with Life" and comes naturally to childhood. She writes of Eliot; "the gift of belief which her greatness denied her, I trust she receives in the childhood of the kingdom of heaven. As childhood is earth's confiding time, perhaps having no childhood, she lost her way to the early trust, and no later came" (*L*, 3:700). The letter mediates Dickinson's grief for a lost sister and model and hides an anxious sense of identity with her as a fellow rebel and skeptic. From what we already know Dickinson's own childhood was not simply "earth's confiding time" but was also the time when "with inference appalling" she listened to the doctrines of Connecticut Valley Protestantism. Surely she projects her own uncertainty on Eliot as well as bestowing on her a sisterly trust. Nevertheless, the letter confirms both Dickinson's recurring intuitive faith in "the kingdom of heaven" and her often-expressed conviction that children are "intimate with Mystery." What that Mystery is, what childhood precisely confides in, she prefers not to make explicit. Her faith is not a matter of "doctrines."

Yet her vocation is partly to express and share that faith, as an alternative to bugbear Calvinism. In another late letter that expresses faith and proffers consolation she writes to Maria Whitney; "You speak of 'disillusion.' That is one of the few subjects on which I am an infidel. Life is so strong a vision, not one of it shall fail" (*L*, 3:794). In other words, "Life," when we grasp its true intensity, is a powerful stimulus to belief, and if we envision it properly with our imaginations we understand that it cannot fail us. "Life" is always "a magic Prison," an invitation to happiness. This late text makes clear that Dickinson's will to belief persists through all her times of anger, loss, and unbelief. Throughout her career she ruminates in particular poems and letters on the words that give meaning to her faith.

Such a faith in the subliminal presence of "Awe," the persistence of "Spirit," and the visionary character of "Life" is nonpartisan in its theology. These labile words represent a nimble style of having faith that cannot be circumscribed in sectarian categories. Though her faith is certainly unorthodox in its individuality, it also draws on Calvinist images and ideas as materials for poetry. At any point in her career Dickinson can, if it suits her, adopt an orthodox evangelical framework in which to imagine her faith. As her historically minded commentators have abundantly shown, she is a child of Amherst Calvinism even when she professes her skepticism or acts out her rebellion.[18] Whatever innocent piety she may have felt in childhood was reinforced in her schooling. Orthodox teachers at Amherst Academy under the intellectual leadership of Edward Hitchcock taught her to revere the Creator in his works,

a lesson she never rejected.[19] She absorbed enough "natural supernatu-
ralism" from Calvinist sources to last a lifetime, and her specific appli-
cation of this ideology can usually be traced to her early orthodox in-
struction. Her belief in a Christlike renunciation that brings spiritual
power is in accordance with the Edwardsean tradition in which she was
raised.[20] Yet at the same time she tries out ideas from New England lib-
eralism and nineteenth-century sentimentalism to help her imagine her
faith, and sometimes she launches forth on her own in her speculations
on religious questions. Moreover, as an enraptured student of nature
and a believer in the importance of poetry, she is a vehicle for ideas and
images she absorbed from English and American Romantic writings. In-
deed, in her own way she is one of the most incisive and adventurous
Romantic poet-thinkers. The resulting medley of thought makes her
faith difficult to analyze. Nevertheless, in my view her thinking has its
own integrity. I will isolate three elements that she seems persistently to
associate with one another as the grounds of her believing imagination.

First, she has faith in a God who is indeed a "better Friend," a God
of love rather than wrath. When she consoles her correspondents in her
letters, she may well invoke such a God. For example, she writes Mrs.
Holland in 1881, two months after Dr. Holland's death, "God bless the
hearts that suppose they are beating and are not, and enfold in His
infinite tenderness those that do not know they are beating and are" (L,
3:721). She would share here a God of infinite tenderness. Sometimes
she simply assumes the existence of a benevolent God without trying to
justify him. Considering her hostility to "the Father" elsewhere, such an
unqualified assumption is remarkable. In "Publication – is the Auction
/ Of the Mind of Man" (P 709), in which her main business is to ration-
alize her decision to keep her poetry to herself, she invokes a familiar
God as her support as if questions concerning his benevolent effective-
ness never entered her mind. After claiming her readiness to go "White
– Unto the White Creator," the speaker explains; "Thought belong to
Him who gave it – / Then – to Him Who bear / It's Corporeal illustra-
tion." The Creator, it seems, has given the poet "Thought," of which he
(she) is its earthly vehicle. The speaker pronounces this sentiment in a
tone of perfect conviction. Faithfully she voices a Neoplatonic humility
before a divinity who is the fount of all creative expression.

Dickinson frequently turns to Jesus as the congenial friend whom
she can extract from her local theology. She expresses at times a faith in
his exemplary saving power that is quite within the bounds of evangel-

ical Protestantism in nineteenth-century New England.[21] This Jesus is a
tender savior who loves humankind, who died to redeem us and infuse
us with love. In a letter of 1862 she uses the example of Jesus to illustrate
her idea of gratitude for the Norcross sisters. "Gratitude is not the men-
tion of a tenderness, but its mute appreciation, deeper than we reach –
all our LORD demands, who sizes better than we. Willing unto death, if
only we perceive He die" (L, 2:417). As usual, Dickinson makes an orig-
inal adaptation of a story she tells. This Jesus is a teacher of isolated
hearts (like the Dickinsons and the Norcrosses) asking for the acknowl-
egment of his humanity. He seeks their "mute appreciation" and en-
gaged perception, their poetic interest in his example and fate. Yet in or-
thodox capitals she also calls him "our LORD," a loving God who died
as a man that we might know and trust him.

One of Dickinson's most trusting celebrations of Jesus even goes so
far as briefly to countenance something somehow like a doctrine of In-
nate Depravity and Original Sin.

964

"Unto Me?" I do not know you –
Where may be your House?

"I am Jesus – Late of Judea –
Now – of Paradise" –

Wagons – have you – to convey me?
This is far from Thence –

"Arms of Mine – sufficient Phaeton –
Trust Omnipotence" –

I am spotted – "I am Pardon" –
I am small – "The Least
Is esteemed in Heaven the Chiefest –
Occupy my House" –

Not only does this Jesus identify himself with "Omnipotence," but he
also thinks of himself as "Pardon," as the Pardoner. When the speaker
calls herself "spotted," she implicitly asks that she may be forgiven, an
indulgence in orthodox humility that Dickinson nowhere else permits
her surrogates, as far as I know. The thought is not typical of her, even
when she depicts a loving Christ.[22] As we will see in the next chapter,

however, she experiments with several images of Jesus. His character is not fixed any more than is God the Father's in her imagination. She can be as questioning of tradition in dramatizing him as she is here orthodox. Her poetry of faith remains flexible and heuristic, a poetry that experiments with beliefs as well as expressing them.

Second, Dickinson often dramatizes the presence of divinity in her perceptions of nature. As we will see in detail in chapter 4, her sense of nature as unknown stimulates her faith. A straightforward early work that displays her preoccupation with divinity in nature is Poem 155.

> The Murmur of a Bee
> A Witchcraft – yieldeth me –
> If any ask me why –
> 'Twere easier to die –
> Than tell –
>
> The Red upon the Hill
> Taketh away my will –
> If anybody sneer –
> Take care – for God is here –
> That's all.
>
> The Breaking of the Day
> Addeth to my Degree –
> If any ask me how –
> Artist – who drew me so –
> Must tell!

This is one of the early Dickinson's songs of innocence, with its biblical resonance of idiom, its deliberate simplicity of sentiment, and its projection of a landscape where one encounters God as a friend. The speaker assumes the wondering openness of a child and invokes a God in whom she confides without hesitation. Her confiding generosity is what makes the poem work, along with its metrical subtlety, especially in the last stanza, where the modulation of open half-rhymes intimates the presence of the sophisticated poet behind the childlike speaker. The thematic emphasis on inner transformation following on natural delight, voiced simply here, persists through all of Dickinson's poems of faith in the experience of nature. What moves the speaker is the "internal difference" (P 258) she feels in herself. She has these responses because she is constituted to have them, created to grow in "Degree" (and in grace) when "The Red upon the Hill / Taketh away my will." An "Artist drew" her so that she would be capable of what Dickinson elsewhere calls transport. The witchcraft is in her, not in the bee.

Dickinson's faith in nature is fundamentally a faith in the imagination of nature. However much she valued the stimulus of the external embodied world, she understood clearly that the divinity she perceived there had meaning only in consciousness. The search for divinity in the self is the subject of one of the most adventurous of her prose fragments.

> Paradise is no Journey because it (he) is within – but for that very cause though – it is the most Arduous of Journeys – because as the Servant Conscientiously says at the Door We are (always – invariably –) out – (*PF,* 99; *L,* 3:926)

Dickinson accepts the Miltonic injunction to labor for "a paradise within thee, happier far"[23] but understands better than Milton how internally arduous that labor must be, given the insights of her Romantic century. We do not have easy access to the within; "we are invariably out" when we seek it. A condition of the journey is that the paradise we would discover is unknown to our ordinary selves. Yet she has faith in its existence and in the human capacity to journey toward it. All the more reason, then, to accept the intimations of divinity and paradise that occur in our experience of nature, a key dimension of our embodied journey.

As this fragment suggests, a third article of Dickinson's intuitive faith is her belief in the human capacity to imagine a paradise, in our life on earth and sometimes beyond it. This power she also sometimes associates with childhood. In one poem she follows Wordsworth's *Intimations* ode in mourning a lost "Dominion" and recalling the "Delinquent Palaces" whence she came. I quote the first two stanzas.

959

A loss of something ever felt I –
The first that I could recollect
Bereft I was – of what I knew not
Too young that any should suspect

A Mourner walked among the children
I notwithstanding went about
As one bemoaning a Dominion
Itself the only Prince cast out –

She appropriates the *Intimations* ode like a typical reader-poet of her American Romantic age, drawing in her own way on the age's belief in the poetic child's closeness to Eden and Eternity. Characteristically, Dickinson's speaker recalls that she did not know the something she felt she had lost. The poem conveys to her reader the speaker's baffled solitary sense of the unknown.

If on this occasion Dickinson regrets the loss of her vision of paradise, she is more often prone to write as if such a vision were perpetually available. In early poems, again, she evokes the vision lyrically and unselfconsciously, as if to confirm that faith in paradise is a gift of childhood that survives in the writing of poetry. Such a faith is manifested in this poem transcribed in 1858.

7

The feet of people walking home
With gayer sandals go –
The Crocus – till she rises
The Vassal of the snow –
The lips at Hallelujah
Long years of practise bore
Till bye and bye these Bargemen
Walked singing on the shore . . .
. . . .
My figures fail to tell me
How far the Village lies –
Whose peasants are the Angels –
Whose Cantons dot the skies –
My Classics vail their faces –
My faith that Dark adores –
Which from it's solemn abbeys
Such resurrection pours.

(st. 1 and 3)

This too is a "song of innocence" with a childlike speaker and a vision of communal happiness in a landscape of paradise that fuses earth and heaven. Here the "people walking home" or "singing on the shore" seem transfigured familiar Saints who walk in grace and are bound for heaven, emblems of happiness nurtured in a Calvinist imagination. Characteristically, however, Dickinson moves in and out of the familiar

imaginative structures of Calvinist culture. She presents a feudally con-
ceived heavenly "Village" with angels as peasants (she likes feudal dis-
tinctions in her imaginary realms), and she insists even this early that
the mysteries she covets be available to the imagination but unknown
to the intellect. "My faith that Dark adores," she asserts in an eloquently
brooding line. She prefers her classics veiled and her figures luminously
obscure, prefers not to know the precise contours of the poetic paradise
she envisions.

A poem transcribed in 1860 draws similarly on images of heaven
assumed by her culture.

157

Musicians wrestle everywhere –
All day – among the crowded air
I hear the silver strife –
And – waking – long before the morn –
Such transport breaks upon the town
I think it that "New life"!

It is not Bird – it has no nest –
Nor "Band" – in brass and scarlet – drest –
Nor Tamborin – nor Man –
It is not Hymn from pulpit read –
The "Morning Stars" the Treble led
On Time's first Afternoon!

Some – say – it is "the Spheres" – at play!
Some say – that bright Majority
Of vanished Dames – and Men!
Some – think it service in the place
Where we – with late – celestial face –
Please God – shall Ascertain!

Here it is still clearer that the speaker herself has felt the transport im-
manent in her atmosphere and that she entertains traditional explana-
tions for these perceptions of divinity without necessarily endorsing
them. She *thinks* it "that 'New Life'" because the language of revival-
ism helps her form a conception of the experience, yet the music "is not
Hymn from pulpit read" nor even the rejoicing of the morning stars at
creation (see Job 38.7). "Some say" it is the music of "the Spheres," but

theirs is only an inspired guess. All the speaker distinctly acknowledges is her own experience of hearing the silver strife in the crowded air, along with her wish to know the meaning of that music if she gets to heaven. Yet she makes use of the language of Protestant hymns and the Bible to communicate her faith in a paradise unknown.

In another poem transcribed in 1858 Dickinson envisions paradise without benefit of Christianity. As Sandra Gilbert and Susan Gubar have argued, this image of paradise can be read as Romantic and feminist, even as pagan.[24] I quote the first two stanzas:

24

There is a morn by men unseen –
Whose maids upon remoter green
Keep their Seraphic May –
And all day long, with dance and game,
And gambol I may never name –
Employ their holiday.

Here to light measure, move the feet
Which walk no more the village street –
Nor by the wood are found –
Here are the birds that sought the sun
When last year's distaff idle hung
And summer's brows were bound.

This echoing green, on which dancing maids celebrate their happiness on a May morning, appears quite unencumbered with the trappings of Calvinism. Yet it still bears a family resemblance to the other images of paradise the early Dickinson entertains. As no one can "tell" why the murmur of a bee yields "A Witchcraft" to a receptive observer, so this speaker "may never name" the gambol she envisions. However pictorially vivid, the dance is purely imaginary; like "the silver strife," it is an image for the unknown joys of a paradise within or for the pleasures of a personal kingdom of heaven. It takes place "unseen," upon a "remoter" or "mystic" green. Perhaps it represents an encounter in imagination with the dead, with those who "walk no more the village street," or with "vanished Dames and Men." Taken together with these other early poems, "There is a morn" confirms Dickinson's readiness to have faith in her own intimations of divinity and displays her ability to find a rhetoric that will convey her enthusiasm for them. If Calvinism lent itself to the expression of these intimations, she would use it, but she would not bind herself inside it. Indeed, she might for the nonce be a faithful pagan if that better expressed the music she heard.

In these early undoctrinal poems, then, Dickinson experiments with the textual traditions of her culture and ornaments them with discoveries of her own imagination. In all of the poems a speaker draws images of paradise from her experience of earthly life yet also envisions a paradise that is a foretaste of a heaven after death. Dickinson's faith in paradise often brings to her mind the possibility of heaven. Sometimes her confidence in heaven seems another article of her faith, as famously in "I never saw a Moor – ":

> I never spoke with God
> Nor visited in Heaven –
> Yet certain am I of the spot
> As if the Checks were given –
>
> (P 1052)

Yet the speaker of these lines is a child in her simplicity, a representative of only one side of the poet, whose views of heaven were far from simple or certain. Heaven is perhaps the preeminent unknowable subject in which Dickinson is ready to believe and disbelieve alternatively over the course of her career. She is repeatedly obsessed with the possibility of an afterlife without definitively deciding on its nature or even its reality.

Dickinson can be quite traditional in her imagination of the afterlife. In "You'll know it – as you know 'tis Noon – " (P 420), for example, she encourages her reader to anticipate the knowledge of a traditional and familiar heaven with serene confidence. She also celebrates an entirely different conception of the Father and the Son from the appalling version of them she presents in more skeptical writings. Yet at the same time she remains true here to the tenets of her intuitive faith.

> You'll know it – as you know 'tis Noon –
> By Glory –
> As you do the Sun –
> By Glory –

As you will in Heaven –
Know God the Father – and the Son.

By intuition, Mightiest Things
Assert themselves – and not by terms –
"I'm Midnight" – need the Midnight say –
"I'm Sunrise" – Need the Majesty?
Omnipotence – had not a Tongue –
His lisp – is Lightning – and the Sun –
His Conversation – with the Sea –
"How shall you know"?
Consult your Eye!

In other texts in which she quarrels with God as the author of death, she distrusts his very omnipotence. Here she celebrates it, and only a sublime creativity flows from it. Similarly, the poem looks forward to heavenly "Glory" as rapturously as a revivalist hymn. Yet, though the poem's framework is orthodox, its chief thematic point is one congenial to her undoctrinal faith. One knows "Mightiest Things" by intuition: God Himself, the Sun he creates, and the unnamed "it" that is the initial subject of the poem, whose meaning we divine only by analogy.[25]

At other times, however, her conceptions of heaven can be gently or wildly heretical, as in her many poems in which she envisions a reunion with a lover she has been forbidden fully to love on earth. Such a heaven for lovers is a special development of her imagination of paradise. The marvelous poem "There came a Day at Summer's full" (P 322), for example, is gently heretical in its projection of the lovers' salvation.

There came a Day at Summer's full,
Entirely for me –
I thought that such were for the Saints,
Where Resurrections – be –

The Sun, as common, went abroad,
The flowers, accustomed, blew,
As if no soul the solstice passed
That maketh all things new –

The time was scarce profaned, by speech –
The symbol of a word

Was needless, as at Sacrament,
The Wardrobe – of our Lord –

Each was to each The Sealed Church,
Permitted to commune this – time –
Lest we too awkward show
At Supper of the Lamb.

The Hours slid fast – as Hours will,
Clutched tight, by greedy hands –
So faces on two Decks, look back,
Bound to opposing lands –

And so when all the time had leaked,
Without external sound
Each bound the Other's Crucifix –
We gave no other Bond –

Sufficient troth, that we shall rise –
Deposed – at length, the Grave –
To that new Marriage,
Justified – through Calvaries of Love –

In incantatory language and imagery the poem evokes a personal gospel of justification through suffering and aesthetic sensitivity.[26] The lovers commune in a divine and supernatural light that only they can receive and recognize. The speaker sets herself apart from "the Saints" and makes her summer's day an exclusive personal possession, a day that "came . . . Entirely for me."

Yet in order to imagine this paradisial experience Dickinson appropriates Protestant language and ritual. The poem's Protestant idiom is concentrated but idiosyncratic. The solstice of souls "maketh all things new." The lovers "commune," even if not "At Supper of the Lamb." Most interestingly, speech between the lovers is "needless, *as at* Sacrament, / The Wardrobe – of our Lord – " (my emph.). In such phrasing the poem wavers between conformity and distanced bemusement. It reverences "our Lord" but uses "Sacrament" only as an explanatory metaphor for the feeling the lovers share in their wordless epiphany. And when Dickinson calls the sacrament a "Wardrobe," she teases the reader with a flicker of ironic hilarity. The idea is familiar—the service of Holy Communion assumes that Christ dressed himself in flesh and blood—but the phrasing is archly bemused at itself. Yet in context Dickinson's touch is so light that her speaker's archness dissolves noiselessly into reverence. She hopes convincingly for her own resurrection and marriage to the lover in heaven. At the poem's end the lovers (eccentrically but reverently) exchange crucifixes instead of rings as tokens of their bond.

> Sufficient troth, that we shall rise –
> Deposed – at length, the Grave –
> To that new Marriage,
> Justified – through Calvaries of Love –

Again Dickinson plays tricks with conventional Christian language and imagery. The pun on "Deposed – at length" (meaning both "dethroned at last" and "laid flat at length") subtly undercuts the narrative in these lines and redeems them from their ardent sentimentality. However crucial the experience on which the poem is based may have been for her personally, Dickinson keeps her distance from the speaker, who as in all her best dramatic poems is "a supposed person" (*L,* 2:412).[27] The poem celebrates and also contemplates a fantasy of heaven that Dickinson can nevertheless put aside when she next writes a poem in which heaven is treated skeptically.

The advantage Dickinson has poetically in not definitively believing or disbelieving in heaven is that she can entertain a variety of ideas concerning the afterlife and represent them in a variety of separate dramas with points of view sufficient unto themselves. On occasion she may try out several scenarios for the afterlife in the course of a single poem. "I cannot live with You" (P 640), one of her greatest poems, is constructed not only to express the speaker's passionate love and intimate despair but also to represent her vacillation among different images of heaven. As she projects a life for herself and her lover after death, she is moved to invent a series of scenes in which their intimacy is frustrated.

> Nor could I rise – with You –
> Because Your Face
> Would put out Jesus' –
> That New Grace

Grow plain – and foreign
On my homesick Eye –
Except that You than He
Shone closer by –

They'd judge Us – How –
For You – served Heaven – You know,
Or sought to –
I could not –

Because You saturated Sight –
And I had no more Eyes
For sordid excellence
As Paradise

And were You lost, I would be –
Though My Name
Rang loudest
On the Heavenly fame –

And were You – saved –
And I – condemned to be
Where You were not –
That self – were Hell to Me –

(st. 6–11)

"I cannot live with You – " is grandly heretical in its transfiguration of
the lover, whose "Face / Would put out Jesus'" and eclipse such a "sor-
did excellence / As Paradise." Yet it too relies on the familiar myths of
Dickinson's religious upbringing in order to deviate from them. Ac-
cording to this teaching, the dead will "rise" after death to face God's
judgment. The saved will enjoy eternal happiness in heaven, while the
damned will suffer eternal torment in hell. In addition, the saved will
be rewarded with a gracious vision of Christ's godly face, which on
earth would have "saturated Sight"; as Dickinson writes elsewhere,
"None see God and live" (P 1247). All this scenario Dickinson here
refigures dramatically to exalt the lover and the beloved. Heaven and
hell become states of mind the speaker imagines for herself. Paradise be-
comes a hypothetical realm she can celebrate, exploit, and renounce for
the sake of her heretical passion.

Liberalism

Dickinson is a child of her questioning age as well as of Congregationalist orthodoxy. As one might expect of a person with spiritual gifts and literary ambitions growing up in Amherst before midcentury, she was deeply affected by the currents of liberal religion that seeped even into such a backwater conservative stronghold. In her writing she uses liberal ideas not only as weapons with which to combat local conservatism but also as a means to her own faith. She is not a student of only one particular variety of liberalism such as Transcendentalism, nor exclusively a follower of one individual thinker like Emerson. Instead, liberalism came to her from many sources: from liberal-minded novels she read as an adolescent such as Longfellow's *Kavanagh*;[28] from liberal periodicals such as the *Atlantic Monthly;* from her readings in Emerson, Carlyle, Thoreau, and Theodore Parker; from women's texts such as Barrett Browning's *Aurora Leigh* that emphasize women's capacity for independent speculation; from her readings in other intellectually adventurous British writers like George Eliot; from relatively open-minded Congregationalist friends like Dr. and Mrs. Holland; and from Unitarians she knew—in particular, Benjamin Newton, who first believed in her as a poet and gave her Emerson's *Poems,* perhaps Mary Bowles, with whom she shared her rebellious appreciation of Parker, certainly Thomas Wentworth Higginson, to whom she confided her religious differences with her family in early letters.

All of these influences helped to open the fortress of thought constructed by Connecticut Valley Calvinists such as Jonathan Edwards, Noah Webster, and Mary Lyon—and not only for Dickinson herself. Under the stress of liberal influences the intellectual climate of Amherst was more variable than it seems at first glance.[29] Even other members of her family, though adhering to the Congregational Church, were not immune to liberalism. Austin and Susan entertained Emerson at the Evergreens and gloried in it (respectability papered over intellectual differences in New England towns). Austin in particular as a young man was as troubled as his sister by the doctrine of Limited Atonement (Christ died to redeem only the Elect) and late in life continued to be a closet skeptic. Dickinson's father himself, just before he died, gave her copies of George Eliot's *Poems* and Frothingham's *Life of Theodore Parker.* Such a gift belies his reputation for inflexible conservatism and even suggests that he occasionally listened to her.

Of course, Dickinson's openness to liberalism did not remove her from the New England Calvinist sources of her imagination. She knew the Bible far more intimately than most of her liberal contemporaries. She used the language of revivalism far more immediately and naturally than might easterners like Thoreau or Higginson. She imagined Christ and heaven in ways that Emerson would certainly not have chosen for himself. Nevertheless, especially in her young womanhood she was on the lookout for friends and writers who would mitigate the rigors of her ancestral religion. After Dr. Holland's death in 1881 Dickinson recalled for his wife her first visit to the Hollands in 1853: "I shall never forget the Doctor's prayer, my first morning with you – so simple, so believing. *That* God must be a friend – *that* was a different God – and I almost felt warmer myself, in the midst of a tie so sunshiny" (*L*, 3:713). "A different God," a God who "must be a friend"—that was what she wanted from liberalism.

Dickinson was drawn to liberal-minded spokesmen such as Dr. Holland or to ministers who might represent authority differently from the clergymen whom she had heard preaching doctrines she disliked. Sewall relates how in 1854 "when Dr. Holland lectured in Amherst on 'Manhood' . . . a reporter in the *Hampshire and Franklin Express* scolded him sharply for his 'creedless, churchless, ministerless christianity, so called.'"[30] Such a Christianity appealed to Dickinson. In 1861, when the Norcross sisters apparently shared with her their enthusiasm for a new liberal clergyman in Cambridge, Dickinson wrote; "I regret I am not a scholar in the Friday class. I believe the love of God may be taught not to seem like bears. Happy the reprobates under that loving influence" (*L*, 2:372).[31] She too was a self-proclaimed reprobate who prospered under kindly influences. Similarly, in 1877 Dickinson wrote Mrs. Holland, "I am glad if you love your Clergyman . . . God seems much more friendly through a hearty Lens" (*L*, 2:576). Of course, sympathetic Congregationalist ministers like Edwards Amasa Park, Charles Wadsworth, and Jonathan Jenkins might deeply engage her so long as they left her intuitive faith more or less undisturbed; she was ecumenically open to "masters" of different persuasions and especially susceptible to the imaginative appeal of Calvinist enthusiasts. Yet throughout her life her writings attest to her resentment at sermons that "condemned" rather than "captivated" (P 1545) and attest also to her welcoming interest in alternatives to a censorious Calvinism.

What did liberalism do to and for Emily Dickinson? To speak generally, it encouraged her to discover a more open-minded religious outlook, while at the same time it unsettled her, made her beliefs more volatile. Liberalism liberated her from terror but also opened up a Pandora's box of contradictory possibilities. She was subject to contradictory strains within it. I have sketched her "liberalism" broadly, because it seems to me that all of these strains—sentimentalism, "ministerless christianity" like Dr. Holland's, Unitarianism, Emersonian Transcendentalism, the Christian feminism of Barrett Browning, and the free-thinking of George Eliot—tended to dislodge her from her Calvinist roots and to encourage her in her own religious speculations, tended above all to help her make her own moral argument against Calvinism and formulate alternative and more sympathetic ideas of God.

Yet different historical movements sometimes pulled her in different directions. Sentimentalism allowed her to make her religion more tenderly emotional. She conspired in her own way in "the feminization of American culture,"[32] preferring emotional appeals to doctrinal rigor in sermons, participating in the cult of a tender-hearted Jesus, asserting the saving innocence of children—especially dying children. In other ways, however, liberal influence made her more hard-headed and rationalistic. We will see in the next chapter how she struggled with the implications of "the Higher Criticism" of the Bible, the movement to scrutinize more precisely its claims to literal and historical truth. To her friends she sometimes paraded her openness to such unorthodox ideas. For example, in 1880 she whimsically related an anecdote to Mrs. Holland showing how much more "advanced" she and Austin were than their benighted mother.

> Austin and I were talking the other Night about the Extension of Consciousness, after Death and Mother told Vinnie, afterward, she thought it was "very improper."
> She forgets that we are past "Correction in Righteousness–"
> I dont know what she would think if she knew that Austin told me confidentially "there was no such person as Elijah." (L, 3:667)

Such an excerpt demonstrates sufficiently what a swirl of speculation she entertained in her liberated mind: "the Extension of Consciousness, after Death" instead of mere salvation or damnation; a Bible whose truth was to be conceived imaginatively rather than literally. No wonder she was prone to "believe and disbelieve a hundred times an Hour."

Yet if her intellectual liberation led to uncertainties, it also opened up imaginative possibilities. The skeptical strain within liberalism, for example, reinforced her resolute this-worldliness that competed throughout her career with her imaginative interest in the afterlife. Like Thoreau, she wished to celebrate "the gift of life."[33] She shared with him an anger at institutional religion that denies this life, and harbored on her own an anger at the God of Calvinism for taking life from us. Yet her affirmation of this world did not stem only from her dislike of a doctrinal system that treated it contemptuously. We recall that she wrote, "Life is so strong a vision, not one of it shall fail." She believed imaginatively in the human and natural world in which she lived her "Life," however much she may have cut herself off from human society and however often she turned to images of a paradise after death. Her adherence to this world, not the next, gets expressed as early as 1859, in a poem where she discounts the idea of "going to Heaven":

I'm glad I dont believe it –
For it would stop my breath,
And I'd like to look a little more
At such a curious Earth!

(P 79; text of copy to Sue)

And again as late as 1885, when she thanks friends for a Christmas letter by sharing with them a spinsterly Promethean sentiment: "A Letter is a joy of Earth – It is denied the Gods – " (L, 3:855).[34]

Such this-worldliness surfaces several times in Dickinson's letters of the early and middle 1870s. In April 1873, for example, after claiming blasphemously that George Eliot is a "mortal" who "has already put on immortality," she adds, "The mysteries of human nature surpass the 'mysteries of redemption,' for the infinite we only suppose, while we see the finite" (L, 2:506). She not only prefers human nature here to redemption in another world but undermines Paul, who could rejoice only in the prospect of immortality after the trumpet sounds at the Last Judgment. Paul's text is: "The dead shall be raised incorruptible, and we shall be changed. For this corruptible must put on incorruption, and this mortal must put on immortality" (1 Cor. 15.52–53). Dickinson expresses her readiness to reconceive this same text in another letter of 1873, to Mrs. Holland. Before she wrote Vinnie had just returned from a visit to the Hollands:

Vinnie says you are most illustrious and dwell in Paradise. I have never believed the latter to be a superhuman site.

Eden, always eligible, is peculiarly so this noon. It would please you to see how intimate the Meadows are with the Sun. . . .

While the Clergyman tells Father and Vinnie that "this Corruptible shall put on Incorruption" – it has already done so and they go defrauded. (*L*, 2:508)

Father, Vinnie, and the Clergyman "go defrauded" because they are misled by their beliefs to shut their eyes to the holiness of what they can see around them.[35]

Sometimes her this-worldliness could generate an abrasive skepticism toward the very idea of a paradise with "a superhuman site." In 1877 she sent her fellow skeptic Austin a short poem that bristles with outraged contentiousness. It is the only later poem that we know she addressed to him; perhaps she assumed that he would agree with it.

1408

The Fact that Earth is Heaven –
Whether Heaven is Heaven or not
If not an Affidavit
Of that specific Spot
Not only must confirm us
That it is not for us
But that it would affront us
To dwell in such a place –

The emphasis on "Fact" here reminds us that Dickinson could voice a defiant empiricism when she chose. She virtually moves into the House of Prose to vent her exasperation. More often, instead of scornfully condemning the notion of a heaven beyond, she lyrically evokes the heavenliness of earth, especially in poems that intimate the divinity latent in a human perception of nature.

I will focus on a well-known poem that seems to me to express such a vision. It illustrates how Dickinson could touch base with Transcendentalist ideas in poems of faith in nature.[36]

1241

The Lilac is an ancient shrub
But ancienter than that

The Firmamental Lilac
Upon the Hill tonight –
The Sun subsiding on his Course
Bequeathes this final Plant
To Contemplation – not to Touch –
The Flower of Occident.
Of one Corolla is the West –
The Calyx is the Earth –
The Capsules burnished Seeds the Stars –
The Scientist of Faith
His research has but just begun –
Above his synthesis
The Flora unimpeachable
To Time's Analysis –
"Eye hath not seen" may possibly
Be current with the Blind
But let not Revelation
By theses be detained –

detained –] profaned –

Implicit in the serene opening is an Emersonian sentiment. As Dickinson writes in an Emersonian vein in one of her letters; "I saw the sunrise on the Alps since I saw you. Travel why to Nature, when she dwells with us? Those who lift their hats shall see her, as devout do God" (*L,* 2:455). In the poem the speaker hardly needs to travel beyond her window to find the ancient lilac in the sunset. Dickinson, however, is much readier than Emerson to transfigure what she sees with the eye of imagination and dissolve the outlines of objects by making them fugitive items in continually shifting analogies: the lilac as shrub expands magically into a firmamental lilac that encompasses the whole horizon. Yet she uses this analogical style for a Romantic Transcendentalist purpose, to envision the unity of nature in its particular details. Her style gives credence to her sentiment that nature is a living whole when it is perceived imaginatively, while at the same time she grounds that sentiment in the detail of her orthodox botany textbook.[37] The sunset transforms the envisioned world to the likeness of a single flower, displayed in its botanical elements. Such a "Flora" is not available to ordinary scientific "Analysis," bound as it is by a merely empirical conception of time.[38] In a liberated age we need science, but let it be a science of faith, the science of Emerson's "best read naturalist" who learns of "his relation to the world . . . by untaught sallies of the spirit,"[39] a science "the research" for which we have "just begun."

Yet orthodox readers of the Bible, detained by "theses," are as blind as mere empiricists to what is before them. They "profane Revelation" (as the variant reading suggests) and fail to understand that in the sunset a revelation is sweetly bequeathed to their contemplation. One has only to open one's contemplative eyes to see the revealed holiness. Dickinson's sentiment can be glossed by Blake's in *The Marriage of Heaven and Hell:* "If the doors of perception were cleansed every thing would appear to man as it is, infinite."[40] Indeed, Dickinson comes still closer to Blake in a well-known passage from a letter to Higginson of 1863. "I was thinking, today – as I noticed, that the 'Supernatural,' was only the Natural, disclosed –

> Not 'Revelation' – 'tis – that waits,
> But our unfurnished eyes – "
>
> (*L,* 2:424)

The faith expressed in "The Lilac is an ancient shrub" epitomizes the syncretic alternative religion Dickinson sometimes adopted for herself. Though in her language and imagery she draws on the Bible and on scientific terms she learned at school, her thought partially coincides with that of earlier Romantics like Emerson and Blake. Yet she did not need to go to them for the conviction that "Eden" was "always eligible," much less for the hymn meter and revivalist idiom that measure and color her thought. Her tone is bemused and serenely persuasive here in differentiating her views from those of her local culture, as if she would invite even her Calvinist readers to share her pleasure in her imagination of this world.

Since "childhood is earth's confiding time," it is significant that Dickinson in her last years tried to pass on her alternative faith in a loving Jesus, an approachable God, and an imaginatively transfigured nature to Austin and Susan's two sons and daughter, the children with whom she was most comfortable and intimate. She could hardly be systematic or philosophical with the six-year-old Gilbert Dickinson when she (reportedly) sent him a dead bee along with a poem, "The Bumble Bee's

Religion," that makes fun of "Industry and Morals / And every right-eous thing." Nevertheless, she added a postscript that shows her in-stilling her private sectarian opinions in him as early as possible.

> "All Liars shall have their part" –
> Jonathan Edwards – [41]
> "And let him that is athirst come" –
> Jesus –
>
> (*L*, 3:701; ca. 1881)

To the seventeen-year-old Mattie Dickinson (and her friend Sally Jenk-ins) she expressed herself more ecumenically, in a poem that allowed for "the Heaven of God" (P 569) as well as for her own earthly paradise. Yet the poem is also idiosyncratic in its theology. Affectionately and con-cisely, it voices a familiar variation of Dickinson's alternative faith.

> Who has not found the heaven – below –
> Will fail of it above –
> For Angels rent the House next our's,
> Wherever we remove –
>
> (*L*, 3:787; ca. 1883)

The Dickinson who learned belief as a child "met no one but Angels" when she walked in her imagined woods (*L*, 2:415), and their presence enabled her to project a heaven above when she chose to and share it here with her beloved fellow children.

To Ned, her older nephew, Dickinson was more expansive in voic-ing her liberalism. She sent him her anti-Calvinist satire, "'Heavenly Fa-ther' – take to thee / The supreme iniquity" as well as her "Diagnosis of the Bible, by a Boy –," a playful synopsis of the stories of Scripture as she reconceived them that begins, "The Bible is an antique Volume – / Written by faded Men," and ends:

> Had but the Tale a warbling Teller –
> All the Boys would come –
> Orpheus' Sermon captivated –
> It did not condemn –
>
> (P 1545)

In one of her last letters to Ned she expresses her satisfaction that he is happy "among . . . speechless Mountains" and that he "find[s] no treason in Earth or Heaven." Ned was vacationing in the Adirondacks, and his aunt rejoiced in his this-worldly contentment. She adds, "Your intimacy with the Mountains I heartily endorse – Ties more Eleusinian [intimately mysterious] I must leave to you – Deity will guide you – I do not mean Jehovah" (*L*, 3:880). As she separated her Jesus from Jonathan Edwards, so she distinguished her "Deity" from "Jehovah." In these messages to a younger generation she articulates her personal views and passes on her faith. As explicitly as anywhere, she makes clear that she has her own God who is not the God of her fathers.

Intimations of Beyond

Yet we should not leave the impression that Dickinson comes to anything like a single, clear resolution of her religious dilemmas.[42] Up to the end of her life she perseveres in a dialectic with herself, balancing her intuitive faith in human love, in natural renewal, and in a God of tenderness against her hostility to a God of sickness and death, "the enemy, 'eternal, invisible, and full of glory'" (*L*, 3:851). Her faith always gets expressed in the context of a world in flux. Even what she writes to Gilbert or Mattie or Ned in these late letters is occasional in import. Her messages in them are familiar; they reflect her passionate adoption of favorite attitudes; but on other occasions she may cast off these attitudes and struggle with despair or loss or unbelief. Moreover, always in the background of her affirming messages is her anxiety about death. While she may need the unknown hauntedness of nature or the unknown mysteriousness of God to stimulate her poetic expression, death is the terrifying unknown that challenges all faith and all expression.

Late in her life especially, Dickinson meditated on "the Extension of Consciousness, after Death." Since such a prospect is necessarily uncertain, it brings a new uncertainty to some of Dickinson's late writings that gives them in turn a new kind of expressiveness. In these particular poems and letters her lifelong dialectic between her intuitive faith and her quarrel with Calvinism subsides into the background. She is neither so infatuated with the "Eden always eligible" in earthly life nor so angry with a Calvinist God who causes death. Rather, she accepts that death must come. The mode of her writings on the extension of consciousness is questioning rather than angry. These late texts also dispense with playful or serious references to a conventional heaven. Dickinson is here no longer preoccupied with the destiny of "the Saints," nor does she focus on the private heaven she once imagined for herself and her lover. Instead, she contemplates and dramatizes a final encounter with the unknown as simply unknown. Earlier myths, whether those of her culture or of her own invention, are sacrificed to a preference for uncertainty.

At times Dickinson voiced a deep consolation at the prospect of an extension of consciousness. For example, in a letter of June 1878 she wrote Mrs. Holland; "How unspeakably sweet and solemn – that whatever await us of Doom or Home, we are mentally permanent. 'It is finished' can never be said of us" (*L*, 2:612). Though she does not here gainsay "Doom," she essentially counts on her belief in mental permanence to tide her over it. Similarly, after the death of her mother she could write to the Norcross sisters:

> She slipped from our fingers like a flake gathered by the wind, and is now part of the drift called "the infinite."
> We don't know where she is, though so many tell us.
> I believe we shall in some manner be cherished by our Maker – that the One who gave us this remarkable earth has the power still farther to surprise that which He has caused. Beyond that all is silence. (*L*, 3:750)

In this eloquent, shifting meditation Dickinson refuses to heed the insistence of "many" that her mother has gone to a conventional heaven; as she stubbornly insists, "we don't know where she is." She also makes frighteningly disparate the distance between living human beings, metonymically represented in "our fingers," and the infinite in which her mother is lost. Yet she offers in place of the usual heaven a consolation the more interesting for its originality. She chooses to believe in an unspecified continuum between earthly life and the afterlife and supposes the distance between them bridged by God's Emersonian "power still farther to surprise."[43] Moreover, God here is "our Maker," to whom she is grateful for "this remarkable earth"—she remembers her affection for this world even when she contemplates the uncertain beyond.

As we are permanent, so is God. In another letter of June 1878 she consoled Thomas Wentworth Higginson for the loss of his wife: "With the bloom of the flower your friend loved, I have wished for her, but God cannot discontinue himself" (*L*, 2:610). Though Mary Channing

Higginson can no longer be in touch with the joy of blooming things, Dickinson implies that she will somehow be sustained in the presence of an everlasting God. Yet in other writings God's mere permanence could seem a bleak prospect. In a prose fragment found in her papers Dickinson contemplates this prospect with ambivalence. She writes; "God cannot discontinue [annul] himself. This appalling trust is at times all that remains – " (*PF*, 34; *L*, 3:916). Such a God offers only "an appalling trust," not an assured belief in his remarkable creativity.

Dickinson may vacillate as she grapples with her future possibilities, but she comes back repeatedly to assertions such as "we are mentally permanent." The key to her power of recovery as she faces the unknown in these texts is her wish to say "we," to share a chastened and abstract but still consoling conception of the afterlife with those she loves. Her expression of this conception, however, includes an acknowledgment of our human uncertainty. As she writes enigmatically in a late letter-poem to Sue, "Faith is *Doubt*." The only way this speaker can have faith in "Eternity" is by questioning it. Yet she will not "foreclose Faith" because she trusts in the visionary permanence of her love for Sue and in the permanence, or "infinity," of Sue's being.

> Sister –
> Show me
> Eternity – and
> I will show
> you Memory –
> both in one
> package lain
> And lifted
> back again –
>
> Be Sue – while
> I am Emily –
> Be next – what
> you have ever
> been – infinity –[44]

The wish to connect "Eternity" to "Memory," to human life as remembered in the heart, is characteristic of a last group of poems I will now consider. All the poems are included in letters; hence all represent

Dickinson's intention to share her final questioning imagination of eternity with others. As a group, these poems vacillate repeatedly between doubt and faith in a precisely unspecific and abstract afterlife. Yet they also show Dickinson's determination to connect this world with the next and to affirm both worlds while not hiding her ignorance of the character of their connection. Thus she combines faith with doubt as she looks toward the end.

The first of the poems is a message of consolation, of scarcely perturbed faith in God's permanence. Dickinson sent the poem to several correspondents to reassure them of immortality after the death of a dear friend. It is the most grandly affirmative of the poems, though laced with its own complexity.

> Though the Great Waters sleep,
> That they are still the Deep,
> We cannot doubt –
> No Vacillating God
> Ignited this Abode
> To put it out –
>
> (P 1599; text from a letter to Sue, *L*, 3:828)

In "the Great Waters" Dickinson offers an image of immortality reflecting God's creative power, as often in the Psalms and originally in Genesis, where God divided the waters to make the world. They "sleep" by projection; humankind sleeps but also survives after death. Moreover, when the speaker asserts that "they are still the Deep," she suggests that the waters lastingly embody a spiritual mystery, as in the Psalmist's "Deep calleth unto deep" (Ps. 42.7). Having summoned the Great Waters as an image of permanence, however, Dickinson moves away from them. In the last three lines a world of waters becomes a world of fire in a deftly "sceneless" transformation,[45] the effect of which is to confirm that the poem is a personal mental construction, not a transparent statement of the way things are. The God of Genesis becomes the God who "Ignited this Abode," a God of Vulcanist geology.[46] Dickinson's duplex image of immortality is thus based on a scientific theory she adopted from the local arch-scientist Edward Hitchcock as well as on her poetic memory of the Bible. It synthesizes the actual world as we understand it naturalistically with a world beyond we can only know through imagination. Whether conceived as water or as fire or both, however, "this Abode" survives. The speaker conveys her passionate conviction of its living permanence.

Another poem of 1884 is expressive of her wondering doubt rather than her would-be-consoling faith. Dickinson sent it to the Norcross sisters in her first letter to them after a seizure that portended her final illness. On June 14 she blacked out and "saw a great darkness coming and knew no more until late at night. I woke . . . and supposed I was dying or had died" (*L,* 3:826). The poem seems prompted by such a foretaste of death.

> The going from a world we know
> To one a wonder still
> Is like the child's adversity
> Whose vista is a hill,
> Behind the hill is sorcery
> And everything unknown,
> But will the secret compensate
> For climbing it alone?
>
> (P 1603; text from *L,* 3:827)

Especially in a biographical context, what strikes one about the poem is its consciously voiced ambivalence concerning the afterlife. The speaker holds to her belief in another world without in any way ignoring her fear of the transition to it. The world we do not know is "a wonder still," which the speaker likens to the unseen farther side of a hill where a child may delight in "sorcery" and "secrets." Dickinson perseveres in imagining the world beyond as enchanting. Yet the solitary awareness of death, as for the younger Dickinson, is profoundly frightening as well as adventurous; it remains the "most profound experiment / Appointed unto Men" (P 822). The encounter with "everything unknown" may be magical or ghastly. Despite the poem's winsome idiom, the ending conveys a tremor of anxiety.

A somewhat earlier poem (ca. 1879), one of the best examples of Dickinson's late elliptical manner, combines affirmation and uncertainty in a delicate synthesis. This poem, signed "Easter," was in all likelihood sent to Sue, perhaps to convey Dickinson's own faith in a possible resurrection.[47]

1454

Those not live yet
Who doubt to live again –
"Again" is of a twice
But this – is one –
The Ship beneath the Draw
Aground – is he?
Death – so – the Hyphen of the Sea –
Deep is the Schedule
Of the Disk to be
Costumeless Consciousness –
That is he –

The meaning seems clear enough, though the idiom is gnomic, as if to advertise to the reader that the afterlife is a mystery best evoked mysteriously. The speaker first claims that faith in immortality is necessary to a full existence in this world. Then she corrects herself, illustrating Dickinson's penchant for exhibiting thought in process, and asserts that the life that spans present existence and whatever comes afterward "is one." Her image of present existence as part of a ubiquitous sea of immortality recalls the Great Waters that "are still the Deep."

Yet, despite this speaker's profession of faith in the oneness of all life, she is nagged by the awesomeness of the transition between life now and life "again." The imagery suggests human ignorance of this transition as well as of the afterlife itself. "Death" is "the Hyphen of the Sea – ." A hyphen is an inscrutable signifier in itself, even if one trusts that it leads beyond itself. Similarly, one cannot know but can only trust that "the Ship beneath the Draw" still survives and moves while it is blanked out from perception. Indeed, what is beyond the draw is itself inscrutable. "The Disk to be," like the hyphen, is a purposely opaque image, a mere geometric shape that follows an obscure "Schedule." With Charles Anderson it is helpful to identify the disk with the sun, summoning up the hope of resurrection promised in such an image as well as in the poem's subtitle. Then, however, one should respect the poem's language and put all such associations under erasure, since Dickinson only writes, "Disk," and keeps her sea of afterlife obscure, "deep" in that sense.[48] Unlike a sun a disk is bodiless, or at least one cannot know what bodily form it may take. Thus analogically "the Disk to be" can be translated into "Costumeless Consciousness"—both are analogies in words for an unknowable future state. The phrase "Costumeless Consciousness" is sybylline and eerie, yet the speaker affirms her faith in just such a bodiless and unknowable extended consciousness. One sacrifices the natural happiness of the bodily imagination in order to reach for an imagination of an undefinable immortality.

Yet the possible bodilessness of immortality could trouble Dickinson and her nostalgia for nature cling to her, impel her on another occasion to write a more troubled if still celebratory poem. Such a poem she sent to Charles H. Clark in 1883, ostensibly to commemorate their mutual friend Charles Wadsworth—but, indeed, Dickinson articulates here questions that are implicit in a number of her late texts. She begins her letter with an explanatory comment and then transcribes the poem.

Dear friend.

These thoughts disquiet me, and the great friend is gone, who could solace them. Do they disturb you?

> The Spirit lasts – but in what mode –
> Below, the Body speaks,
> But as the Spirit furnishes –
> Apart, it never talks –
> The Music in the Violin
> Does not emerge alone
> But Arm in Arm with Touch, yet Touch
> Alone – is not a Tune –
> The Spirit lurks within the Flesh
> Like Tides within the Sea
> That make the Water live, estranged
> What would the Either be?
>   (P 1576, ll. 1–12; text from *L,* 3:801–2)

These lines take for granted that "Spirit lasts." They restate, if with a difference of connotation that seems unimportant, Dickinson's belief that there is an "Extension of Consciousness, after Death." Yet, even while they look toward an afterworld, they celebrate the world of art and life that Dickinson has known. The speaker questions whether a disembodied spiritual existence has any attraction for her. Dickinson does not always show such a commitment to the importance of the body. At times she views the activity of the mind as wholly autonomous, as when she writes Higginson, "a Letter always feels to me like immortality because it is the mind alone without corporeal friend" (*L,* 2:460). In one late poem she can even indulge in what seems a conventional religious scorn for mere "Dust."

> The spirit looks upon the Dust
> That fastened it so long
> With indignation,
> As a Bird / Defrauded of it's song.

(P 1630)

Yet such lines basically illustrate her lifelong penchant for intellectual role-playing. Whatever positions she might temporarily take, her dependence on the bodily expression of spiritual longing remains profoundly central to her art and life. Her muted but still sensuous pleasure in music in "The Spirit lasts – " is of a piece with the "erotics of reception" that kept her going during her crisis years. Over and over in poems and letters from all periods she longs for the absent face of a friend. Separated from a lover, her speaker only wishes for "the looking in his Eyes" (P 398). She grieves that her dead mother cannot feel the touch of "our fingers." Her poems exist to realize embodied agonies and ecstasies. As Dickinson wrote to Maria Whitney in 1880, she was "constantly more astonished that the Body contains the Spirit" (*L,* 3:661). Their interconnection is not easy for human nature, as she recognized. Yet I think she believed in the astonishing tie between the body and the spirit as in a miracle of creation.[49]

The opening lines of Poem 1576 are a distilled reaffirmation of the spirit and the body's mutual need for each other, conveyed through two analogies the likes of which I have not found elsewhere. Dickinson shows no interest elsewhere in "the Music in the Violin"—*in* rather than *of* to enforce the idea that music on earth has its life in a physical instrument. Moreover, as she wittily puts it, this music emerges "Arm in Arm with Touch"; its expression is inevitably corporeal. Yet "Touch / Alone" is nothing. The poem keeps reasserting the fragile balance of interdependent equals necessary to spiritual and artistic embodiment. In the next analogy Dickinson thinks as so often of "the Sea" as the scene of her immortality-long spiritual adventure, but the beautiful figure of the spirit as "Tides within the Sea / That make the Water live" is a unique discovery of this particular poem. The conspicuous enjambments in lines 7–12, especially those after "Touch," "Sea," and "estranged," mirror the effort of thought to work itself out as it strikes its difficult balance. In its unusual metaphors and its metrical subtlety the whole passage conveys the effort to discover a truthful expression for troubling thoughts.

After these splendid lines the poem loses its way in obscurity, at least temporarily.

> Does that know – now – or does it cease –
> That which to this is done,
> Resuming at a mutual date
> With every future one?

The speaker seems to ask whether the spirit knows or ceases to know the fate of the body after death and also whether they "resume" their unity at the last judgment, when the body is restored to the soul. The resurrection of the body was a subject of supreme importance for Dickinson. She passionately wanted to see her loved ones again—that would be the "Wild Prosperity" she hopes for later in the poem. Yet it was also a subject of which she was aware that she knew nothing. Hence, perhaps, it suited her to be obscure, the better to convey the trouble of her questions.

Human ignorance of the future state of human being is eloquently conveyed in the poem's last four lines.

> The Rumor's Gate was shut so tight
> Before my Mind was sown,
> Not even a Prognostic's Push
> Could make a Dent thereon –

She used these lines (with some variant readings) on three other occasions in 1883, one a consoling poem she sent to Sue after Gilbert's death ("Expanse cannot be lost – " [P 1584]), the second a poem attached to a letter to Maria Whitney recalling her mother's death,[50] the third an anxious contemplation of the uncertainty she would face after her own death ("This Me – that walks and works – must die," [P 1588]). The repeated lines summarize her sense of utter ignorance when faced with the blank prospect of the afterlife. Yet "The Spirit lasts" also keeps true to Dickinson's intuitive faith even in such an uncertain context. The speaker reminds us that she is a created being in a mysterious universe. "My Mind was sown" by God, the creator of this remarkable earth and the sower of souls, all marked in particular ways for unknowable destinations.

3

Bible Stories and Divine Encounters

Bible

More than any other book, the King James Bible helped make Emily Dickinson a poet. Through much of her life she heard it read aloud daily–by her ministers, her teachers, or her father. Not content with her culture's version of it, she studied it and made it her own book as well. Her poems and letters suggest that she knew much of it by heart. She quotes and misquotes it freely, alludes to it reverently or frivolously, reconceives it over and over for her own personal or philosophical reasons.[1]

In this chapter I will first present an overview of various ways she puts the Bible to use and then focus on a group of narratives she writes about Jacob, Moses, and Jesus Christ. These figures from her religious tradition are all dramatic characters in the private epic she constructs in her imagination. Because they loom so significantly in her experience of religion as well as in her reading, she returns to them repeatedly in the course of her career. She varies the stories she chooses to tell about them. Jacob, Moses, and above all Christ represent for her different potentials at different times. She "believes" in them as religious figures and human representatives, but flexibly. She dramatizes them in variable, original images rather than in fixed, received ones, in order to give poetic form to her nimble belief. At the same time, these figures embody enacted values she persistently cherishes: constancy, bravery, reverence for awe, the willingness to love and suffer for it, and the capacity to bless one's loved ones. She put her faith in these active virtues as well as in her own preferred versions of God and paradise. She believed in the human capacity to live bravely and to embrace "Life" as "so strong a vision" it will not fail us in the encounter with the divine. Such values are more reminiscent of Unitarian and liberal writing and preaching than of the doctrines of Connecticut Valley Puritanism, yet the ease and seriousness with which she imagines them acted out in biblical dramas sets her apart from Emerson or Parker or George Eliot. Moreover, her sense of the workings of the human heart is based profoundly in the ethics and the metaphorical language of the New Testament. However various and unorthodox her reading of the Bible, it helped keep her grounded in her own local religious culture, and fed her soul and imagination so that she needed no other scriptural authority or competing mythology.

Just as Dickinson prefers not to codify her religious doctrines, so also she has no single doctrinally consistent view of the Bible. It was a resource for her because it could meet so many of her needs, both ideological and poetic. Her attitudes toward it appear in flux in her writings, as if it had a living presence to which she responded differently at different times. It was not merely a source of language and a storehouse of narrative for her but also a compendium of religious possibilities. Its diverse presence stimulated her own varying religious orientations by turns. Thus my survey of her attitudes in the previous chapter should help to organize her many responses to the Bible.

I begin with Dickinson's rebelliousness. Embedded in the Bible are vivid illustrations of a forbidding God and salient evidences for the Calvinist doctrines that outraged her. Especially in the Old Testament, she finds traces of a Father God she would unmask. For example, this is her rendering of the episode in which God restrains Abraham from sacrificing Isaac.

1317

Abraham to kill him
Was distinctly told –
Isaac was an Urchin –
Abraham was old –

Not a hesitation –
Abraham complied –
Flattered by Obeisance
Tyranny demurred –

Isaac – to his children
Lived to tell the tale –
Moral – with a Mastiff
Manners may prevail.

Compared to her poems on Jacob and Moses, this is a relatively straight-forward exercise in rewriting biblical narrative. It reconceives the psy-chology of the Genesis account (Gen. 22.1–14), casting Abraham as a vessel of unthinking obedience rather than a man of reverent fear. It mimics the action of the episode at a fast clip and in impudent trochaic meter. Unlike the narrator in Genesis, this Dickinson shows no wonder at God's miraculous act of mercy.[2] Nor does she treat divine power with conventional deference, or even the unconventional deference she might show elsewhere: God is "a Mastiff," tyrannical but neither awe-some nor luminous. With incisive skepticism her speaker exposes the action of the episode in Genesis as typical of a familiar pattern in do-mestic and political psychology.

In this poem Dickinson attacks the oppressive conception of God she found in the Genesis story with mordant wit. Her speaker maintains a cool distance from the fable she satirizes.[3] Nevertheless, God's tyranny here and elsewhere in the books of Moses was real and ap-palling to her. As she read Exodus or Deuteronomy, Jehovah was a name for the omnipotent tyrant she knew from her childhood who enacted "His Perturbless Plan" by letting women suffer and children die. She kept the story of Abraham and Isaac in her mind throughout her life as scriptural evidence for the power and capriciousness of such a God. In August 1885, nine months before her own death, she wrote Judge Lord's niece Abbie C. Farley on the occasion of the drowning of Miss Farley's cousin Mary in Walden Pond. Much of the letter is an attempt to com-fort a bereaved survivor and tenderly ease her mind. Yet it also contains this contentious two-sentence paragraph: "Isaac pleads again, 'But where is the Lamb for the Sacrifice?' The Clock's sweet voice makes no reply" (L, 3:883). Even so late in life Dickinson will advertize her dread of an inexorable and unresponsive Providence, a God who causes all, including Mary Farley's death.

Dickinson's hostility to one Old Testament version of God is con-sistent with her occasional skeptical attitude toward the Bible's preten-tions to sacred authenticity. When she chooses, she can strike out com-batively against its authority, as in a pronouncement in a letter of 1882:

"The Fiction of 'Santa Claus' always reminds me of the reply to my early
question of 'Who made the Bible' – 'Holy Men moved by the Holy
Ghost,' and though I have now ceased my investigations, the Solution
is insufficient – " (*L,* 3:756). Dickinson alludes pointedly here to the third
of the "Articles of Doctrinal Belief" reprinted each year by her own Con-
gregational Church, according to which "the Scriptures of the Old and
New Testaments . . . were composed by holy men as they were moved
by the Holy Ghost."[4] In the language of a determined rationalist, she
claims to have carried on a lifelong skeptical study of the Bible's claim
to truth, pitting her investigations against her culture's solutions. Other
statements she made about the Bible are by no means so skeptical. Yet
the seemingly all-encompassing scope of her pronouncement implies
that with part of her mind she felt it necessary to assume a distance from
the most important book in her life. She was aware of other "investiga-
tions" about who made the Bible, aware of the higher criticism emanat-
ing from Germany and spread in New England by (among others)
Theodore Parker, whose "poison . . . I like very well" (*L,* 2:358).[5] Though
she has not left many specific traces of her familiarity with this scholar-
ship, she seems to have accepted the idea that the Old Testament was
largely fictitious. We recall that she assented conspiratorially when
Austin told her, "there was no such person as Elijah." In poems she play-
fully assumes as current opinion the notions that "Ararat's a Legend"
(P 403) and "Eden – a legend – dimly told – " (P 503), that "in soberer
moments – / No Moses there can be" (P 597). The figures in stories she
knew from the Old Testament still have vital poetic significance for her,
as we shall see, but at the same time she understood that they were los-
ing their currency as historical persons to be believed in literally. Even
the New Testament she treated highly selectively, satirizing what she
disliked while celebrating what still moved her to assent with a ques-
tioning reverence. Her absence of certainty might threaten her with
emptiness or, alternatively, encourage her to take pleasure in her own
enlightenment, but in either case she accepted the loss of the Bible's un-
questioned truth as a fact of her times.

    Dickinson the rebel projects a mood of cheerful enlightenment or
even impudence in writings where she affirms her human experience of
this world. When she rejoices in the beauty of her natural existence she
has no need of an elaborate conversion experience to prepare her for a
world to come. She reconceives biblical passages to support this natu-
ralism. When Mrs. Joseph Sweetser sent her some thoughts on lilies (or

a gift of bulbs) in the spring of 1884, Dickinson answered, "Thank you for 'considering the Lilies.' The Bible must have had us in mind, when it gave that liquid Commandment. Were all it's advice so enchanting as that, we should probably heed it" (*L,* 3:821). In June that same year Dickinson claims that "Consider the Lilies" is "the only commandment I ever obeyed" (*L,* 3:825).[6] In an early poem (transcribed 1859) she has her own this-worldly answer to Nicodemus's question to Jesus, "How can a man be born when he is old?" (John 3.4).

An altered look about the hills –
A Tyrian light the village fills –
A wider sunrise in the morn –
A deeper twilight on the lawn – . . .
An axe shrill singing in the woods –
Fern odors on untravelled roads –
All this and more I cannot tell –
A furtive look you know as well –
And Nicodemus' Mystery
Receives it's annual reply!

(P 140, ll. 1–4, 11–16)

Like other poems of the late 1850s (e.g. "The feet of people walking home"), this is an open invitation to share her imaginative world. Dickinson makes no idiosyncratic difficulties for the reader, who like her is a potential this-worldly poet and ought to be aware from his or her experience that "Eden" is "always eligible." The speaker puts herself on the reader's level; "you know" the furtive look of spring as well as she. Quietly, however, Dickinson dislodges one from intellectual complacency even in this inviting poem. She reconceives a biblical episode to make it conform to her this-worldly stance, thereby requiring the reader to consider how such a stance reorients the received text. In the Gospel of John a man is born again when he accepts Christ as his savior; in the poem rebirth happens annually and naturally if we are receptive to it.[7]

Like the story of Abraham and Isaac, Jesus' exchange with Nicodemus reminded Dickinson until the end of her life of her differences with conventional Protestant readers of the Bible. A comment in a letter of 1885 or 1886 to Mrs. George S. Dickerman is a well-meditated gloss on "An altered look about the hills"; the very late comment clarifies the early poem but also enlarges its meaning: "If we love Flowers, are we not 'born again' every Day, without the distractions of Nicodemus? Not to outgrow Genesis, is a sweet monition – " (*L*, 3:899). How beguilingly ironic are some of Dickinson's heretical expressions! Distractions afflict Nicodemus, she implies, when he worries about the meaning of Jesus' message. But we need not be distracted by Christian doctrine to be born again; all we need do is "love Flowers." Yet this love implies a grander commitment, in that it is a synechdoche for sustaining in ourselves a Romantic vision of innocence. The flowers sweetly advise us "not to outgrow Genesis," not to succumb to the received idea that Eden is lost, and not to lose our innocent faith that we can be renewed in spirit "every Day" when we love the world's beauty.

However revisionary in their treatment of Nicodemus, both poem and letter are themselves expressions of faith in "the Maker who gave us this remarkable earth" (*L*, 3:750). They do not dispense with Jesus, whom Dickinson revered, so much as forget him temporarily so that she can worship him elsewhere. They suggest how elastic the categories of our dialectic must be if we are to follow the motions of Dickinson's mind. Her conviction that life is fundamentally sacred can emerge whether she is indulging in rebellion or experimenting with a version of orthodoxy, if in both instances she means to voice her intuitive faith.

Dickinson adopts Scripture not only to combat it but also to stimulate her faith in God the Creator and in the sacredness of life. Especially the language of the Psalms or of Revelation helps her convey the awe that she finds latent in her experience. Since, as Blake says, "every thing that lives is Holy,"[8] she seeks support in the Bible's sacred language for her appreciations of the holiness repeatedly surfacing in her life. Twice in 1883, for example, she quotes a phrase from Revelation 19.11, "And I saw the Heavens opened," first to express her "rejoiced surprise" at receiving a letter with a gift from James Clark, the friend of Charles Wadsworth, the second time to commend books, "those enthralling friends," to Maria Whitney (*L*, 3: 762, 771). In both instances the heavens open for her when she responds to human spiritual activity in the life she knows here on earth.

In the letter to Maria Whitney, Dickinson also draws on the Bible in order to rescue herself from grief over her mother's death, "grief of wonder at her fate," as she puts it. "Seeking what it means," Dickinson looks to Scripture for words that will in some way explain the loss and give her images for the home in the afterlife where she imagines her mother rests. The Bible offers a language of faith in immortality that consoles her for this inscrutable loss. Dickinson seems to convey such a faith when she quotes from Saint Paul elsewhere in the letter: "The sunshine almost speaks, this morning, redoubling the division, and Paul's remark grows graphic, 'the *weight* of glory'" (*L,* 3:771). "Paul's remark" appears in 2 Corinthians 4.17, "For our light affliction, which is but for a moment, worketh for us a far more exceeding and eternal weight of glory." As I read her, Dickinson finds the promise of glory not only in Paul's words but also in the speaking sunshine itself. True, like many of her messages of consolation this passage has an ambivalent edge to it. She could well mean that she feels oppressed by the sense of separation she projects on the sunshine as well as enthralled by the morning's glorious light. Yet, despite her division from her mother, with part of her mind she would overcome her affliction by a faith in a glory that manifests itself in the heaven below as well as the heaven above.[9]

In this letter the Bible brings an ambivalent Dickinson something like a traditional Christian assurance. Indeed, in some moods she will have nothing to do with liberal skepticism and presents herself as a traditional reader of Scripture. In 1873 she writes to Mrs. Holland:

> Science will not trust us with another World.
> Guess I and the Bible will move to some old fashioned spot where we'll feel at Home.
>
> (*L,* 2:511)

Especially when she looked toward "another World" where she might encounter her lost loved ones, she clung to biblical passages that sanctified such longings. In 1883, after Gilbert Dickinson's death, she recalled his last words for Mrs. Holland: "'Open the Door, open the Door, they are waiting for me,' was Gilbert's sweet command in delirium. *Who* were waiting for him, all we possess we would give to know" (*L,* 3:803). Then, as she ends the letter, a phrase from the Bible prompts her to this afterthought:

> How lovely that you went to "Church"!
> May I go with you to the "Church of the first born?"
>
> Emily –

The quoted words are from Hebrews 12.23, in which Paul envisions "the heavenly Jerusalem," with "an innumerable company of angels," "the

general assembly and church of the firstborn," and "the spirits of just
men made perfect." Dickinson supposes that Mrs. Holland is to belong
in this hierarchy of God's servants and asks that she be allowed to join
her. Perhaps she surmises that Gilbert would also be there. If the king-
dom of heaven existed, she was quite ready to imagine that one entered
it by becoming as a little child.

Dickinson was intensely curious about passages in Paul's epistles
where he gives hints concerning another World, as we have seen a sub-
ject about which she kept an anxiously open mind. She came back re-
peatedly, for example, to 1 Corinthians 15, a chapter in which Paul spec-
ulates extensively concerning the resurrection of the dead but leaves the
form of resurrection "a mystery." Though Dickinson may well have
longed to see the faces of these she loved after death and dramatizes
such longings in some poems, she was perfectly aware that Paul's prom-
ises concerning the resurrection of the body were indefinite. In a letter
of 1878 to an unknown recipient she quotes 1 Corinthians 15.51: "Were
the Statement 'We shall not all sleep, but we shall all be changed,' made
in earthly Manuscript, were his Residence in the Universe, we should
pursue the Writer till he explained it to us" (L, 2:621). Dickinson is ob-
sessively interested in what happens to human beings in death but also
realizes that one can know nothing about it.

Dickinson's responses to the Bible, then, cover a spectrum from rebel-
liousness to conforming faith. It was at once a vital source of comfort, a
stimulus to her imagination of paradise, and a provocative goad to her
sense of independence. She maintains an ambivalence concerning its sa-
cred authority. On the one hand, she is ready to assume with her local
culture that the Bible is more than an "earthly Manuscript." On the other
hand, she is not satisfied with what her culture has told her, that it was
made by "Holy Men moved by the Holy Ghost." Her uncertainty gives
her Bible a fluid and changing character. It is something else she cannot
take for granted. At the same time, its openness to mystery in its narra-
tive and doctrine is exemplarily instructive. It offers a fund of language
and stunning examples of dramatic representation to a writer who
would wrestle with the unknown. Given her historical and cultural sit-
uation, it is not suprising that she shows a curious combination of close-
ness to it and detachment from it. Figures like Abraham and Isaac or
Nicodemus or even Paul are intimately familiar acquaintances whom
she summons easily to illustrate or amplify her aphorisms, but at the

same time she preserves a contemplative distance from them. For her Paul is the writer of a manuscript rather than a father of the church, a fellow writer whom she berates or praises but also calls on when she feels the need for him.

Dickinson's most extensive single comment on the Bible suggests her intimacy with it along with her adopted distance from it. The comment appears as an excerpt from one of her later letters to her childhood friend Joseph Lyman. Richard Sewall estimates that this particular letter was probably written "in the mid-1860s"[10] but infers that Dickinson recalls in it her reading of the mid-1850s. If so, she deliberately made a study of her culture's chief book at about the same time that she began to embark in earnest on her vocation as a poet.

Bible

> Some years after we saw each other last I fell to reading the Old & New Testament. I had known it as an arid book but looking I saw how infinitely wise & how merry it is.
> Anybody that knows grammar must admit the surpassing splendor & force of its speech, but the fathomless gulfs of meaning – those words which He spoke to those most necessary to him, hints about some celestial reunion – yearning for a oneness – has any one fathomed that sea? I know those to whom those words are very near & necessary, I wish they were more so to me, for I see them shedding a serenity quite wonderful & blessed. They are great bars of sunlight in many a shady heart.[11]

This is a passage that reflects several entangled moods. Sewall rightly observes that Dickinson's praise of "the splendor & force of its speech" and her comment on "how infinitely wise & how merry it is" constitute "a quite secular response"[12] to the Bible. By endeavoring to assess its aesthetic character, she assumes a distance from it. I would also argue that the passage contains an element of defensive posturing; she defends her adult, poetic self against memories of her childhood. Some pronouncements and episodes in the Bible seemed not arid but terrifying to her as a child and then dogged her into her last years. She testified in 1882, for example, "No Verse in the Bible has frightened me so much from a Child as 'from him that hath not, shall be taken even that he hath'" (*L*, 3:751). Neither this verse nor Revelation 21.8, which relegates "all liars" to the flames of hell, was ever "merry" to her. Moreover, despite her initial distanced appreciation, Dickinson shows as she continues her nimble meditation that she is not so disengaged emotionally from the Bible as she seems to claim. It reminds her inevitably that she is different from her loved ones, to whom Christ's words are "very near & necessary." Her difference from them is poignant to her, as it was also in her youth when she would not participate in revivals while her friends and relations were flocking to give themselves up to Christ. Yet she has her own ways of using the Bible as a medium of faith. Her evocations of Christ's words as "hints about some celestial reunion – yearning for a oneness" describe with poetic uncertainty her own longings for immortality. She makes Christ's image of heaven suggestive but unknowable—"has any one fathomed that sea?" She lays special emphasis on "the fathomless gulfs of meaning" abiding in his words and in the Bible's "speech." In effect she reimagines and revises Christ's message to make it better suit her sense of the soul's desires. She approaches the Bible in a revisionary spirit even when she is trying to do it justice. She also implies that, despite her effort at distancing, the Bible is a living presence for her, as it has been and will be all her life.

Jacob

In fragmentary form at least, we have seen how Dickinson retells episodes from the Bible to reflect her sense of human needs and possibilities. When she finds her own answer to Nicodemus' question to Jesus or when she reimagines Isaac on the altar, she not only rewrites these episodes but also uses biblical figures to represent personal lessons she discovers in them. In this perspective the Bible is a vast symbolic and moral drama, with a host of characters and incidents that bring instruction and delight to Dickinson as a reader. When she reads the Bible as such a source of dramatic examples, she follows but also transforms the practice of many Amherst generations, brought up like her on verses from the New England Primer:

> *Job* feels the Rod
> Yet blesses GOD.
>
> *Peter* denies
> His Lord and cries
>
> *Rachel* doth mourn
> For her first born.[13]

Figures like Job, Peter, and Rachel are "correlative types" a pious reader might store in the imagination for quick reference; they furnish examples of behavior to be imitated or shunned or at least observed with fellow feeling.[14] Dickinson makes use of this mode of reading but as a nonconformist. The lessons she draws from Nicodemus or Isaac are heretical and revisionary. She adopts them as types to help her revise the text as traditionally received.

This revisionary spirit gives Dickinson's use of biblical characters and incidents its intellectual excitement. Her aphorisms and fragmentary sermons (for in effect that is what she sometimes composes) also differ from the conventional sermons she heard in that for her Scripture is in the process of becoming legend, while it nevertheless retains the persuasive interest of an ancient sacred text and has the potential to illuminate modern existence. As we shall see, she writes of Moses as if he did not exist historically but were still passionately important to her. She writes of Moses and Jacob as if key dramatic incidents in their stories not only had traditional mythical resonance but also had new lessons to impart to the modern reader. Her Jesus is different in that many of her poems that invoke him imagine an unparalleled intimacy with him and reverence for him. In many writings he is her "Lord" and "Saviour," a real divine and human presence her speakers believe in and draw comfort from, and a figure of exemplary courage in his willingness to face death.

> He – would trust no stranger –
> Other – could betray –
> Just His own endorsement –
> That sufficeth Me –
>
> (P 698, st. 2)

Nevertheless, like Moses and Jacob, Jesus Christ is still a creature of her reading and subject to her reinterpretations and reinventions. Moreover, all three of these figures seem to have special significance for her because she imagines them as facing the unknown and surviving the encounter.

Dickinson's retelling of the story of Jacob wrestling with the angel is one of the most striking and intriguing of her early poems.

59

A little East of Jordan,
Evangelists record,
A Gymnast and an Angel
Did wrestle long and hard –

Till morning touching mountain –
And Jacob, waxing strong,
The Angel begged permission
To Breakfast – to return –

Not so, said cunning Jacob!
"I will not let thee go
Except thou bless me" – Stranger!
The which acceded to –

Light swung the silver fleeces
"Peniel" Hills beyond,
And the bewildered Gymnast
Found he had worsted God!

One can be put off by the poem at first. The speaker's manner is oddly comic, arch, and self-bemused compared to that of the narrative voice in Genesis: "And Jacob was left alone; and there wrestled a man with him until the breaking of the day" (Gen. 32.24). When Jacob becomes "a Gymnast" in the poem, the reader assumes an ironic distance from him. But that seems to be the point of Dickinson's stylization. Rather than the reader's getting lost in an ancient myth, he or she is asked to hold up Jacob's story for personal contemplation. Moreover, Jacob is made a modern type (a gymnast) while still retaining his ancient identity (cunning Jacob). Thus we interpret him through alternating filters of mediation. Similarly, his opponent is "an Angel" yet asks to be allowed to return "to Breakfast." The cuteness of the phrasing creates an alienation effect that not only changes one's perspective on the angel but also provokes one's uncomfortable curiosity about what will come next. For this dynamic toying with gymnast and angel is part of the narrator's waiting game before she springs her most interesting surprise.

All the narrator's cuteness is startlingly displaced when she quotes without warning from Jacob's words in Genesis 32.26, "I will not let thee go / Except thou bless me." Dickinson cites the biblical text word for word, without revision. The quotation gives the poem a sudden mythical seriousness. As in Eve's confession to Christ after the fall in Milton's *Paradise Lost* or Cain's encounter with the Angel of the Lord at the end of Byron's *Cain,* the voice of an ancient text enters a modern reimagination of it.[15] The words from Genesis endow Dickinson's poem with a difficult awesomeness, because the reader cannot quickly understand what this mixing of styles portends—the text has a writerly multiplicity of voices. The intensity of the mixture is heightened in Dickinson's next word, "Stranger!" She adds the word as her interpretive gloss on the biblical text she quotes while setting it off by leaving it outside the quotation and marking it as an exclamation.

The gloss brings out an idea latent in the Genesis narrative—Dickinson was a careful as well as imaginative reader. Jacob does not know who the "man" is who wrestles with him, nor does he realize that his opponent is an angel. He is understandably "bewildered," as Dickinson puts it. Moreover, Dickinson may remember Jacob's question, not answered by the angel in Genesis, "Tell me, I pray thee, thy name." One could infer from such a question and from the narrative as a whole that the angel is a "Stranger." Yet Dickinson's use of "Stranger" also emphasizes the angel's and Jacob's isolation from one another, a kind of nineteenth-century isolation not conveyed in Genesis. Jacob does not know the angel; he is estranged from the angelic and divine.

To sharpen the point, Dickinson omits any recollection of a key moment in Genesis, when the angel renames Jacob "Israel" and thus makes him a founding father of his people ("for as a prince hast thou power with God and with men, and hast prevailed"). The angel in the poem shows no such inclination to congratulate Jacob or give him a social mission. Dickinson's Jacob is not a tribal prince but a mere wrestler, a man alone. His solitude is reemphasized in the final lines of the poem, when Dickinson hones in on Jacob's paradoxical situation. The angel leaves him surrounded by silver-fleeced clouds, victorious but "bewildered"—both isolated and baffled. More, he finds he has "worsted God!" By contrast, the biblical Jacob, though certainly bewildered by his encounter with the divine, is relieved and thankful afterward. He calls the place of the encounter "Peniel" (i.e., "Face of God"), "for I have seen God face to face, and my life is preserved." Now he can return to his wives, his children, his brother, his birthplace. Moreover, he has come into a new, if mysterious, relation with his God. Dickinson's Jacob has overcome God, but the price of his victory is that he faces a void. He has put God out of his presence and senses that he no longer knows him.

As I read Dickinson, I see her lifelong dilemmas as a religious writer prefigured in such a poem. By 1859 she had struggled with Calvinist orthodoxy and had "prevailed," at least to the extent that she preserved her independence. Yet her situation as a religious poet and protagonist was fundamentally unstable. She did not need to wait until after she had absorbed Darwin[16] to recognize that she faced estrangement in her universe and had to find strategies to deal with it. Sometimes she writes as if she has found an independent way to love God and to wrest a blessing from him. In such writings, if in her own style, she resembles "Amherst Trinitarians" who "construed Jacob's wrestle with God as the archetypal model for every man and woman who sincerely strove for belief."[17] More often, however, she writes as if she too has worsted God and feels bewildered with the results, or as if she is God's victim, or as if God looms over his world but cannot be seen behind his mask. In all these cases she imagines the place in which one finds oneself struggling or recovering as awesome and inscrutable. Yet whether Dickinson believed or disbelieved, rejoiced or despaired, she imagined the effort to make the unknown speak as a wrestling, a trope in numerous poems for the efforts of longing or love or natural need for expression, revelation, or fulfillment.

1255

Longing is like the Seed
That wrestles in the Ground,
Believing if it intercede
It shall at length be found.

The Hour, and the Clime –
Each Circumstance unknown,
What Constancy must be achieved
Before it see the Sun!

This is an example of Dickinson's poetry of analogy, to use Robert Weisbuch's key conception.[18] The poem has no subject except the analogy itself: "Longing is like the Seed / That wrestles in the Ground." Yet it is open to various readings that focus on the struggle of desire to express itself. It might be interpreted as a poem about a lover's wish to be acknowleged and fulfilled; or a poem about the imagined desire of nature for fruitfulness; or a poem about religious conversion, the wrestling of the soul for illumination; or a poem about the desire for immortality, the desire to see the "Sun" not through a glass darkly but face to face. This multiple potential of meaning suits Dickinson's poetry of nimble believing, in which belief is a living process rather than a set of finished assumptions.

One way of reading "Longing is like the Seed" is as a rewriting of the Jacob story, a hopeful completion of "A little East of Jordan." The seed that wrestles in the ground refuses to be bewildered by the unknown dark, the absence of (angelic) illumination. Its belief in itself brings it to the light. Its struggle has an ethical significance: belief enables the wrestler to persevere through each unknown circumstance. Longing is transformed to constancy as the speaker works out the terms and the plot of the analogy. As the poem itself exemplifies, constancy is one of Dickinson's strategies for addressing the unknown and persevering in belief even under the pressure of bewilderment and estrangement.

Dickinson was constant in her effort to reimagine the Bible and make it yield meanings she could use to give wisdom to her writing and impose her changeable sense of things on her audience(s). As with other biblical figures, Jacob stays in her imagination through the course of her career but takes on different meanings when she considers him anew. Three times in texts of her last years she remembers the Bible's narrative of his wrestling with the angel. In the last two of these recollections, she experiments with the story in different ways, offering alternative versions of the human struggle to come to terms with divine power. About 1881 she transcribes on a stray piece of paper without comment the angel's exclamation in Genesis 32.26, "Let me go for the day breaketh" (L, 3:705).[19] In March 1886, two months before her death, she reconsiders Jacob's willful response to the angel. Now at the end of her career she has moved beyond bewilderment (at least temporarily), but to show this she engages in a genial revision of the original narrative. To end a letter of consolation to her dear friend Mrs. Edward Tuckerman, she quotes Jacob's answer she had quoted unrevised in "A little east of Jordan" but reverses the pronouns: "Says the blissful voice, not yet a voice, but a vision, 'I will not let thee go, except I bless thee'" (L, 3:898). As I read her, she here ascribes Jacob's answer to the angel. A vision that turns into a blissful voice might well be a figure for the angel as he fades from mortal view. It also seems to point to the change Dickinson imagines for herself from life with friends to the solitude of death. As Johnson comments, Dickinson's letter "seems to be in the nature of a farewell." She herself will hold on to her friend and bless her before she leaves her. As a poet she can assume the prerogative of an angel, confidently bestowing her vision of a divine presence as well as her love.[20]

In another very late letter, this one to Thomas Wentworth Higginson, Dickinson draws on Jacob's exchange with the angel for a last time, using the same reversal of pronouns but with a different significance. Though she sends two briefer messages to Higginson after this, the end of the letter seems to be her considered testament of what she would say to him at the end of her life.

> I have been very ill, Dear friend, since November, bereft of Book and Thought, by the Doctor's reproof, but begin to roam in my Room now –
> I think of you with absent Affection, and the Wife and Child I never have seen, Legend and Love in one –
> Audacity of Bliss, said Jacob to the Angel "I will not let thee go except I bless thee" – Pugilist and Poet, Jacob was correct –
> > Your Scholar –
> > (*L*, 3:903; spring 1886)

Her report of her illness to him is straightforward, without the indirections that could prompt him to describe her to his sisters as "my eccentric" or "partially cracked poetess" (*L*, 2:518, 570). She seems to say, while offering him the friendliest affection and courtesy, "I may not write you again, so please attend to what I say." Then she quotes Jacob's words in Genesis, but in another eccentric revision. Jacob wrestles not in order to be blessed but to do the blessing himself. More, Jacob is pugilist as well as poet, a representative man who takes on the authority and power of the angel to fight and to bless and bring inspiration through his words. Poetry requires pugilism, a struggle with the divine, in order to have the power to bless. She insists in a last word to Higginson (whether he understands it or not) that she is not only a poet but one with a vocation of power. She identifies with Jacob, hence also with pugilism, even as she expresses her desire to bless in life as in art. For as a final gesture to Higginson she blesses him as she has blessed Mrs. Tuckerman, affectionately and forcefully: "I will not let thee go except I bless *thee*." Yet, despite her self-assertion she is still his "Scholar," deeply grateful to him in her constancy. Her culminating word to him, like her writing as a whole, includes both blessing and wrestling in a vital synthesis.

Moses

Dickinson wrote a number of poems in which she either makes Moses her protagonist or dramatizes in passing an episode from his saga. She adopts at least three different approaches to him. In two early poems, "Where bells no more affright the morn – " and "If the foolish, call them 'flowers' – " (P 112 and P 168; transcribed 1859 and 1860), she remembers the moment before Moses' death when he looks out over the promised land of Canaan from the top of Mt. Nebo. She assumes, as did her local Calvinist culture, that Moses is a type of visionary whose beholding of the landscape anticipates the vision of the saints in God's heaven. She returns to the subject of Moses's final sight of Canaan in a questioning and rebellious spirit in "It always felt to me – a wrong" (P 597; transcribed in 1862). Here she remembers God's refusal to allow Moses to enter Canaan after many years in the wilderness. In this poem his glimpse of that land is only a kind of grudging compensation for his magnificent service. God's unfairness to Moses is also mentioned with focused bitterness in "So I pull my Stockings off" (P 1201), a poem of 1871 in which Dickinson adopts the voice of a defiant child.

> Moses was'nt fairly used –
> Ananias was'nt –

"No man saw awe" (P 1733), probably written in the mid-1870s, departs radically in its subject and tenor from all the earlier poems on Moses. Dickinson imagines him reflecting on his encounter with the divine in the burning bush on Mt. Horeb. He is neither a unique beholder of God's glory nor a personal victim of his injustice but a representative of humanity in general in his experience of God's terrifying but illuminating mysteriousness.

These poems, then, represent significantly different religious attitudes Dickinson takes as she contemplates the story of Moses. Each of these attitudes—willfully innocent hopefulness, rebellious skepticism, inquiring wonder—figure typically in different phases of her experience as a religious poet.

Johnson calls Poem 112 "a lighthearted plea for early morning quiet."[21] It makes fun of Dickinson's father's habit of peremptorily rousing up his household.

> Where bells no more affright the morn –
> Where scrabble never comes –
> Where very nimble Gentlemen
> Are forced to keep their rooms –
>
> Where tired Children placid sleep
> Thro' Centuries of noon
> This place is Bliss – this town is Heaven –
> Please, Pater, pretty soon!
>
> "Oh could we climb where Moses stood,
> And view the Landscape o'er"
> Not Father's bells – nor Factories,
> Could scare us any more!

An obviously occasional poem like this in which Dickinson's imagined audience is apparently her family circle as well as herself makes use of the language, the texts, and the opinions the family presumably shares without thinking about them. Just as the Dickinson daughters would be well aware of the danger of "nimble Gentlemen" in Amherst, Dickinson children (or adults posing as children) would seek relief from morning bells and factories by projecting a "Heaven" where one can "placid sleep" one's life away. When life on earth seems annoying, Dickinson as an Amherst daughter can facetiously ask "Pater" (God the Father confused with Edward Dickinson) to take her to heaven. Nevertheless, she also remembers a grander and less domestic idea of heaven in the poem, one drawn from the fourth stanza of Isaac Watts's well-known hymn "There is a land of pure delight":

> Could we but climb where Moses stood,
> And view the landscape o'er,
> Not Jordan's stream, nor death's cold flood
> Should fright us from the shore.[22]

Dickinson invokes Watts's image of Moses playfully. By alluding to it, however, she makes use of the earnest inherited assumption that in the land of Canaan Moses saw the likeness of heaven. Read typologically, his was a vision all the saved might share, and it stands also for the superior vision of enlightened Christians as compared to the shadowed understanding of the unregenerate.

Dickinson remembers Watts's conception of Moses also in Poem 168, in which an innocent orthodox speaker prefers the wisdom vouched for in "the 'Revelations'" to the knowledge offered by classifying "Savans," merely empirically minded scientists.

Could we stand with that Old "Moses" –
"Canaan" denied –
Scan like him, the stately landscape
On the other side –

Doubtless, we should deem superfluous
Many Sciences,
Not pursued by learned Angels
In Scholastic skies!

The poem ends with an enthusiastic prayer for heavenly translation; the speaker asks to be a star "amid profound *Galaxies* – / At that grand 'Right hand'!" The heavenly vision that Moses scanned she would behold also, not as he did in an earthly image but immediately, at God's "Right hand."

Yet, despite the speaker's zest for traditional wisdom and her longing for a conventional heaven, the poem is curiously divided against itself. Dickinson seems to call the Watts view of Moses into question even while she represents it enthusiastically. All those quotation marks surrounding "Revelations," "Moses," "Canaan," and "Right hand" convey the implication that this biblical and theological language is that of remembered texts rather than of reported facts. Moreover, the speaker recalls significantly that Canaan was "denied" to Moses, as if to undercut her orthodox use of his example. She seems thereby to indicate in passing that there is another way to read the episode of Moses on Mt. Nebo than the way one learned in church and school. God's denial of Moses's wish to die in the Promised Land does not figure in "There is a land with pure delight." In standard Protestant interpretations Moses is denied only that he may later be appropriately rewarded, when he beholds Canaan as a man of spiritual vision. Poem 168 records the denial without interpreting it but raises the question of what it might mean to a less innocent-eyed speaker.

In Poem 597 Dickinson elaborates on the possibility of reading the episode heretically.

> It always felt to me – a wrong
> To that Old Moses – done –
> To let him see – the Canaan –
> Without the entering –
>
> And tho' in soberer moments –
> No Moses there can be
> I'm satisfied – the Romance
> In point of injury –
>
> Surpasses sharper stated –
> Of Stephen – or of Paul –
> For these – were only put to death –
> While God's adroiter will
>
> On Moses – seemed to fasten
> With tantalizing Play
> As Boy – should deal with lesser Boy –
> To prove ability.
>
> The fault – was doubtless Israel's –
> Myself – had banned the Tribes –
> And ushered Grand Old Moses
> In Pentateuchal Robes
>
> Upon the Broad Possession
> 'Twas little – He should see –
> Old Man on Nebo! Late as this –
> My Justice bleeds – for Thee!

Though the poem responds to the larger biblical narrative of Moses as a man of struggles and sufferings, its germ is Deuteronomy 3.25–27, in which Moses reminds the people of Israel how he asked God to be allowed to enter Canaan and was denied. The excerpt begins with Moses' quoting his own plea then has him report the Lord's answer.

> I pray thee, let me go over, and see the good land that is beyond Jordan, that goodly mountain, and Lebanon. But the Lord was wroth with

me for your sakes, and would not hear me: and the Lord said unto me,
Let it suffice thee; speak no more unto me of this matter. Get thee up
into the top of Pisgah, and lift up thine eyes westward, and northward,
and southward, and eastward, and behold it with thine eyes: for thou
shalt not go over this Jordan.

Pisgah is a plateau adjacent to Mt. Nebo, overlooking the Promised
Land. Later, shortly before Moses' death, God repeats his injunction/
prohibition to him: "Get thee up . . . unto mount Nebo, which is in the
land of Moab, that is over against Jericho; and behold the land of Canaan
. . . but thou shalt not go thither unto the land which I give the children
of Israel" (Deut. 32.49, 52).

Dickinson seems to have taken to heart Moses's impassioned plea,
"I pray thee, let me go over, and see the good land that is beyond Jor-
dan." In this poem she makes nothing of God's promise of a Pisgah-
sight but focuses instead on his angry prohibition, "thou shalt not go
over this Jordan." Her sense of God's injustice may well stem from her
reading of the whole story of the wandering of Moses and the tribes in
the Books of Exodus, Numbers, and Deuteronomy.[23] She would have
found there no clear basis for God's anger against Moses. In Exodus
17.1–7 and again in Numbers 20.1–13 the children of Israel are desper-
ate with impatience because they have no water, and they cry out
against Moses because he brought them out of Egypt into the wilder-
ness and the desert. Moses (along with Aaron in Numbers) appeals to
the Lord, who tells Moses to take a rod and smite a rock in the midst of
the people, that water may come forth abundantly and his glory may be
revealed. Later God holds Moses' supposed uncertainty in this episode
against him. Yet neither here nor elsewhere in the surviving narrative
does Moses show any clear indication that he doubts the Lord. Instead,
he calls on him, trusts him, does his bidding, and worships his glory.
"The tribes," in contrast, complain, disobey, and even turn to other gods
in the course of their wanderings. But the Lord reproves Moses and
Aaron and rewards Israel. "Because ye believed me not, to sanctify me
in the eyes of the children of Israel, therefore ye shall not bring this con-
gregation into the land which I have given them" (Num. 20.12).

Such a God (or Jehovah) conforms to the conception of an arbitrary
God in the Shorter Catechism who "out of his mere good pleasure" re-
wards and punishes whom he will.[24] The Lord's arbitrary punishment
of Moses might be covered up in traditional readings and glosses, but
Dickinson went back to the original story and reread it independently.

Just as in their treatments of the story of Jacob and the angel nineteenth-century evangelical readings bypassed the bewildering fact—patent in Genesis—that Jacob had "worsted God," so in the story of Moses evangelical tradition obscured Moses' expression of sadness at the frustration of his desire. Responding to the poignancy of that frustration, Dickinson gives voice to a rebellious and experimental speaker who pits her own morality against Jehovah's. This speaker arrogates "justice" to herself, since in her view the God of the books of Moses was patently unjust. The Lord acted like a bully or a tribal boss to Moses, as he had acted like a mastiff to Abraham. Better to be put to death, like Stephen or Paul, than suffer this "tantalizing Play."

As the speaker of Poem 597 is skeptical of the orthodox moral attached to Moses' sight of Canaan, so is she skeptical also of its historical truth: "in soberer moments – / No Moses there can be." Yet she clings to the incident as to an episode in "Romance." "Late as this" her "justice bleeds for" Moses. His story still moves her even if she understands that it is only a story. In Harold Bloom's terms the poem presents a "belated" reading of an Old Testament text—ironic and multilayered yet still marked with the desire for original and originating feeling.[25] It is belated also in that Dickinson dispenses, as she does in Poem 59, with the social and tribal dimension of the Old Testament narrative. She would "ban the tribes," make Moses into a theatrical individual sufferer and hero, and clothe him in his text, "in Pentateuchal Robes."

In her playful bitterness the speaker even implies a fleeting doubt about the truth of Christian history. Her skepticism spreads to Stephen and Paul, whom she also regards for the occasion as figures of Romance rather than of history. I would fill in the ellipses in lines 7–10 as follows: "I'm satisfied – the Romance [of Moses] surpasses [the] sharper stated [Romances] of Stephen – or of Paul." Their deaths are "sharper stated" endings in the plots of stories rather than actual events in a history we accept on faith. True, such a skeptical implication is an effect of the syntax and is offered as an idea to be entertained rather than as a firm persuasion. The speaker does not say "No Stephen there can be." Yet, whatever the status of his story, she questions God's role in it. For this poetic occasion the historical Stephen and Paul are yoked together with the legendary Moses as victims of God's injustice. If God's will dictated the fate of Moses, so did it also decree the deaths of these two martyrs. In both cases this is a God of power who deals with representative human sufferers as if they were "lesser boys." One hears Shakespeare's

Gloucester in the background: "As Flies to wanton Boyes, are we to th'Gods, / They kill us for their sport."[26]

As *King Lear* does not rest in Gloucester's despair but includes it as but one strand in its tapestry of feeling, so Dickinson's composite portrait of Moses extends beyond her image of him in Poem 597. He is more than just an old man unfairly used by a bullying God. What seems to be her last reckoning with the saga of Moses presents a different God and a different Moses. If one of her projects is to free herself and her reader from the authority of a Bible that seemed to sanction an unjust and all-powerful Jehovah, another project is to come to terms with her own equally biblical conception of an inscrutable divinity at the heart of experience.

A key word Dickinson uses to convey her sense of this frightening divine power is "awe." Significantly, she identifies divinity with the feeling she has for it. "Awe" in her writings is fundamentally a human feeling including terror as well as reverence. Sometimes, especially in earlier poems, she uses the word without a religious connotation. It helps convey moments of involuntary terror before an abyss, sudden rushes of human fear when a speaker is faced with chaos or death. For example, the speaker in "I Years had been from Home" (P 609), after returning to her "House" of earlier memories, conveys her moment of uncertain fear by the door of the house as follows:

> I leaned upon the Awe –
> I lingered with Before –
> The Second like an Ocean rolled
> And broke against my ear –

Such an example suggests that already in the early 1860s Dickinson enjoys playing with "awe," making it a nimble abstraction in her idiosyncratic lexicon and dramatizing it variously to suit her inner occasions.

One poem of the same period shows that Dickinson already thought of awe not only as a state of fear but also as a positive capacity of the soul. In "She rose to His Requirement" (P 732), a fine poem that summarizes the spiritual costs to a woman who chooses marriage rather than solitude, the speaker speculates on what gets inwardly obscured by such a choice. "If ought She missed in Her new Day, / of Amplitude, or Awe – . . . It lay unmentioned." The wife's remnant of awe has become imperceptible, like a pearl or weed in the depths of the sea.

Only in Dickinson's later writings, however, does she allegorize the capacity for awe and project it apart from herself as a separate being, for example when she writes, "Awe is the first Hand that is held to us" (*L,* 3:800), or, more famously, "I always ran Home to Awe when a child, if anything befel me. He was an awful Mother, but I liked him better than none" (*L,* 2:517–18). Once awe is personified as a being with power of its own, the way is open for Dickinson to use it as a name for God. Yet the word itself reminds us that hers is a deity that "reside[s] in the human breast."[27] In reimagining divinity, Dickinson aligned herself again with Romantic writers, embarked once more on an internal quest to find her way to faith.

We recall that Dickinson at one point called her God "A Force illegible" (P 820); it was fundamental to her spiritual psychology that this superhuman power be mysterious. Awe she associated with the human capacity to respond to this power, and by projection she used it as a word for the divinity itself. In order to reach out or reach within to this divinity, she made her business "circumference," meaning in Jane Donahue Eberwein's careful definition the "ultimate boundary between the finite and the infinite, the known and the mysterious, the human and the divine."[28] Dickinson seems to have preferred such a God, a power that solicits awe, to the God sometimes preached in Amherst churches, a God who punishes and rewards humankind arbitrarily. To quote Eberwein again, a God of awe had "no involvement with man's troubles or aspirations."[29] "It" or "he" could not be mistaken for the bully who frustrated Moses. Such a God reflects a Puritan conception of divinity shaken loose from its dogmatic framework. Though not "like bears," this God is no nineteenth-century sentimental friend either. Indeed, the fear of a God of impersonal dynamic force is for Dickinson a fount of her inspiration and, in that sense, the beginning of wisdom. He is like lightning that dazzles and strikes but leaves behind the reverberations of a baffling grace. For this "waylaying Light" Dickinson is enthusiastically grateful: "I would not exchange the Bolt / For all the rest of Life" (P 1581). He is an unknown God who yet communicates dynamically with human nature. He is illegible and inscrutable; he cannot be described in human language; but nevertheless the experience of encountering him can be conveyed, poetically and dramatically.

One of Dickinson's most interesting attempts to represent this experience of divinity is also one of her most daring distortions of a story from the Bible. Poem 1733, "No man saw awe," is to my mind Dickinson's most creative treatment of the story of Moses. Probably it is also her last, at least the last of those that have survived. If so, it would accord well with my ordering of her poems concerned with Moses. She begins by using him rather lightheartedly as a type of a saintly visionary, then sees him more earnestly as God's victim, but at last dramatizes him as a man whose encounter with the face of awe is representative of something only dimly understood but nevertheless powerfully felt by "human nature." The only version we have of the poem is a copy made by Mrs. Todd.[30]

> No man saw awe, nor to his house
> Admitted he a man
> Though by his awful residence
> Has human nature been.
>
> Not deeming of his dread abode
> Till laboring to flee
> A grasp on comprehension laid
> Detained vitality.
>
> Returning is a different route
> The Spirit could not show
> For breathing is the only work
> To be enacted now.
>
> "Am not consumed," old Moses wrote,
> "Yet saw him face to face" –
> That very physiognomy
> I am convinced was this

"No man saw awe" is an obscure poem and can use a strenuous reading. The poem culminates in a reconsideration of Moses, but it touches earlier on other concerns much brooded over in Dickinson's writings. It begins with deliciously brazen awkwardness: "Saw awe," indeed! one focuses on the sounds as if trying out strange vowels in a foreign language. Moreover, if seeing awe is already a peculiar conception, the reader should be still more disconcerted and bemused to learn that awe has an "awful residence." Not for the last time, Dickinson parades this juxtaposition of "awe" with "awful" to give her metaphysics a colloquial intonation.[31] One point of these oddities is to call attention to the strange yet powerful and inevitable existence of awe as a feature of human experience. Sometimes, when Dickinson wishes to clue in her reader concerning those features of her "real life" not generally acknowledged by common sense, she puts her idiom through amiably jarring contortions. Yet she also insists here that the experience she represents is one humans partake of generally. "By his awful residence / Has human nature been." She insists that there is more to human nature than common sense perception, philosophy, and syntax allow for. Common sense ignores these secrets because, like Horatio, it can neither dream of them nor deal with them when they emerge into experience.

The second and third stanzas of this poem hint at why we creatures of common sense ordinarily prefer not to think about awe. As her earlier writings testify, awe involves sudden terror; one comes upon "his dread abode" without warning. Then one feels caught, frozen, terrified, like the speaker of "I Years had been from Home." Something takes hold of one's "comprehension," a grasp that obsesses the understanding, and this moment of terrified stasis suspends one's "vitality," one's vital life force. From such terror one "flees," but the intensity of the experience is too much for consciousness: one "covers the Abyss with Trance" (P 599). "Breathing is the only work" for human nature now. In one's stunned condition one can "breathe," go through the motions of physical life, yet at least for "now" one is numb to the memory of awe, in its intensity, terror, and numinousness. The spirit cannot return to "his awful residence," cannot reenact this fundamental inner journey.

If the poem stopped after the third stanza, its story would seem a later, if differently developed, version of a psychological story presented in numerous poems of the 1860s, such as "There is a pain – so utter – " (P 599), or "I tie my Hat – I crease my Shawl – " (P 443), or "After great pain, a formal feeling comes – " (P 341), where the speakers are reduced by pain or terror to a state of numbness in which only mechanical activity is possible. Yet, though Poem 1733 certainly harks back to these expressive dramas, already there are hints that "seeing awe" is something different from feeling great pain and its aftereffects or observing that one's "Existence" has "stopped" while one goes on emptily living. One might infer, for example, that, though "the Spirit cannot show" itself the route, it nevertheless wants to find how to return to the house of awe. To be "by his awful residence" might be a human privilege as well as an experience of breathtaking consternation. Moreover, the poem's opening playfulness complements its memory of sheer dread, and the combination of playfulness and remembered dreadfulness beckons toward a further resolution.

What happens next, however, is still surprising. Dickinson works out her psychological speculations by moving far away from her initial imagery and plot (the house, the journey, the breathing afterward) to reimagine an episode from the Bible that the reader must relate to the rest of the poem. In the last stanza she takes as her point of departure the story of Moses encountering God in the burning bush at the beginning of his career as a prophet of the Lord. Her specific subtext is Exodus 3.2: "And the angel of the Lord appeared unto him in a flame of fire out of the midst of a bush: and he looked, and, behold, the bush burned with fire, and the bush was not consumed." In God's fiery presence the bush nevertheless lived on, its life a token of God's awesome but profoundly life-giving and preserving energy. But the Moses of Exodus was overcome with dread. He "hid his face; for he was afraid to look on God" (Exod. 3.6). Dickinson's Moses, in contrast, "saw him face to face." For her Moses represents in the poem the potential of human nature to experience awe and survive the encounter. She rewrites the biblical story to give human nature greater power and dignity. Not only is her Moses "not consumed." If we subliminally remember the angelic fire, we may picture him as illuminated by his vision. Like Jacob in Genesis 32.30 (but unlike the biblical Moses in his various encounters with the Lord) he can unmistakably assert, "I have seen God face to face, and my life is preserved."

Yet in the poem as a whole Dickinson is idiosyncratically faithful to the larger Old Testament story of Moses encountering God. In Moses' several meetings with Jehovah in Scripture the narrators imply alternatively that Moses sees God and that he doesn't.[32] For example, in Exodus 33.20 the Lord says to Moses, "Thou canst not see my face: for there shall no man see me, and live." Then the Lord puts Moses in "a clift of a rock," where he may see his "back parts" but not his face. On the other hand, the narrator of Deuteronomy asserts of Moses after his death, "And there arose not a prophet since in Israel like unto Moses, whom the Lord knew face to face" (Deut. 34.10; see also Exod. 33.11). If the Lord knew Moses face to face, one infers that Moses saw him. The speaker of Poem 1733 brings out a similar contradiction more starkly and concisely. At the start she asserts, "No man saw awe," presumably including Moses. Then at the end she has her Moses say, "yet saw him face to face," and comments, "That very physiognomy / I am convinced was this." Despite the intentional vagueness of "this" (Dickinson means to convey that what she evokes is beyond rational definition), the speaker clearly implies that the "face" or "physiognomy" that Moses "saw" was awe.

Moses as a man could not have seen awe, and yet he saw it. If Moses is a type of the visionary in all of us, as Dickinson apparently means him to be, we too as participants in that human nature he represents have the potential to see awe. We too have been by his awful residence. At the very least we take a participatory satisfaction in Moses' vision. Yet at the same time the poem also says that awe is too overpowering for us to know face to face. The experience of awe, Dickinson implies, can only be rendered by means of such a contradiction. It is both beyond our understanding and within our experience.

Finally, it is significant that "*old* Moses" remembers seeing awe, a reminiscence that justifies his later life and gives him his reason for being. The speaker of this poem treats her old friend not as a victim but as a vessel, an illuminated recipient of awe. But, if Dickinson reconceives Moses she reconceives God also, as an inscrutable divinity she hesitates to name but nevertheless believes in for this poetic occasion, a divinity of power and mystery she associates with Moses' God who spoke from the burning bush, a God who illuminates and terrifies but does not consume the Spirit. This was a form of Jehovah she was happy to countenance.

Dickinson's Moses is lucky in this poem. Normally she assumes that in this life one cannot endure the sight of God's face. Given human nature, the privilege she allows Moses in "No man saw awe" is rare, unaccountable, and expressible only through contradiction. Yet she also wishes to affirm the human potential to enjoy that privilege. Seeing God face to face is one of her key tropes for encountering the boundary between the human and the divine. If the Bible makes this form of knowing awe dangerous, it also makes it entrancing.

A key complementary poem to "No man saw awe" uses similar language and imagery in its final lines but makes no provision for a Moses to exemplify human nature's readiness to survive the encounter with the divine. Yet it too ascribes value only to such all-consuming experiences.

1247

To pile like Thunder to it's close
Then crumble grand away
While Everything created hid
This – would be Poetry –

> Or Love – the two coeval come –
> We both and neither prove –
> Experience either and consume –
> For None see God and live –

In her fine reading of this poem[33] Cristanne Miller emphasizes how Dickinson's language and syntax help to represent the tentativeness with which she approaches the experiences of poetry, love, and the divine. One cannot "know" these essences in themselves, since in this life at least one knows them only by their effects. Moreover, "the expression of creativity, or love, or deeply religious experience of any kind involves the release of potentially destructive power."[34] If one confronted any one of these experiences fully and directly, one would not survive it, "For None see God and live –." Yet the poem also makes such experiences powerfully inviting and leaves ambiguous whether one can have them in actual life. As Miller points out, "consume" is an uninflected verb that in this context can mean either "are consumed" (are destroyed) or "consume" (take in).[35] In the conjectured world of Dickinsonian abstract ideas we are consumed by the divine. Awe and love and poetry are too much for us. Yet in the actual world of human feeling we regulate our responses; we die and become again; we survive spiritually by consuming. In "No man saw awe" Moses both sees awe and doesn't. In "To pile like Thunder" "we" experience poetry and love and yet fail to experience them. "We both and neither prove – ." Dickinson resorts openly to contradiction to exhibit the paradoxical nature of what goes on at circumference.

In "To pile like Thunder" Dickinson also zestfully eliminates the boundaries between poetry and love and then between them and "seeing God." The very fact that these are distinct activities when symbolized in ordinary language makes her amalgamate them all the more readily. Like Thoreau, she would overpower ordinary language by means of "extra-vagance" to tell her volatile truth.[36] Dickinson posits love and poetry as interconnected limit experiences that "together come," that happen simultaneously when one of them happens. She prefers not to fixate her beliefs and experiences but, like Emerson, to illustrate their fluidity. As for Emerson, so also for Dickinson, human nature has access to the divine through diverse but analogous experiences of vastation and illumination, analogous because each is a specific analogy for the fundamental experience of circumference she made it her business to know and articulate. Yet, as the poem suggests, it is "poetry" that makes other experiences of circumference available to Dickinson. Through her conversation, her letter writing, and her responsiveness to the language of body and spirit, she knows what love is. In reading the Bible she finds awe dramatized and made credible. By tasting "this loved Philology," she can also taste her Christ, the divine analogue, "a Word made Flesh" (P 1651).

Jesus Christ

As "To pile like Thunder" and "No man saw awe" suggest, seeing God face to face is analogous in Dickinson's writing to other ways of going "out upon Circumference" (P 378), analogous not only to "Poetry" or "Love" but also to tasting "A Word made Flesh" or to confronting the "awful Mother" within. Hence her Bible stories about Jacob and Moses are in part occasions to tell a story she told over and over with differing emphases, the story of human nature's experience of the beautiful dark, the awesome unknown. In fact, her narratives of Jacob's and Moses' en- counters with the divine change to suit the occasions she finds for them. Jacob and Moses do not stay the same in her mind but are biblical types to whom she gives varying meanings over the course of her career. Yet, if she meditated on them in different ways at different times, their im- portance to her as exemplary dramatic figures in her Bible was sus- tained and crucial.

Still more crucial in Dickinson's religious imagination and her read- ing of the Bible is the figure of Jesus Christ. Her imagination seizes on him as the chief source of comfort in the Christian tradition, while with part of her mind she assumes a critical detachment from him. The Christ she reveres is not only the Christian God as a friend, a divine Pardoner of human weakness. He is also the exemplar of those active human virtues that we have seen her celebrate: constancy in loving and long- ing, courage in facing the unknown, the willingness of a Jacob to strug- gle with the divine, the persistence in vision of a Moses, and her own in- sistent generosity in blessing her loved ones. As Dickinson sees it, precisely because Jesus was so fully human in his virtues is proof of his divinity.

Dickinson liked to think of Jesus as a God who chose to be human and who was willing to renounce life and die as a man to test his human love. Indeed, in a letter of September 1877 she could write to Higginson:

"To be human is more than to be divine, for when Christ was divine, he was uncontented till he had been human" (*L,* 2:592). At such times she was ready to enlist Christ as a partisan of her own this-worldliness. Yet in November of that same year, as if to correct a balance and reaffirm Christ's divinity, she wrote to Richard H. Mather, a professor of classics at Amherst: "That the Divine has been human is at first an unheeded solace, but it shelters without our consent – " (*L,* 2:594). The story of Jesus in the Bible is proof that the divine can exist in the human world, can even "shelter" us without our knowing it. Both these sentences appear in letters of consolation to men who have lost their wives, as if to intimate that Christ's readiness to face death allows one to hope that by dying these women too may partake of the divine as they encounter the circumference of their human lives. He is a model for all humans as we come to the time of trial.

A significant group of Dickinson's poems, especially from the crisis years, enact her version of an *imitatio Christi,* imagine Jesus Christ as a divinely human model of courage and tenderness whom her speakers find solace in imitating. In a phrase rightly celebrated by Dorothy Huff Oberhaus, Dickinson calls Christ a "Tender Pioneer,"[37] a man whose boundless compassion for his fellow humans and whose utter confidence in exploring the unknown realm of death set a standard the speaker holds up for herself and her readers, to inspire them with their own adventurousness and tenderness.

698

Life – is what we make it –
Death – We do not know –
Christ's acquaintance with Him
Justify Him – though –

He – would trust no stranger –
Other – could betray –
Just His own endorsement –
That – sufficeth Me –

All the other Distance
He hath traversed first –
No New Mile remaineth –
Far as Paradise –

>   His sure foot preceding –
>   Tender Pioneer –
>   Base must be the Coward
>   Dare not venture – now –

In this poem it is clear that Dickinson means seriously to play the role of a Christian pilgrim herself and to express her spirit of devotion traditionally as well as personally. Clearly also, she imagines a like-minded audience for her Christian message. "We" as her readers may not know death but would not be so "base" as to fear it now that Christ has shown the way to journey through it.

What "justifies" Christ for this loving pilgrim is his "acquaintance with" death and his assured temper of mind at the Crucifixion. The orthodox Dickinson passionately and repeatedly commemorates Jesus' exemplary willingness to die as a vulnerable human being like herself. This willingness presumably helped Dickinson to contemplate her own death and to console her for the deaths of others. As she claims was also true of her "dearest earthly friend" Charles Wadsworth (*L*, 3:764), Jesus' "personal Expanse," his individual human grandeur, sustained him through his dying and death, the "most profound experiment / Appointed unto Men – " (P 822).

>   Obtaining but his own extent
>   In whatsoever Realm –
>   'Twas Christ's own personal Expanse
>   That bore him from the Tomb.
>   (P 1543; text from letter 776, a eulogy of Wadsworth [*L*, 3:745])

Dickinson's persistent adoption of Jesus as a source of comfort and a heroic exemplar, however, still gives her latitude to vary her treatment of him. True to her nimble belief in him as well as to her sense of the changeableness of all inner experience, she kept dramatizing him differently, with great variety throughout her career. If Jacob and Moses are variable types in Dickinson's rewritings of Bible stories, Jesus Christ is a variable antitype, a lasting archetypal model for all humans whose image nevertheless changes to suit her poetic needs. There are occasions when she manifests hostility to received conceptions of Christ, as when she remembers him as a bogeyman of her childhood, or dismisses him as a figment of the Calvinist imagination, a "Prince" who is "Son of

None" (P 721). Especially in a few poems of the 1860s (e.g., Poems 497, 502) her speaker berates him as a divine figure who will not answer her prayers, because (like the Calvinist Father) he seems not to be listening. Yet Dickinson also writes many devotional poems to Christ that follow rather than violate the expectations of her Protestant culture. Or she experiments with devotions of her own. In at least one poem, we shall see, she celebrates Christ as wholly divine, a companion and antagonist to God the Father. Often she prefers to write of him in generously human terms as the Jesus who "yearns for a oneness" and "hints of a celestial reunion"[38] or as a shepherd of souls who proclaims, "And let him that is athirst come" (L, 3:701).

Dickinson expresses a more detached and critical synthesis of attitudes toward Jesus in a late letter to her neighbor, Mrs. Henry Hills. "When Jesus tells us about his Father, we distrust him. When he shows us his Home, we turn away, but when he confides to us that he is 'acquainted with Grief,' we listen, for that also is an Acquaintance of our own" (L, 3:837). It is worth stressing that the Jesus of this fragment is a creature of Dickinson's reading. He is the confessional narrator of his own story who "tells," "shows," and "confides" to "us," meaning to Dickinson as our representative reader. Though the Jesus she imagines elsewhere is not always obviously biblical, this letter suggests that her complex of views concerning him derives essentially from the Gospels. Because she has formed her image of him through reading, she feels freer to manipulate that image to suit the varying contexts in which she turns to Jesus. Here she discriminates between three of her views.

First, as in "Who were 'the Father and the Son,'" she is wary of a conception of Jesus that couples him with a sovereign God read Calvinistically. She cannot reach a Jesus who is only a duplicate sky-god, a "Jesus – in the Air" (P 502). Her second implicit view is more intriguing because so heretically unfamiliar. I read "When he shows us his Home" as her periphrasis for Jesus' allusions to his resurrection in heaven. She uses "Home" elsewhere as a metonymy for "Paradise," as in the pronouncement, "whatever await us of Doom or Home, we are mentally permanent" (L, 2:612; see also L, 2:329, 635). The late Dickinson, as we have seen, developed her own more hypothetical imagination of the afterlife and avoided aligning her eschatology with her culture's. Yet, while she "distrusts" a Jesus of authoritarian belief and "turns away" from a Jesus of other-worldly legend, she "listens" to a Jesus "acquainted with Grief"[39] like herself. "Grief" meant many things to Dickinson, but it seems especially to have meant the grief of coping with death.

The image of Jesus Dickinson here prefers is that of a human being who struggles in this world, who is willing to grieve and die as a man. Yet her preference does not imply an exclusion; she gives equal attention to the other-worldly Jesus she "distrusts." Moreover, Dickinson's three Jesuses are grammatically the same, even if engaged in differing acts. In other words, despite what I take to be her humanist disposition, Dickinson here makes no attempt—as Theodore Parker might—to sift a historical and merely human Jesus from the Gospels. In her grammar she implies her intimacy with a Jesus who is both historical and divine, however much she may distrust his words on suitable occasions. She assumes through her style of projection a closeness to him that nineteenth-century liberals have lost, while at the same time assuming a reader's equality with him that would be a scandal to nineteenth-century orthodoxy.

Commentators on Dickinson's use of Christ have either tried to present a unitary conception of him they extrapolate from her writings or acknowledged her variety but treated it as chaos.[40] I would argue that when she turns to Christ she always has a design but that her designs vary not only because she inhabits a transitional period in intellectual history but also because she prefers to vary them. Her unusual combination of belief in him and contemplative distance from him generates new opportunities for a writer of fictions that are her way of giving Jesus his deserved importance. I will read four of her Christ poems, all of which in different ways recall his encounter with the unknown divine in and after death. Two poems celebrate his exemplary courage in dying on the Cross: one is an imagined narrative of his interaction with God in eternity, and the last is an evocation of the dying and redemption of a beloved friend who is also a type of Christ. All four poems experiment with the limits of orthodoxy: they ennoble the human by associating it with Christ or present fables of divinity not found in any catechism or put Christ in the shadow of a human friend. Together the poems give a sense of the variety of Dickinson's Christ-centered imaginings and bring us back to her apprehensions of the divine and her struggles with the unknown.

The first of these poems is one in which Dickinson appeals to Christ as an exemplar of courageous active humility. Like other New Englanders before her, she applied her reading of Jesus' life typologically to her own experience, not in a public or political context but privately. Her Jesus here is the antitype of suffering love in her "private typology of personal affairs."[41]

833

Perhaps you think me stooping
I'm not ashamed of that
Christ – stooped until He touched the Grave –
Do those at Sacrament

Commemorate Dishonor
Or love annealed of love
Until it bend as low as Death
Redignified, above?

Just what the speaker literally means by her own "stooping" is impossible to say; on a personal level the poem is a passionate plea to an unidentified friend, and its private context remains veiled.[42] Yet when the speaker likens herself to Christ in the wonderful line "Christ – stooped so low until He touched the Grave – ," she makes transcendent all loving self-sacrifice, her own as well as Christ's. By means of an unstated analogy between "stooping" and "touching the grave," the poem imagines Christ as both human and divinely more-than-human. He "stooped" to become human in the first place and stooped even more grandly to die, touch the circumference of life, and encounter the beyond. Only by means of such a renunciation of life could he be "redignified above," take on divinity again. When the speaker suggests that her stooping is like Christ's, she implies that she too is willing to die, to meet that circumference. The second stanza implies as well that she is willing to melt and "be annealed of love"—tempered and strengthened through love as Christ was. As a type of Christ, the speaker undertakes to love, die, be annealed, and be transfigured—her stooping potentially entails all this. Moreover, when she celebrates Christ's humanity and her own, she implicitly repudiates Paul's claim that humankind is "sown in dishonour" (1 Cor. 15.43; see P 62). Not Total Depravity, but the human capacity to stoop with humility, melt with love, and be thereby annealed and strengthened, makes the imitation of Christ possible.

Christ is again a figure of heroic renunciation in a companion poem that also implies Dickinson's freedom to read his heroism according to her own lights rather than those of her religious tradition.

527

To put this World down, like a Bundle –
And walk steady, away,
Requires Energy – possibly Agony –
'Tis the Scarlet way

Trodden with straight renunciation
By the Son of God –
Later, his faint Confederates
Justify the Road –

Flavors of that old Crucifixion –
Filaments of Bloom, Pontius Pilate sowed –
Strong Clusters, from Barabbas' Tomb –

Sacrament, Saints partook before us –
Patent every drop,
With the Brand of the Gentile Drinker
Who indorsed the Cup –

partook] indorsed   indorsed] enforced
Brand] Stamp

This is a poem of faith in Christ's divine humanity, a meditation on "the Son of God" who also manifested human energy and felt human agony. As in "Perhaps you think me stooping," Christ's act of renunciation is uncanny and unknowable, while it is also supremely exemplary and helps the speaker to sustain her own immortal longings. "To put this World down, like a Bundle – / And walk, steady, away," requires a miracle of fortitude the speaker nevertheless aspires to. It is like poetry, love, and seeing God face to face—too much for human nature. Yet Christ did it and made it an achievement for human imitation.

Christ's renunciation was beyond comprehension even for the writers of the Gospels, the first of his "faint Confederates" who "Justify the Road." We who come much later can only get a sense of his story from "Flavors, Filaments, and Clusters"—atmospheric essences and stray threads we apprehend through the mediation of earlier justifications. The "Confederate" largely responsible for our (mis-)understanding is "the Gentile Drinker," who seems to have predetermined the Christian way as we know it. This preemptive interpreter, I think, is the Apostle Paul. Paul was no Gentile, but as apostle to the Gentiles Dickinson is likely to have identified him as such for poetic purposes.[43] She was knowingly skeptical of the "Brand" of Pauline Christianity she inherited from Calvinist "Saints" who came before her. Whoever the Gentile Drinker, he stands between us and Christ. The end of the poem insists with quiet irony on our distance from Christ, whose uncanny stooping passes understanding.[44] The speaker would restore divine mystery to Jesus while vividly recalling his human striving, his energy and agony.

Once she concludes that the Saints have misread Christ and imposed their distortions on his gift of himself in the "Sacrament," the way is open for Dickinson not only to celebrate his miraculous renunciation anew but also to reimagine him in different ways. One of Dickinson's most surprising Christ poems celebrates his prowess not as God's incarnate son on earth or as a courageous exemplary man facing death but as God's divine antagonist in heaven. The poem seems invented to answer the question, what fiction would I come up with if I made the risen Christ into a heavenly Jacob.

865

He outstripped Time with but a Bout,
He outstripped Stars and Sun
And then, unjaded, challenged God
In presence of the Throne.

And He and He in mighty List
Unto this present, run,
The larger Glory for the less
A just sufficient Ring.

Dickinson does not name her hero—it is part of the tact of the poem to focus on his astounding action rather than his identity—but it seems to me plainly evident that "He" is the Son of God transfigured. This is the Christ who overcame death, harrowed hell, and ascended into heaven. No longer bound by time or subject to a natural universe of stars and sun, he assumes his place by the throne of God. But the companionship of Father and Son is presented not as a serene conversation, as in Milton, but as a struggle, a "mighty List." Christ is thus the antitype of Jacob, the wrestler who "worsted God" in Dickinson's poem. More remotely, he is connected to the Dickinson who would "*harass God*" until he let a beloved friend into Paradise (*L,* 2:393—the phrase is from a poem addressed to Samuel Bowles). Dickinson liked the idea of challenging God; it meant pushing against human limits and wresting from the deity an acknowledgment of human needs and aspirations. Yet only in this poem does she make Christ into a vehicle for this impulse and even transports him beyond the human realm to confront God "in presence of the Throne." Gentle Jesus is absent in such a conception of Christ's and God's Glory as an eternal "Ring," an arena for struggle. Such an image of divinity is dynamic but impersonal, as if Dickinson gravitates once again toward a vision of God as "a Force illegible" and also imagines a place for Christ in such a quasi-Calvinist cosmology.

At an opposite extreme from "He outstripped Time with but a Bout" is a poem that—as I read it—conflates Christ on the Cross with a dying mortal man, affectionately remembered.[45] Rather than a wrestler, this man is a weakened sufferer. Here the Christ the poem dramatizes is at first wholly human. Yet the speaker of the poem has faith that the consciousness of the dying man, like Christ's, will be divinely changed, will survive death to participate in the fullness of God's glory.

622

To know just how He suffered – would be dear –
To know if any Human eyes were near
To whom He could entrust His wavering gaze –
Until it settled broad – on Paradise –

To know if He was patient – part content –
Was Dying as He thought – or different –
Was it a pleasant Day to die –
And did the Sunshine face His way –

What was His furthest mind – Of Home – or God –
Or what the Distant say –
At news that He ceased Human Nature
Such a Day –

And Wishes – Had He Any –
Just His Sigh – Accented –
Had been legible – to Me –
And was He Confident until
Ill fluttered out – in Everlasting Well –

And if He spoke – What name was Best –
What last
What One broke off with
At the Drowsiest –

Was He afraid – or tranquil –
Might He know
How Conscious Consciousness – could grow –
Till Love that was – and Love too best to be –
Meet – and the Junction be Eternity

This remarkable, sentimental, and reverent poem has been little no-
ticed.[46] To my mind the speaker's affectionate voice, craftily modulated
through variations in the meter, makes her sentiment not maudlin
but expressive in an intelligent total structure. The pentameter lines
in the first stanza and in significant junctures later, along with the
open vowels of line endings (*dear/near, wavering gaze/Paradise, die/
way/say*), help convey the speaker's serene concern about the dying
man's state of mind, a mind that she cannot know but in which she
deeply trusts. The more truncated two-, three-, and four-beat lines
within the poem suggest the dying man's and the sympathizing
speaker's questionings, yet these short-breathed units issue in pen-
tameter lines containing unanswerable affirmations: "Everlasting
Well," "Love too best to be," "Eternity." Hardly another poem Dickin-
son wrote seems so confident about "the Extension of Consciousness,
after Death."

The confidence stems partly from the presence of the Christ story as
a subtext to a story of human dying and redemption. In one of its di-
mensions, reinforced by the capitalization of "He" throughout, the poem
expresses the speaker's effort to imagine Christ's human suffering, iso-
lation, and uncertainty on the Cross until "He ceased Human Nature"
and "His wavering gaze . . . settled broad – on Paradise." (The "broad-
ness" of the gaze finely anticipates the growth of divine love at the end

of the poem.) The speaker's perfect assurance of her friend's salvation suggests that she envisions him as a type of Christ who illustrates how Christ's agony and triumph might repeat themselves in her own circle of loved ones. It is the Christ in him that suffers but also loves and survives, "until / Ill fluttered out – in Everlasting Well." Such a faith-inspired vision provides her with a wishfully serene consolation for his dying.

The speaker's distance from the departed friend (or her still greater historical distance from Christ on the Cross) is overcome by her powerful wish to "read" him. "Just His Sigh – Accented – / Had been legible – to Me." Her voice is balanced between questioning uncertainty and confidence that she can make that sigh legible, can transport herself to the scene of Christ's (or the friend's) agony and understand it, can by means of her sympathy get through the veil of inscrutability covering another's soul. Moreover, since the friend she cherishes is sure to join with God in love, God himself is accessible and indirectly legible to the speaker.

The final stanza reinforces the friend's likeness to Christ and links the poem to other poems we have been reading. The friend might be both afraid *and* tranquil, as Christ was in different phases of his agony. Yet, despite the dying man's imagined fear, the speaker is certain that his "personal Expanse" will "bear him from the Tomb"; "Consciousness" can "grow" until it joins with God in love. Like Moses, the dying man sees awe but is not consumed. I read "Love that was" as Christ's human love, or as Christ's indwelling love in the friend. "Love too best to be" is a divine love that humans can acknowledge but cannot experience in human life, a love that will nevertheless be joined with "the Love that was" in "Eternity." Dickinson thus retells in a key of serenity how "the larger Glory" of God blends in eternity "with the less," with the human glory of Christ. Eternity is imagined here as an infinite ring of love, not as the terrifying "odd fork in Being's Road" the speaker meets in "Our journey had advanced – " (P 615) or as the "Maelstrom – in the Sky –" of "Before Me – dips Eternity –" (P 721). And consciousness is a secret capacity in the soul for personal expansion, not an "awful stranger" who waylays a terrified speaker (P 1323). With the example of Christ to encourage her, Dickinson dramatizes a confident attitude toward the terror of death with all the affectionate seriousness she can muster.

These poems movingly suggest how central Jesus Christ on the Cross was for Dickinson, while at the same time she imagined him as a "nimble centre" with "circumference elastic."[47] They bring us up against a series of paradoxes that are essential to her poetics of the unknown. First, her imagination of Christ, as of Jacob and Moses, is essentially of a human figure in a poetry that focuses on the trials of human nature in "the world we know," yet Christ has supreme value in her writing because he dared to enter the world that is "a wonder still," the unknown world of death where he found God's glory. Her private typology allows her to move flexibly between these two worlds. Second, while Dickinson implies that the experiences she evokes in all her biblically or typologically based poems are common to human nature, she also stretches the conception of human nature so that "common sense" no longer meaningfully applies to it. Encounters with angels or with awe or with God require a new language that departs from common-sense assumptions. At circumference ordinary conceptual language falters, and one resorts to fluid contradictions—one sees God face to face and one doesn't; one dies in the act of love or the practice of poetry and also survives. Similarly, Christ knew God and transcended humanity, yet his value lies in the fact that "he was uncontented till he had been human." In nearly all her writings Dickinson wanted him to be a human Christ, a friend in need, not a merely transcendent divinity. At the same time, she wanted him to remain a divine and human mystery. As she saw it, the intellect needs the unknown, in human nature, in the natural world, and in the divine.

4

The Unknown as Needed
and Dreadful

Circumscribing the Unknown

> Vinnie has a new pussy the color of Branwell Brontë's hair. She thinks it a little "lower than the angels," and I concur with her. You remember my ideal cat has always a huge rat in its mouth, just going out of sight – though going out of sight in itself has a peculiar charm. It is true that the unknown is the largest need of the intellect, though for it, no one thinks to thank God. (*L*, 2:559)

This passage from a letter of 1876 to the Norcross sisters is the surprising context for Dickinson's surprising claim that "the unknown is the largest need of the intellect." This pronouncement is the catalyst for the following chapter. In her letter Dickinson informs her cousins that her sister Vinnie has still another cat, and that she [Emily] agrees with Vinnie that it is "a little lower than the angels." (Probably she means a lot lower—Emily was perpetually disenchanted with Vinnie's cats.)[1] Yet, though Dickinson pictures her "ideal cat" as "going out of sight" with a rat in its mouth, this grisly image also reminds her whimsically that she cherishes the charm of "going out of sight in itself," cherishes the principle of evanescence. Such a principle, I take it, is part of what "the intellect" needs from "the unknown." The intellect needs not to know definitively and permanently the things it observes because they exist in time and space and disappear into an unknowable realm. It seems to be Dickinson's considered opinion (the aphorism reads like one she has meditated and stored away) that not only do we as humans live surrounded by the unknown, but also, given the nature of our minds and our desires, we are better off for it and ought to "thank God" that so much is undisclosed to us.

It is useful to have Dickinson's well-known aphorism before us in context for several reasons. First, the context illustrates that for her thinking is a temporal process of casually surprising associations rather than a systematic working out of "timeless" arguments. Her sense that we live and think evanescently in time contributes to the value she gives to the unknown—thoughts go out of sight as well as cats. Second, for Dickinson the unknown-as-needed is not far away in the passage from the unknown-as-dreadful. What goes out of sight here is a representative predatory animal in a brutal world in which God's creatures kill and die. One thanks such an unpredictable and unknowable God warily as well as gratefully. Later in this same letter Dickinson will tell the Norcross sisters that she dreams differently every night of her father, dead now two years—he too has gone out of sight. Death, here as elsewhere, is the frightful unknown in her mental universe. The quoted passage as a whole balances the dread Dickinson conjures up at the grisly cat against the gratitude humans owe God for his unknown gifts, an incongruous balancing of terror at her world and affection for it one finds sometimes in her reflections. In this case gratitude prevails, and dread is in abeyance. The passage suggests that Dickinson has (for the moment) come to terms with her condition as one of God's creatures observing the vanishing unknowableness of life. The mood changes from bemusement at her sister's foibles to mock horror at her own ideal cat to the intelligent serenity of a writer of challenging aphorisms. I think Dickinson means it when she implies that one should thank God for the unknown. She may well express anxiety about the unknown at many points in her writing, yet fundamentally she means to accept it and relish it. I see no sign whatsoever that her state of mind in the aphorism is "that of the temporarily enervated, disconsolate quester,"[2] as one critic writes. Instead, it is one more illustration that Dickinson accepts her vocation as a poet of intellect whose special province is the unknown—in God and God's creation, in the inner life of human beings, in the human experience of nature, and in the sorcery or chaos of death.

Dickinson's preoccupation with the unknown is pervasive in her work. (As Christopher Benfey points out, next to "to be," derivatives of "to know" are more frequent than any other verb in her poetry.)[3] Yet her conception and treatment of it have proved elusive. One reason for this elusiveness is that the unknown is not so much a subject she takes up as a condition of her poetic existence she perpetually comes up against. Whether it prompts her to reverence or to fear, it is the ground of her poetry, the condition of her being that makes her invent her own poetic worlds. All the general subjects she considers interesting—"God," "nature," ecstasy or "transport," one's beloved friends and other human beings, even one's own "consciousness"—she identifies as "subjects of which we know nothing," or "strangers."

> But nature is a stranger yet;
> The ones that cite her most
> Have never passed her haunted house,
> Nor simplified her ghost.
>
> (P 1400)[4]

> We must travel abreast with Nature if we want to know her, but where shall be obtained the Horse –
>
> (*PF*, 119; *L*, 3:929)

> I do not know the man so bold
> He dare in lonely Place
> That awful stranger Consciousness
> Deliberately face –
>
> (P 1323)

> His mind of man, a secret makes
> I meet him with a start
> He carries a circumference
> In which I have no part
>
> (P 1663)

The last two of these texts suggest how often Dickinson focuses on an unknown inner life, her own or that of stranger-friends she meets and observes. Her "haunt and the main region of her song" is the life within, yet, as Sharon Cameron says, "we have few words, if any, for what happens inside us."[5] Finding a language of names and metaphors for the inner life is an ongoing challenge for Dickinson. She feels challenged, for example, to write a poetry of pain, "the most excruciating interior experience, and perhaps the most inherently nameless."[6]

955

The Hollows round His eager Eyes
Were Pages where to read
Pathetic Histories – although
Himself had not complained.
Biography to All who passed
Of Unobtrusive Pain
Except for the italic Face
Endured, unhelped – unknown.

But she is also challenged to express the success of her efforts to live introspectively, to evoke, for example, the steadfastness of emotional and personal "growth," a name for an unknowable private process that cannot be shared, except intuitively.

Growth of Man – like Growth of Nature –
Gravitates within –
Atmosphere, and Sun endorse it –
But it stir – alone –

Each – it's difficult Ideal
Must achieve – Itself –
Through the solitary prowess
Of a Silent Life –

(P 750, st. 1 – 2)

As with her interior world, so also with her exterior. Dickinson's sense that we live surrounded by the unknown is exacerbated by her suspicion that our perceptions do not put us directly in touch with the world we perceive. According to her radical idealism, the very act of perception divides what is perceived from the perceiver: "Perception of an object costs / Precise the Object's loss – " (P 1071). The "object" in this poem recedes into the distance, a "Perfectness" by virtue of being perceived, but also "Heavenly far."[7] Though "Perception in itself" is "a Gain," though we take in what we perceive and have it available for contemplation, the object perceived has gone "out of sight" and into the mind. True, Dickinson's idealism was in the philosophical air in her New England. She could have found an awareness of the epistemological problems of the isolated self in articles she read in the *Atlantic*

Monthly,[8] in Emerson's "Experience," in the chapter "Solitude" from Thoreau's *Walden*, or in the play of characters in Hawthorne's *The Scarlet Letter* or *The Blithedale Romance*. For these last three writers as well as for Dickinson, "souls never touch their objects. An innavigable sea washes with silent waves between us and the things we aim at and converse with."[9] But, though Dickinson certainly responds to Emerson and his school, she insists more consequentially on the separateness of the self and the pervasiveness of the unknown than any of her predecessors and contemporaries. As we have seen, this obsession draws strength and intensity from her religious upbringing.

Throughout this study I have been concerned with Dickinson's fascination with the unknown as a gift or burden that came with her religious inheritance. I have stressed that the Calvinist tradition she was raised in was especially hospitable to the idea of God as unknowable. Calvinist doctrines of predestination and sanctification tended to make the Calvinist God less approachable through intermediaries than the God of other conservative traditions such as the Roman Catholic and more a distinct mysterious being than the transfigured human God of late-nineteenth-century liberals and Unitarians. A sovereign God who elects and sanctifies whom he will out of his mere good pleasure is not bound by human expectations. Similarly, the Calvinist conception of the sacrament of Holy Communion puts God at an intellectual distance from the believing communicant. For Calvin when Christ said, "This is my body," his expression was "metonymical"; the bread at the Supper is thus a corporeal "sign" of a spiritual mystery but is not "the thing signified," not the mystery itself.[10] In Dickinson's use of sacramental imagery she draws freely on this distancing poetic conception of God's workings. On the one hand, she identifies key experiences as sacramental, hence giving them a living and corporeal religious significance, like the wordless communication of lovers in "There came a Day at Summer's Full" (P 322) or the "Sacrament of summer days" in "These are the days when Birds come back – " (P 130). On the other hand, her sacramental moments point to an unknown beyond themselves and are shadowed by her consciousness of their evanescence. They are seldom if ever moments of lasting fulfillment, like Herbert's "So I did sit and eat" ("Love" 3). For her "A Word made Flesh" is emphatically a word, a sign, an instance of "loved Philology" (P 1651), recalling Christ or the body of Christ only by analogy.

When Dickinson rejected the Calvinist God of her local tradition,

the appalling Father of "Who were the Father and the Son," the God or
spirit she chose in some moods to replace him with was equally in-
scrutable. The God of "awe" that old Moses sees and survives is no more
knowable than the "Eclipse - whom they call their 'Father'" (L, 2:404)
or the distant God one of her earlier speakers petitions for temporary
relief, a Being "too vast, for interrupting – more – " (P 293), or the ab-
sentee God who "remembered" at last so "the Fiend" finally let go of its
distraught victim (P 414). In all these instances Dickinson's speakers
imagine God as "a Force illegible" (P 820). Dickinson's projected strug-
gles with a sadistic Jehovah are dramatized differently from her over-
whelmed contemplations of God as an awesome Stranger, but in
both cases her intellect needs an unknown divinity to make its dramas
effective.[11]

Though Dickinson certainly had gentler forms of faith in an un-
known Creator than she presents in any of these texts, even when she is
"better Friends" with the divine she does not deprive it of its mystery.
As we recall, the late poems in which she tries out her faith in the per-
manence of the spirit are markedly abstract, as if by means of a new ap-
propriate style to represent the unknowableness of "costumeless Con-
sciousness" (P 1454). In another late poem of faith in a mysterious
divinity she writes, "The Star's Etruscan Argument / Substantiate a
God – " (P 1528). By "Etruscan" she means that God's language of in-
struction as written in the stars is remote and illegible. Similarly, her Je-
sus is not merely the gentle Jesus preferred by her contemporary culture
but is also a hero of consciousness who confronted the unknown. She
identifies with him particularly because he had the courage to face
death, the ultimate unknown. And his presence in the Bible moves her
because "the words He spake" are meaningfully obscure; they contain
"fabulous gulfs of meaning."

Dickinson's reading of the Bible, as we have seen, often focuses on
encounters with the unknown: on Jacob's wrestling with the angel or on
Moses's astonishment at the burning bush that was not consumed or on
Christ's miraculous stooping to touch the grave and survive. Moreover,
her historical position allowed or forced her to contemplate the Bible as
a multiply indeterminate and thus unknowable text. For her orthodox
ancestors and neighbors it was a vehicle of certain truth and knowledge,
"composed" as it was "by holy men as they were moved by the Holy
Ghost." For her those "men" were "unknown" or "faded" (P 1545).[12]

Because its authority was questionable, much of the Bible might be legend. Given her sense of its multiple indeterminacy, she felt at liberty to revise or rethink or divide it up as suited her. Some of its words she attributed to "Jonathan Edwards," others to "Jesus." Even Jesus himself was masked for her by Christian tradition and knowable only in imaginative conjecture. Her recognition of the Bible's indeterminacy did not make it any less compelling for her; on the contrary, she felt compelled to keep responding to it. Yet her continuing engagement with it as a text she knew in intimate detail led her to both believe and disbelieve in it, painfully or nimbly.

In what follows, I will stress the ways in which Dickinson's intellect needs and values the unknown. It seems to me that her enthusiastic interest in it has baffled readers less apt to be fond of it themselves. Yet I will also underscore how enthusiasm can modulate into dread or at least mock dread in her texts, as in her reflections on Vinnie's cats with which I began, and how fear of a meaningless unknown perpetually threatens her speakers even in the midst of poems and passages of faith or gratitude. I will start with two poems that dramatize dynamic spiritual change, an unknown inner process she represents as an alternative to Calvinist conversion. Then I will address her preoccupation with death and how that gives urgency to her latent fear of the unknown. Next, I will move back to Dickinson's appreciation of the unknown and to a topic seemingly undisturbed by the dread of death, her aesthetic interest in the remote and the undisclosed, in distant landscapes that pass and "go out of sight" even as they are apprehended. This focus on the distant unknown leads into a consideration of Dickinson's use of nature, both as an unknowable subject and as a storehouse of metaphors for human concerns. I will conclude with three poems based in natural imagery that in different ways balance terror or estrangement in the presence of the unknown with faith or interest in it.

As should already be apparent, one difficulty in broaching such a subject is that "unknown" shifts its meaning according to its context in Dickinson's writing. If it refers to spiritual change or poetic inspiration, she is prone to celebrate the unknown even while such changes may leave her speakers devastated as well as uplifted. If it refers to God's inscrutability, her texts may reflect her mixed response to a post-Calvinist God of awe and power. If she contemplates the unknowableness of

death, her speakers struggle to allow for it and still persist in their be-
ing. If nature is unknown, it can provide Dickinson with a poetic op-
portunity to invent a host of responses to it.

Dickinson's unknown, then, appears variously in various contexts.
Yet, despite the diversity of its manifestations, it needs to be grasped as
a single entity as well as examined for its different meanings. Sometimes
one can distinguish sharply between a chaotic, impenetrable unknown
implicit in death:

> Death is the supple Suitor
> That wins at last – . . .
> It bears away in triumph
> To Troth unknown
> And Kinsmen as divulgeless
> As throngs of Down –
>
> (P 1445)

and a mysterious and lovely unknown implicit in human and divine
creativity:

> So of the Flower of the Soul
> It's process is unknown.
>
> (P 945)

Dickinson herself, however, does not reflect analytically on this distinc-
tion. The unknown is a single flexible abstraction for her that attracts or
appalls her speakers depending upon their moods and circumstances.
She seems to have preferred to keep a spectrum of meanings available
for reflection on the subject, meanings that she does not differentiate
from one another. One needs to allow her the play of her different re-
sponses to the unknown in order to understand her sensibility and her
will to experiment with uncertainty.

Grace and Change

Throughout her career Dickinson is attracted to a dynamic spirituality
that evades the categories she learned in church and school.

673

The Love a Life can show Below
Is but a filament, I know,
Of that diviner thing
That faints upon the face of Noon –
And smites the Tinder in the Sun –
And hinders Gabriel's Wing –

'Tis this – in Music – hints and sways –
And far abroad on Summer days –
Distils uncertain pain –
'Tis this enamors in the East –
And tints the Transit in the West
With harrowing Iodine –

'Tis this – invites – appalls – endows –
Flits – glimmers – proves – dissolves –
Returns – suggests – convicts – enchants –
Then – flings in Paradise –

"That diviner thing" transforms and enhances human existence pre-
cisely because it cannot be analyzed or named or known. It is unknow-
able in large part because it is continually "going out of sight." Nowhere
in Dickinson is her attraction to evanescence more dynamically con-
veyed. Even before the astonishing last stanza the poem is full of verbs
of epiphany: Divine love "faints," "hints," "sways," and "enamors."
Moreover, it operates in an imagined landscape that expands the scope
of evanescence. The circumference of the poem is a "sceneless" fusion
of distant cosmic horizons. That diviner thing moves dynamically and
elastically back and forth between the mind and the horizon, passing
from "the face of Noon" to "the Sun," to the hindered flight of an angel,
to "far abroad on Summer days," to an enamored East, and to a transi-
tory harrowing sunset in the West. The scope and the rapid transitions
of this love imply its power—we recall that Dickinson preferred the
Power to the Kingdom and the Glory. Love powerfully "smites the Tin-
der in the Sun," bringing the brightness of day to the speaker. The ex-
perience of love here is implicitly erotic as well as dynamic, both in its
endlessness of feeling and in its linking of pleasure to pain. The power

of love "Distils uncertain pain – " and reminds the speaker of death as
figured in the "harrowing Iodine" of the sunset. Thus the poem also
brings out the painfulness and dread with which one experiences Dick-
inson's religious unknown. Divine love "appalls" as well as "enamors,"
even if it brings one to "Paradise." Dickinson's paradise, we recall, "is
the most Arduous of Journeys" (*L*, 3:926).

"The Love a Life can show Below" is abstract and indefinite in its
theological reference and can be read to suit a variety of religious posi-
tions.[13] Not so another major poem from the same period, the finest of
her elegies for Elizabeth Barrett Browning.

593

I think I was enchanted
When first a sombre Girl –
I read that Foreign Lady –
The Dark – felt beautiful –

And whether it was noon at night –
Or only Heaven – at Noon –
For very Lunacy of Light
I had not power to tell –

The Bees – became as Butterflies –
The Butterflies – as Swans –
Approached – and spurned the narrow Grass –
And just the meanest Tunes

That Nature murmured to herself
To keep herself in Cheer –
I took for Giants – practising
Titanic Opera –

The Days – to Mighty Metres stept –
The Homeliest – adorned
As if unto a Jubilee
'Twere suddenly confirmed –

I could not have defined the change –
Conversion of the Mind
Like Sanctifying in the Soul –
Is witnessed – not explained –

'Twas a Divine Insanity –
The Danger to be Sane
Should I again experience –
'Tis Antidote to turn –

To Tomes of solid Witchcraft –
Magicians be asleep –
But Magic – hath an Element
Like Deity – to keep –

   In this foundational text the experience of reading Mrs. Browning's
poetry is presented as an outrageous but plausible alternative to a
Calvinist conversion experience. Dickinson makes conscious use of Re-
formed Protestant language and psychology to convey her sense of
Browning's importance for her identity as a poet. According to the pre-
scribed pattern for conversion in the Connecticut Valley tradition, the
mind or understanding turns to God before the will (the affective self)
can be transformed and the soul sanctified. Thus the language of the
poem mimics the stages of conversion.[14] Likewise, the "change" in a tra-
ditional conversion cannot be "defined" or "explained." Both Dickinson
and her orthodox teachers would attach special value to an unknowable
change in the soul. For the poem's speaker the experience of reading a
foreign lady leads to a sustained probing of the unknown. As she recalls,
"The Dark – felt beautiful – "; the somberness of her own feelings were
magically converted to a beautiful but unknowable darkness. Thus she
found herself "enchanted" and transported to a mysterious mental
realm where Nature's "meanest tunes" seemed works of grandiose
imagination. In this "reader's sublime"[15] poetry is analogous in its ef-
fects to that diviner thing in "The Love a Life can show Below." In the
two poems poetry and love powerfully transfigure all of human, natu-
ral, and cosmic existence. "The two coeval come," as Dickinson says
elsewhere, for both are analogous to seeing God (P 1247).
   "I think I was enchanted" makes a large claim for the experience
Dickinson found in poetry. Yet, more clearly and fully than any of Dick-
inson's other poems about poetry, it is a declaration of heresy. This
"Conversion of the Mind" is marked as *like* "Sanctifying in the Soul" (as
"Magic" is "*Like* Deity"), but the two conversions are clearly not the
same. Instead, the speaker's conversion is generated by "Witchcraft"
and leads to "Insanity." The speaker celebrates the remembered inspi-

ration of another woman poet or "witch." She does not obey the prompt-
ing of a man in the pulpit, as did Sarah Edwards or Dickinson's sister
Lavinia.

This witch's magic is unpredictable and scary in its workings – or
at least mock-scary. The speaker not only remembers experiencing a
"Lunacy of Light," but her narrative exhibits an exaggerated lack of con-
trol in her responses to the experience. Yet, when David Porter writes,
"the poem is on the verge of hysteria in its joined urgency and ecstasy,
art and sainthood,"[16] he misreads its mood and design. The poem
means to convey not only the speaker's gratitude to "that Foreign Lady"
and her own wonder at her "Conversion," but her ironic retrospective
awareness that she became a holy fool in the throes of a crazy enchant-
ment. Dickinson's control of tone is the very opposite of hysterical. The
tone moves from that of a grateful recollection that is also a confessional
invitation to Dickinson's own reader (st. 1), to a wildly self-mocking yet
celebratory narrative of what poetry did to her (st.2 – 4), modulating to
the earnestness of her statement of conversion (st. 6), and returning to
the paradox—an occasion for further self-mockery and celebration—
that this conversion and sanctification felt insane (st. 7 – 8). Then the
final two lines are like a benediction, not only for Barrett Browning but
also for the community of readers persuaded by the poem.

In the early stanzas the speaker parodies with enthusiastic hyper-
bole the way a poet's figurative language transforms natural objects.
When "The Bees – became as Butterflies," we may take the outland-
ish comparison more or less straight, but when "The Butterflies – as
Swans – / Approached – and spurned the narrow Grass – " we have to
smile at the ballooning of the butterflies into swans and at the solemn
cadence with which they spurn the pathetic grass, somehow still stuck
in ordinary nature. Yet, by means of such Romantic irony, Dickinson
makes her claim for the experience itself convincing. She reinforces the
point that the change that comes with poetic inspiration happily distorts
the perceived world, in that sense makes it unknown as well as surreal.

The weaving of different tones culminates in the final two stanzas,
in which the speaker admits to insanity but gratefully stands her
ground. The revelations of Browning's poetry are "Tomes of solid
Witchcraft." The paradox is zestfully accurate: there is magic in the ma-
terial pages of these books. Moreover, it is a magic to be shared. Though
Browning is "asleep," she has passed on her probing of the unknown to

Dickinson, who as "witness" of what is "not explained" will share it with her readers. The magic that survives in these pages "hath" permanence, like God. The biblical idiom expresses the speaker's conviction that poetic witchcraft is a viable alternative to other forms of conversion. It sustains the speaker and keeps her happily insane in a lasting communion with the poets and sisters who have come before and will come after her.

These two poems exemplify how Dickinson's attempts to convey a religious feeling for the unknown are pitched to a community of readers invited to understand a mystery. That is, she does not call attention to the peculiar private drama of a protagonist's experience, as she might in poems in which she imagines a speaker in love or dying or recovering from pain. Though I think she still takes for granted in these poems that other persons are strangers, she also surmises that her readers share an attraction to that diviner thing and an intellectual need for the unknown.

Death and Chaos

Dickinson's desire for mysterious spiritual transformation is a central empowering impulse in her writing. Yet it has been relatively neglected. The unnamed power that attracts her imagination in "The Love a Life can show Below" or the indefinable change that Barrett Browning's poetry brings her in "I think I was enchanted" represents aspects of the unknown that critics have tended to acknowledge only in passing.[17] Instead, they have been drawn to poems in which one confronts the unknown in emotional chaos or death, partly because these are among her most powerful poems and also because they resonate with present and recent ontological insecurity. And indeed, Dickinson's concern with death is of overmastering importance throughout her career, whether she has in mind actual death or the temporary chaotic eclipse of self she often connected with it. At the end of her life, as we have seen, she contemplates her own death repeatedly, probing the afterlife's realm of "sorcery / And everything unknown" (P 1603). Earlier, in her prime as a poet, she is especially apt to dramatize conflicts between the soul or consciousness and death, conflicts leading to an uncanny passage into the unknown.

594

The Battle fought between the Soul
And No Man – is the One
Of all the Battles prevalent –
By far the Greater One –

No News of it is had abroad –
It's Bodiless Campaign
Establishes, and terminates –
Invisible – Unknown –

In terms of Dickinson's religious thinking the most dreadful death she can imagine is the annihilation of the spirit, the end of meaning, the utter blankness of spiritless nonbeing. Such an idea can come into her writing when she contemplates her own death or when she projects the death of a friend onto the human condition or when she imagines the death of poetry, of the embodied spiritual Word. She does not deal often with the prospect—she quarantines her fear of it perhaps—but we shall see it emerge in key texts in tension with her spiritual hopes.

One's apprehension of death happens suddenly and mysteriously, just as much as one's apprehension of divine power.

974

The Soul's distinct connection
With immortality
Is best disclosed by Danger
Or quick Calamity –

As Lightning on a Landscape
Exhibits Sheets of Place –
Not yet suspected – but for Flash –
And Click – and Suddenness.

The poem makes an instructive complement to "The Love a Life can show Below." In both poems power moves with ineffable rapidity through an imagined landscape beyond the defining scope of sight. One cannot precisely see "Sheets of Place," though one can certainly apprehend their power and suddenness. In both poems also the experience the speaker contemplates cannot be named, only intimated by analogy.

The effect of the analogy in "The Soul's distinct connection" partly resides in its dynamic inscrutability. Sharon Cameron writes, "Perhaps what is most appalling is the discrepancy between the enormity of the revelation and the blankness of our comprehension of it."[18] I would argue that elsewhere in Dickinson ignorance in the face of revelation is sometimes a requisite for imaginative happiness. We recall how that diviner thing also appalls, partly because it stuns comprehension, but then invites and enchants as well. Dickinson puts herself on the stretch for inscrutable intimations of paradise as well as for disclosures of calamity. Nevertheless, her speakers gird themselves over and over for the anticipation of death, the battle with "No Man" that leads to its blank and unknown termination.

Death for Dickinson is not only the end of human life but, even during life itself, the great opposing force to all "quickness," all lively consciousness; hence it is the fulfillment or antitype of despair, the inevitable outcome of daily entropy, what all reductions of human individuality or exuberance come down to.[19] At times the awareness of death, with all the metaphorical resonance she gives it, imbues her writing with a somber stoicism. One of her fullest and most tenaciously somber meditations appears in a prose fragment, in which she associates death as often with the condition of not knowing.

> Death being the first form of Life which we have had the power to Contemplate, our entrance here being an Exclusion from comprehension, it is amazing that the fascination of our predicament does not entice us more. With such sentences as these directly over our Heads we are as exempt from Exultation as the Stones. (*PF,* 70; *L,* 3:922)

When we come into life we are excluded from understanding our origins, and that exclusion Dickinson implies here is an initial obliteration of the desiring self, a kind of death. Once we "contemplate" this initial ignorance, we feel a terrifying "fascination" that is surely one of the conditions of feeling empowering Dickinson's poetry. David Porter comments; "Exclusion from comprehension: this is the stark vacancy at the center. The disabling, decohering ignorance streams through her entire canon and forms time after time the significance of her allegories."[20] If Porter exaggerates Dickinson's inability over the long run to cope with her condition of ignorance, he is right not to gainsay the bleakness of this late meditation. In its wish not to offer or accept consolation, it is typical of a number of prose fragments Dickinson confided to her own

papers but not to any correspondent, since she regarded all her
friends—all sensitive human beings—as fundamentally in need of con-
solation. Behind the fragment's bleakness and reinforcing its grim tone
is Dickinson's sense of metaphysical injustice. If human beings and nat-
ural creatures die, it is because "an Approving God" licenses their death
(P 1624). If when we consider our beginnings and ends we contemplate
"an Exclusion from comprehension," that too is part of our given con-
dition. All we can do is find ways of living with our anticipation of an
unknown death. But why, under these conditions, does the intellect
need this terrifying unknown? For Dickinson does not exclude the ter-
ror of the unknown when she claims that we should thank God for it.

In her study of Dickinson and Whitman, Agnieszka Salska answers
this question provocatively and clearly. According to Salska, the un-
known is needed in Dickinson's poetics because it continually chal-
lenges the mind to confront it.[21] Dickinson's "aesthetic consciousness"
needs to be tested if it is to "impose its own order" on the chaos of her
experience of the unknown. She does not "incorporate" the unknown
(as Whitman might) but leaves it powerfully "other," a looming dra-
matic antagonist to the mind as it struggles to make its poetic revela-
tions.[22] Hence she explores "the moment when the known is abruptly
brought into the presence of the unknown" in familiar poems such as "I
felt a Funeral, in my Brain" (P 280), "I heard a Fly buzz – when I died"
(P 465), and "Our journey had advanced – " (P 615).[23] Or she "courts self
destruction" in encounters with chaos like "I saw no Way – the Heav-
ens were stitched – " (P 378).[24] Or she sets up dramatic incidents in
which a treasured imagined world is suddenly endangered by chaos or
death. In poems such as "I started Early – Took my Dog – " (P 520) and
"Because I could not stop for Death – " (P 712), the imagination "im-
poses, even if precariously, a wholly domestic order upon the ominous
unknown."[25] Salska is ready to attribute ominousness to the unknown
generally. She writes in summary, "Dickinson's domain is the poem of
critical confrontation between the ordering power of consciousness and
the tumultuous forces of the unknown."[26]

Salska's interpretive dialectic pitting consciousness against chaos
works very well for many poems of Dickinson's crisis years. Along with
Sharon Cameron, David Porter, and Paula Bennett, she has helped to
show graphically what not knowing feels like in Dickinson.[27] Yet the
trouble with Salska's interpretation of the unknown as a category is that
for Dickinson the unknown is not always ominous or tumultuous; it can

also be numinous or mysterious. As a result, Salska's account leaves out key dimensions of Dickinson's poetry and distorts her sensibility. We have already seen how crucial for Dickinson are the unknown transformations of the spirit that she discovers in poetry, in music, or in her intimations of nature, "far abroad on Summer days." The unknown in these changes is exhilarating, if disconcerting. Such moments of transport "distil uncertain pain," but they also flood the mind with temporary "Exultation." They suggest how Dickinson is perennially on the rebound from her own moods of disheartened stoicism.

Distance and Intimacy

The pleasure Dickinson takes in intimations "far abroad" is characteristic of one side of her. A feature of her sensibility that I think becomes especially prominent in some letters and poems of the late 1860s and the 1870s is her wish to keep a saving distance from what she perceives. She prefers at such times not to know but, rather, to sweetly imagine "Reportless Subjects" (P 1048) at a distance. The indescribable character of these experiences is another part of the spectrum she calls "the unknown." This distant unknown is not ominous but comforting. Her pleasure in it is calmer than the ecstasy of enchantment she recalls from Barrett Browning's poetry, and her responses to it are mediated by a controlled reflectiveness. She celebrates such an experience at the start of an 1873 letter to the Norcrosses.

> Sisters,
>   I hear robins a great way off, and wagons a great way off, and rivers a great way off, and all appear to be hurrying somewhere undisclosed to me. Remoteness is the founder of sweetness; could we see all we hope, or hear the whole we fear told tranquil, like another tale, there would be madness near. Each of us gives or takes heaven in corporeal person, for each of us has the skill of life. (L, 2:504)

The passage is a condensed associative summary of some of Dickinson's seasoned conflicting ideas, ideas that pull against one another but also coexist in a spontaneously dialectical relation to one another. The first sentence expresses lyrically her delight in the remote and the undisclosed. The second suggests that we cherish remoteness because if our experience grows too explicit it may overcome us, even drive us mad. (Here again, a fear of experience is recalled in conjunction with

gratitude for its "sweetness.") The third sentence, however, reassures
her cousins that despite our capacity for madness we are created "in cor-
poreal person" to enjoy and impart the "heaven" that is all around us,
an earthly heaven in which Dickinson for the moment clearly believes.
Our bodies as well as our souls participate in this heaven, for as corpo-
real persons we have "the skill of life," the ability to live and share per-
sonally and spiritually. Moreover, we know that we live in such a heav-
enly world partly because we are familiar with the sweetness of
remoteness. This sweetness is precarious; given our psychic condition,
it needs to hurry out of sight into the unknown for Dickinson to cherish
it. Nevertheless, it sustains her as a type of experience and memory in
which she has faith.

I quote the first two stanzas of a poem of the 1870s that illustrates
this faith.

1382

In many and reportless places
We feel a Joy –
Reportless, also, but sincere as Nature
Or Deity –

It comes, without a consternation –
Dissolves – the same –
But leaves a sumptuous Destitution – [28]
Without a Name –

In this peaceful meditation the speaker accepts her own predicament as
a transient and ignorant creature. The mood, reinforced by pauses that
help induce contemplation, is one of measured acceptance of the condi-
tions of perception. The speaker's "Joy" comes and dissolves repeat-
edly. This evanescence is not shocking, as it might be if the experience
were felt as too close, as encroaching on one's privacy. Instead, "It
comes, without a consternation – ." If it then leaves "a Destitution," that
is a feature of its inevitable rhythm. A person made bereft of joy becomes
destitute. Yet the memory of joy's temporary presence and dissolution
is "sumptuous," compensating for joy's loss. The experience the poem
commemorates, though life enhancing, is palpably unknown. The
"places" are "reportless," so is the joy, and the destitution is "Without a
Name." Finally, though this is suggested in a condensed, abstract way,

the speaker's feelings are experienced in nature, in places. Dickinson's account beginning, "I hear robins a great way off," might well be taken as a gloss on the poem and the distant sounds of robins, wagons, and rivers as concrete manifestations of dissolving joy.

The desire for private intimacy with a transient nature perceived at a distance is common in Dickinson.[29] (The privacy of one's intimacy is part of what makes it "reportless.") Here is another fine example.

774

It is a lonesome Glee –
Yet sanctifies the Mind –
With fair association –
Afar upon the Wind

A Bird to overhear
Delight without a Cause –
Arrestless as invisible –
A matter of the Skies.

The speaker's delight in the bird's song is "without a Cause"—spontaneous and inexplicable. Because the experience is also "lonesome," it can "sanctify the Mind." The transition to a mood of holiness takes place in private. The bird, too, she "overhears" privately at a distance rather than confronts openly. Once again, Dickinson delights in distant perspectives in a disappearing landscape. The speaker listens to the bird "Afar upon the Wind." Like the bird's song, the sky is "Arrestless" in its movement and by association partakes of the song's invisibility. "A matter of the Skies" is pleasantly hard to see. (Grammatically, "Delight," too, is "Arrestless as invisible," suggesting a fleeting correspondence between the mind and the landscape it delights in.) Skies often attract Dickinson because they are in motion toward an unknown.[30]

Yet Dickinson does not enjoy the unknowableness of nature only at a distance. To use key terms from a pertinent essay by Roland Hagenbuechle, she requires precision as well as indeterminacy in her translations of nature into her own language, partly because to her way of thinking a precise "world of time and space" impinges on a "timeless realm of 'God.'"[31] While in some texts the indeterminacy of distance helps to sanctify the Mind, Dickinson in other situations imagines and "hallows" the things she cherishes close at hand. Let us turn to a poem that mediates between the closeness of things and the distancing and hallowing of perception.[32]

797

By my Window have I for Scenery
Just a Sea – with a Stem –
If the Bird and the Farmer – deem it a "Pine" –
The Opinion will serve – for them – [33]

It has no Port, nor a "Line" – but the Jays –
That split their route to the Sky –
Or a Squirrel, whose giddy Peninsula
May be easier reached – this way –

For Inlands – the Earth is the under side –
And the upper side – is the Sun –
And it's Commerce – if Commerce it have –
Of Spice – I infer from the Odors borne –

Of it's Voice – to affirm – when the Wind is within –
Can the Dumb – define the Divine?
The Definition of Melody – is –
That Definition is none –

It – suggests to our Faith –
They – suggest to our Sight –
When the latter – is put away
I shall meet with Conviction I somewhere met
That Immortality –

Was the Pine at my Window a "Fellow
Of the Royal" Infinity?
Apprehensions – are God's introductions –
To be hallowed – accordingly –

To be hallowed – accordingly –] Extended
inscrutably –

This is not an easy poem. It has not the measured ease and transparency of "It is a lonesome Glee – ." At points it seems willfully obscure, or the meter seems not only irregular but imperfectly worked out. Yet even these apparent defects are signs of the speaker's mind wrestling with the problem she sets herself, how to express the ways the "Pine" is both physically known and spiritually unknown to its perceiver.

At the start the tree at the speaker's window is not a tree to her but "a Sea – with a Stem –, " the canopy of needles and the tree's trunk "set fair" by perception and transformed by imagination. Dickinson whimsically yokes "sea" and "stem" together, calling attention to their visual incongruity as well as to her own language. The effect of this defamiliarization is eventually to call "Sight" and "Definition" into question. No more than "Melody" can such a sea be defined, because both these objects of perception have a spiritual import for one who perceives them. "The Divine" in them "suggests to our Faith" and can only be apprehended by it. "Dumb" things by themselves—the wind, the odors, the jays, the squirrel, especially the "Pine"—"suggest to our Sight" or to our other senses.[34]

Yet, having reached this point, Dickinson reverses course. In the last stanzas "a Sea – with a Stem – " has become "the Pine at my Window," the pine no longer the property of birds and farmers and no longer placed between quotation marks, as if the speaker accepted its existence as a tree in itself. Why this surprising acceptance of common words for natural objects she had seemed to scorn? Because Dickinson changes her language to suit a willed change of perspective. Thus she changes the "Pine" from a mere dumb thing seen uncritically into a subject for poetic "Apprehension." Indeed, the poem has been about apprehension all along, the speaker's apprehension of things in motion that attract not merely her sight but also her imagination. Everything the speaker observes is moving in time and space: the squirrel and the jays in flight, the fragrance of the leaves carried to her window, the voice of the wind. These things, "Dumb" in themselves, are part of an active, mutable universe that expresses itself in melody, in giddiness, in "Spice," and in "a Sea – with a Stem –, " all of which ideas can only be "inferred" and imagined, not defined. In that sense natural phenomena too "suggest to our faith" and are subjects for apprehension.

In "By my Window have I for Scenery," as we saw earlier in "The Lilac is an ancient shrub," the speaker experiences a current of connecting life moving through the parts of the natural world so that nature temporarily becomes a living whole. Yet, while Dickinson makes use of a Romantic mode of feeling in these poems, especially in "By my Window" she insists on her own understanding of the way we perceive divinity in an unknown nature, distinguishing herself from predecessors like

Thoreau or Wordsworth. In "Spring" Thoreau is obsessed with finding
"*the twig*" the robin sits upon.[35] He pins his faith on a permanently
imagined natural world. For Dickinson, with all her precise appreciation
of phenomena, things as things fade into the mind once they have been
apprehended. These "Objects" are "lost" as objects (P 1071) when per-
ceived by the eye of faith. All the speaker expects to remember of them
when sight "is put away" is a "Conviction" that they became evidences
for her faith and part of her spiritual life when she perceived and imag-
ined them. She can assert her faith here but cannot define it precisely.

The lively ineffableness of the speaker's faith is reinforced by a key
variant in the last two lines of the poem. Moreover, this alternative end-
ing helps to show how the whole poem is concerned with the (religious)
unknown. With the variant the last lines read:

> Apprehensions – are God's introductions –
> Extended inscrutably –

I embrace the implications of both endings. The speaker's "Apprehen-
sions" throughout the poem are "God's introductions" and help bring
her to the conviction that the pine is "immortal" as it stays in her mem-
ory. Accordingly, apprehensions are "To be hallowed" and reverently re-
membered. At the same time, they are offered to human beings ("Ex-
tended") in such a way that they remain unknowable. The whole poem
illustrates the inscrutability and indefinability of the things we appre-
hend, in its irregular form as well as in the story it tells. The metrical ir-
regularities and metaphorical opacities force the reader not to assume
anything about pines and jays. The poem has a structure of nimble be-
lieving, beginning with a whimsical doubt concerning the pine, ending
with a qualified faith in it, but all along insisting that the pine this
speaker sees is a spiritual subject "of which we know nothing."

Nature and Perception

"By my Window have I for Scenery" articulates a faith not only in "the
Divine" but also in human apprehensions of natural beauty. This is an-
other side of Dickinson's personal faith in the spiritual that sustained
her following her retreat from local orthodoxy. The poem is an example
of Dickinson's investment in her experience of nature, an investment ev-
ident in one way or another in hundreds of poems and letters.

Dickinson experiments with a range of attitudes toward nature. If "By my Window" projects her appreciation of it, so in their different ways do "The Love a Life can show Below" or "In many and reportless places" or "It is a lonesome Glee." Her speakers tend to be more detached toward a natural world full of strangers in her numerous poems about bats, rats, frogs, and hummingbirds, the curiosities and eccentricities of nature that she whimsically and affectionately displays to herself and her readers. In dramatic poems she uses the temporary splendor or excitement of perceived landscapes not only as occasions for reverence, as in "The Lilac is an ancient shrub," but also as occasions for fear, as in poems that recall storms or dramatize the invasions of frost. In some poems nature seems to have "an adversarial presence," as Joanne Feit Diehl argues,[36] and I agree that a potential for hostility to nature remains in Dickinson's frame of thinking insofar as she imagines it as the ongoing creation of an indifferent God who "approves" the beheading of flowers and the death of children (P 1624). Yet in most of her imagined encounters Dickinson meets angels in the woods, not frost in the garden. She may entertain an adversarial stance toward nature as an ideological fiction, but in my view she does not hold to such a stance as if to an ingrained conviction.

Whether Dickinson experiences nature as a blessing or imagines herself oppressed by it, through all its permutations her one constant tendency is not to come to a conclusive view of it. However well beloved or warily distrusted, nature is unknown, "a Subject of which we know nothing." Given her conviction that humankind is ignorant of nature, it is hardly surprising that she believes and disbelieves in it by turns and takes a range of attitudes toward it. At the same time, it remains a subject to which she is deeply committed, both as a habitual lover of New England fields and flowers and as a poet who would make use of nature as the lingua franca of her imaginative projections.

Dickinson's sense that nature is unknown is congruent with her usual ideas concerning perception. Given nature's separate, "lost," and unknowable existence, she is not apt to philosophize on its attributes or give it a single, imagined character, except fleetingly or whimsically. She does not attempt, like Thoreau, to give nature coherence by tracing the details and patterns of the seasons, nor like Wordsworth or Tennyson or Whitman does she personify it either as a steadfast comforter ("Tintern Abbey") or as a savage beast ("Locksley Hall") or as a fount of sexual energy ("Song of Myself"). She passes by these images transmitted in texts by male poets of her immediate past to enjoy and reflect on nature as it touches her own sensibility.

While Dickinson stays away from masculine ardors projected toward a feminine nature (even parodies them as in her rewritings of Emerson's "Bacchus" and "The Humble-Bee"),[37] she also avoids familiar traps in nineteenth-century women's poetry of nature, either sentimental overidentification or self-abandonment and imagined death in an encounter with the power of nature.[38] She manages both to keep her distance from nature as a consuming presence and to express her affection for natural things, by a combination of strategies: first, as Margaret Homans has shown, Dickinson is aware from early on that language is fictive and that metaphors for nature as an entity, including "Mother Nature," are fictions. Hence, "Dickinson's sense of the fictiveness of language . . . frees her from [the] problematic [Wordsworthean] tradition" of woman's identification with nature.[39] Second, Dickinson has a precise empirical interest in natural facts, reinforced apparently by her early scientific training. Third, she marries this early interest to a later post-Kantian awareness of the impossibility of knowing natural objects except through the mediation of human perception. Fourth, she habitually plays with what she perceives and imagines—dramatizing changing perspectives toward her experience of nature—and thus practices nimble believing in nature's presence. Some or all of these strategies are at work in "By my Window have I for Scenery," in "I think I was enchanted," and in numerous other poems. They help safeguard her generally affectionate, appreciative, and reverent relation to nature and the details of nature.

As Paula Bennett has persuasively shown, Dickinson is prone like other American women writers to "look to nature's small and seemingly insignificant moments . . . for their intimations of immortality."[40] She looks at common things round her like the pine by her window and apprehends God. Over and over in poems and letters Dickinson sketches with accuracy and delight the details of her experience of landscape. She is more apt to share these sketches—her "cricket," her "bluebird," her "oriole," her "pebble" (Poems 1068, 1465, 1466, 1510)—with her (usually female) correspondents than she is to show them her poetry of death or love or despair or philosophical admonition. Of course, none of these poems is merely a sketch, and some other descriptive poems about "Nature's People" like "A narrow Fellow in the Grass" dramatize a speaker's fear instead of her "transport of cordiality" (P 986). Still,

Dickinson's abiding wish in most of her sketches of nature is to convey a precise intimation of heaven to herself or her friends.

Dickinson adopts a comfortably appreciative persona in much of her nature poetry partly because she is comfortable adhering in her own way to the expectations of nineteenth-century sentimentalism. She often treats the coming of seasons and the appearance of flowers as occasions for sentimental appreciation. Her sentimental enjoyment of natural phenomena is obvious, is even conventional in the work of women poets, artists, and scrapbookmakers of her period. As Bennett stresses, a middle-class New England woman's experience of nature makes her writing about it different even from the nature writing of men whose philosophical preoccupations she may share. Thus Dickinson takes "Mother Nature" for granted as a fictive presence without swearing allegiance to her. Her mode of address to natural things is casual and familiar in most of her poems. She feels no masculine call to make love to nature like Wordsworth or Goethe, whose invocations to a hidden feminine presence are statements of faith grounded in impassioned masculine desire.

Until recently, this sentimental naturalistic side of Dickinson has been downplayed or ignored by critics in the rush to understand her obscurity and enjoy her drama. But it is a side of her consistent with my picture of her as a daughter of New England seeking her own alternative faith. In earlier chapters we have seen a good deal of evidence for her conviction that she felt at home in God's created universe. "Eden" is "always eligible" from her liberal perspective. "Consider the Lilies" is "the only commandment [she] ever obeyed." "Deity," not "Jehovah," guides Ned Dickinson as he wanders among "speechless mountains."

How can one reconcile the sentimental naturalist in Dickinson with her poetics of the unknown? with the Dickinson who wrote famously in "What mystery pervades a well":

> But nature is a stranger yet;
> The ones that cite her most
> Have never passed her haunted house,
> Nor simplified her ghost.

> To pity those that know her not
> Is helped by the regret
> That those who know her, know her less
> The nearer her they get.

(P 1400)

The answer, I think, is that, however affectionately Dickinson regards her neighbors in nature, she assumes behind her affection that as a perceptive human being she is irrevocably other than they are. The creatures and things of God are divine or terrifying because humans perceive them as such. "The Bird would be a soundless thing without Expositor" (*L*, 2:464). Natural creatures in themselves are "inscrutable," like the bat the speaker distances from herself with such relish in "The Bat is dun, with wrinkled Wings" (P 1575). Hence one can only guess unknowingly what natural creatures feel. In 1873 Dickinson wrote her cousin Frances Norcross, "I suppose the wild flowers encourage themselves in the dim woods, and the bird that is bruised limps to his house in silence, but we have human natures, and these are different" (*L*, 2:503). In that unknown difference lies not only our painful sense of loss but also our poetic opportunity. While nature's "Haunted House" is unknowable, the poet creates in her own art "a House that tries to be haunted" (*L*, 2:554) by shrewdly combining countless perceptions of landscapes she has set fair in her imagination.

Moreover, Dickinson's acknowledgment of her ignorance of nature and her awareness of her human difference from it does not preclude her from imagining an intimacy with it. She has other ways of relating to nature than through "knowledge."[41] If at times, as in "What mystery pervades a well," she dramatizes a fear of nature's adjacent strangeness, at other times, indeed rather like Emerson and Thoreau, she cherishes being intimately in touch with its mystery. To use Christopher Benfey's word, she seeks a "neighboring" relation to an unknown nature, as also to her unknown friends and to an unknown God.[42] She is well aware of the paradox of intimacy with nature as neighbor and stranger. Her speaker observes a bird that comes down the walk with detailed accuracy but then surreally projects its utter inhuman strangeness as it flies away from her.

> And he unrolled his feathers
> And rowed him softer home –
>
> Than Oars divide the Ocean,
> Too silver for a seam –
> Or Butterflies, off Banks of Noon
> Leap, plashless as they swim.

(P 328)

She cherishes the pine at her window but also treats it as an inscrutable extension of God's creativeness, as inscrutable in its own way as the arc of a bat's wing in flight (P 1575). The bat may be "empowered with . . . Malignity," while Dickinson's "seraphic" bluebird may "shout for joy to Nobody" (P 1465), but both are intimate strangers in her field of vision. She can be warmly sentimental or whimsically critical toward nature's creatures but always with an underlying awareness of her separation from them.

In summary, then, Dickinson can cherish and accurately observe natural phenomena, while she can also be knowingly distant from them because she carries with her the underlying assumption that they are different from her and unknown to her. By preserving an epistemological distance from her beloved hummingbirds and orioles, she also preserves the integrity of her distinctive consciousness. As a woman poet, she can be an ecstatic receiver of distant or intimate natural impressions, without losing her identity in an imagined death. Her mind is "sanctified" by its "lonesome glee," not submerged in it. Not for her the fate of Wordsworth's Lucy, "Rolled round in earth's diurnal course / With rocks, and stones, and trees."

Moreover, if nature is a stranger, the poet remains in charge of her refigurations of it. The otherness of nature is throughout her poetry a catalyst for her invention. Since she only knows her own perceptions of nature, it becomes a source of enormously varied analogies for the nuances of her own mental experience. Her poetry of an unknown nature is, magisterially, a poetry of analogy. This means, among other things, that some poems with ostensibly natural subjects are primarily concerned with human states of mind. To take a lighthearted example:

1437

A Dew sufficed itself –
And satisfied a Leaf –
And felt "how vast a Destiny" –
"How trivial is Life!"

The Sun went out to work –
The Day went out to play –
And not again that Dew be seen
By Physiognomy.

Whether by Day Abducted –
Or emptied by the Sun
Into the Sea – in passing –
Eternally unknown.

Attested to this Day
That awful Tragedy
By Transport's instability
And Doom's celerity.

(packet version [set 14], Poems, 3:996–97)

The action of the poem certainly takes place "in nature." Morning dew disappears from a leaf it covers when the sun goes "out to work." Humans cannot see and do not know what happens to the dew. "Eternally unknown" sounds ominously final; "unknown" usually signals a tremor of dread when it ends a line or stanza in Dickinson. One might be tempted to infer that Dickinson proclaims here that nature is mortal as well as inhuman, an unknown realm of death. But, since the dew's pretensions to self-sufficiency and permanence are so very human, it functions as a mirror image of an aspect of human being as well as an emblem for nature. Because it is an unknown, because Dickinson cannot really share feelings with it, she plays with it to enforce a human moral. She ascribes human feelings of "transport" to it (feelings she might rejoice in elsewhere) but then treats them ironically. The dew's fate reminds the speaker and the reader that we too will meet death, experience the celerity of doom. This "awful Tragedy," however, is here best taken lightly. What is unknown and evanescent can also be enjoyed.

In this miniature frame Dickinson sounds familiar themes. We live in time and hence are constituted not to hold onto knowledge. Things are unknown because they disappear, go out of sight. When things go out of sight, we are reminded of our mortality; our fate too is eternally unknown. The evaporation of dew on a leaf is an apt analogy for the evanescence of our feelings and ideas, indeed of our lives. Like the dew itself, human transport is "unstable" and evanescent, though while we are in its throes it may excite us to make pontifical pronouncements. Yet, as the poem's bemused cheerfulness implies, the relish of life is in its evanescence and hence in the fact that it is full of the surprise of the unknown. The reader of the poem is reminded of the pleasure as well as

of the foolishness of transport, and reminded also of the temporary nat-
ural splendor of dew on a leaf as well of its inevitable disappearance.

Three Poems

I will conclude by examining three great poems that focus in different
ways on the unknown. Each poem depends for its effectiveness on Dick-
inson's attentive observation of events in nature, even when such events
are partly used to represent the life within human beings or to make con-
nections between the human world and the divine. All of the poems em-
ploy natural images to make a statement about unknowable subjects
crucial to Dickinson's poetic being. At the same time, the poems illus-
trate how Dickinson shifts her approach to the unknown in different
dramatic contexts. Each poem is poised in a different way between faith
in an unknown mystery and fear that the mystery will be lost, or the un-
known turn meaningless and sinister.

The first is perhaps Dickinson's finest poem of "sumptuous Desti-
tution."

812

A Light exists in Spring
Not present on the Year
At any other period –
When March is scarcely here

A Color stands abroad
On Solitary Fields
That Science cannot overtake
But Human Nature feels.

It waits upon the Lawn,
It shows the furthest Tree
Upon the furthest Slope you know
It almost speaks to you.

Then as Horizons step
Or Noons report away
Without the Formula of sound
It passes and we stay –

A quality of loss
Affecting our Content
As Trade had suddenly encroached
Upon a Sacrament.

The poem is believable first of all because we can visualize such fields
and horizons in early spring and imagine the presence of light moving
over them. Even when aiming to represent the unknowable Dickinson
begins with common observation. As from our own experience of the
seasons we feel the despair implicit in a slant of light on a winter after-
noon, from another seasonal experience we recognize here the promise
of March light on "solitary Fields." Though the light in spring cannot be
grasped or "overtaken," it is nevertheless commonly felt by "Human
Nature." The speaker invites the reader to share in recalling it: "It almost
speaks to *you*," and when it is gone the loss affects "*our* Content." As
often, Dickinson says "we" in poems in which she would illustrate her
faith and invites a reader to share a simple natural event with transcen-
dent implications.

Yet the modesty of the natural scene only sets up the demanding
transcendence the speaker discovers there. Light in movement is Dick-
inson's chief symbol for the divine as human beings passingly experi-
ence it.[43] "Light" as perceived often implies mental illumination in her
poems, "this great light upon our Minds" shining at the dying of a friend
(P 1100) or the light that afflicts one inwardly with "Heavenly Hurt"
(P 258) or the "waylaying Light" of "Thought" or inspiration that
"founds the Homes and decks the Days" and gives meaning to "Life's
reverberation" (P 1581). All of these images vividly represent unknow-
able passages in human mental life. Light in each instance generates
"internal difference, / Where the Meanings, are – ."

In "A Light exists in Spring" the light has no named analogue in in-
ner experience like "Thought" or "the Seal Despair." The implicit sub-
ject is unnamed because the strategy of the poem is to leave it unknown.
"Science cannot overtake" or categorize it because it "exists" in a state
of transience and then disappears. The whole poem is an intricate dis-
play of the language of transience. Even in the first stanza we read that
"March is scarcely here" and will soon be gone. In the second stanza the
light has become "A Color," not light itself but a metonymy for it sig-
naling change. It "stands" or hovers over the fields, but "abroad," sig-
naling movement from a familiar to a distant space, the "furthest" slope

or tree of stanza 3. It is moving "a great way off" (*L*, 2:504) into the realm of the distant unknown. "It almost speaks to you" but doesn't, owing to its very nature as light, not sound. Then in the fourth stanza Dickinson executes one of her drastic expansions of poetic space-time that we have come to cherish in her poems of evanescence. "Noons report away" because early March days pass and with them their light. But with this movement "away," specific natural features like solitary fields and the lawn and even "the furthest Tree" dissolve into the expanded indeterminate space of "Horizons" that "step" as if they like the light had angelic being.

The pathos of this unknowable dissolving light is that "It passes and we stay – " as Dickinson writes with simple finality. "The Quality" or essence of loss here is painful to experience. It "Affect[s] our Content" as if we were to be lastingly marked with discontent now that we have perceived the light and then lost it.[44] The impact of loss is figured as "Trade encroach[ing] Upon a Sacrament"—a sudden intrusion, stigmatized with terse scorn, of auctions and hiring and prices in a moment of templebuilding. Yet something like a (Calvinisitic) sacrament has occurred, an outward sign of an inner grace, even while that sign is wordless, transient, and unknowable. As we recall the poem from its end, its focus from the beginning has been on the breathtaking power and commonness of the light, felt by human nature in the simple presence of a color on solitary fields. The intellect needs this unknowable light in early March to give dramatic meaning to its earthly experience of the seasons, however jarring the light's inevitable evanescence.

In "A Light exists in Spring" an ineffable natural light appears on the fields from somewhere beyond them, affecting human nature mysteriously with its presence and then with its disappearance. The following poem represents a mysterious process within human nature. Yet the poem depends for its meaning and expressiveness on Dickinson's manipulation of natural images, on the tact of her language as she recalls the familiar operations of a living and transient nature.

945

This is a Blossom of the Brain –
A small – italic Seed
Lodged by Design or Happening
The Spirit fructified –

Shy as the Wind of his Chambers
Swift as a Freshet's Tongue
So of the Flower of the Soul
It's process is unknown.

When it is found, a few rejoice
The Wise convey it Home
Carefully cherishing the spot
If other Flower become.

When it is lost, that Day shall be
The Funeral of God,
Upon his Breast, a closing Soul
The Flower of our Lord.

The poem is constructed on an analogy between an unnamed expression of the "Brain" and a "Blossom" or "Flower" that grows (or is expressed) on a spot of earth. Robert Weisbuch reads "This" in the first line as "this very poem."[45] I also think that the poem is about an instance of "poetry" in the large sense Dickinson sometimes gives the word, about a dynamic work of the spirit that converts the mind and has an effect on those who experience it analogous to seeing God. Yet it seems truer to Dickinson's analogical poetics not to confine a subject she does not name to one designation. Moreover, "italic" in Dickinson has something of the force of "hieroglyphic" in other American Renaissance writers.[46] It implies that a mark or letter or word is emphatically significant but indecipherable, its meaning vivid but unknowable. In my view, then, "This" might be any work of symbolic expression that develops in the mind and that "the Wise" can find and "convey Home"—"this very poem" to start with but also a poem of Mrs. Browning a creative reader such as Dickinson might find and cherish or a poem or painting "wrought" by a "Martyr Poet" or "Painter" so that "Some" may "seek in Art – the Art of Peace – " (P 544). All these expressions of the spirit can be cherished but not known. As the workings of the poem's natural analogy also suggest, though "This" comes quite specifically from an "italic Seed," it is "a subject of which we know nothing" because it is naturally alive, a blossom then a seed then a flower, then perhaps the site for "another Flower," changing and becoming as one finds and contemplates it.

The living changeableness of "This" is vividly apparent in the second stanza, where it is associated with other images of imperceptibly transient life. We cannot see "the Wind in his Chambers" but can imagine its shyness, its wish not to be known or seen. We cannot hold a freshet but can imagine its swiftness as its "Tongue" laps over a stream bed. Flower, wind, and freshet are features of a living nature, evolving too mysteriously for the categories of scientific knowledge. It can be said of each of them, as of "This," that "It's process is unknown." Yet what the wind and the freshet feel like inwardly to the poetic observer is very specifically evoked, in a narrative of definition that clarifies its mysteries without unveiling them. By the precision of her language drawn from an evasive and changeable nature Dickinson has clearly shown that, while one cannot "know" the internal process of the mind's expression, one can represent it in a metonymic chain of natural images with its own expanding and evanescent life.

In the second stanza "a Blossom of the Brain" has become "the Flower of the Soul," a work of spiritual as well as of intellectual growth and beauty. How the flower came into being in the first place is another mystery. A designing God could have "lodged" the small "Seed" or it could have just happened into its existence—this speaker prefers not to choose a single explanation for it, keeping the flower's origin as well as its "process" unknown. In either case, however, "the Spirit" made it fruitful, by implication though not designation the Holy Spirit. The full-grown flower, like all finished living spiritual beings, needs careful cherishing in order that it may safely survive. Since the other natural images associated with the flower (seed, wind, freshet) convey ideas of emergence, motion, and evanescence, the prospect of the flower's impermanence is already subliminally present in the text. But by the end of the third stanza the reader has no cause to doubt that the flower's life will continue; throughout it has been carefully nurtured in Dickinson's words then cherished and protected at "Home," in the imaginative speaker's own garden of fulfilled expression.

What happens in the final stanza, then, is a wild surprise, one of those melodramatic turns of thought Dickinson enjoys springing on us even in a quiet context. A grandiose doubt enters this poem of faith and leaves its assurance uncertain. "The Flower of the Soul" may have started as a small seed, but by this point the speaker has made it a synecdoche for the soul's work of beauty in the world, and "When it is lost" is hence a "Day" of general calamity. She insists imperatively on the calamity: "that Day *shall be* / The Funeral of God." I would gloss this dire prediction with lines from another of Dickinson's poems that also makes an extreme claim for the importance of poetry as a spiritual activity. "A Blossom of the Brain" is what Dickinson elsewhere calls "A Word made Flesh," a word embodied in poetry presumably but analogous in its living presence to God's incarnation in human life.

> A Word that breathes distinctly
> Has not the power to die
> Cohesive as the Spirit
> It may expire if He – . . .

(P 1651)

Only if the Spirit itself "expires" will "a Word that breathes distinctly" lose its cohesiveness and be annihilated out of memory. Yet, though in Poem 1651 the idea of the Spirit's annihilation is presented only as a remote possibility, it is an idea that seems to haunt Dickinson in key interstices of her writings. In "This is a Blossom of the Brain – " as well, the loss of the flower of the soul stands for the permanent death of the incarnate Word. The three persons of the Trinity are all involved in Dickinson's condensed narrative of loss. When the fruit of the Spirit dies, God dies, and "our Lord" Christ too, the Christ she cherishes as a model and a survivor in her narratives of crucifixion and redemption. If the poetic word, whose "process is unknown," is lost, one is engulfed by another unknown of meaningless continuance she represents as a death so momentous it requires "the Funeral of God." The effect of the last two lines is to have the reader tangibly imagine this day of death, here represented in the actual funeral of a man dressed for burial, and bearing "the Flower of our Lord" on his breast.

Unlike "This is a Blossom of the Brain" and "A Light exists in Spring," "Four Trees – upon a solitary Acre – " is apparently not concerned with a spiritual mystery.

742

> Four Trees – upon a solitary Acre –
> Without Design
> Or Order, or Apparent Action –
> Maintain –

The Sun – upon a Morning meets them –
The Wind –
No nearer Neighbor – have they –
But God –

The Acre gives them – Place –
They – Him – Attention of Passer by –
Of Shadow, or of Squirrel, haply –
Or Boy –

What Deed is Their's unto the General Nature –
What Plan
They severally – retard – or further –
Unknown –

These trees hardly "suggest to our Faith" anything more than their bare existence in a given place. The landscape exposed in the poem is not in motion, as in the previous two poems and in others I have called attention to. The trees do not go out of sight but "maintain" themselves as if riveted for our contemplation. The speaker's ignorance of their purpose stands starkly for human ignorance of the origin and end of nature. The poem reminds us that Dickinson presents herself repeatedly as surrounded by a potentially ominous unknown as if by an atmosphere in which she lives and writes.

"In the homeliest of sites, Dickinson's language could find the great ignorance," David Porter eloquently puts it.[47] Yet it is an open question as to whether the poem makes this ignorance appalling or simply inevitable, a necessary and even welcome condition of human existence. In my view the poem is perfectly poised between potential dread at the prospect of the unknown and tentative appreciation of our human ability to deal with it. This balance of possible implications is played out in the poem's technique. The tone is too cool, the details too spare, and the poem's strategy too dialectical for any single inference as to its meaning. The syntax is full of ambiguous connectives or "disjunctions" that cause "a partial loss of bearings" for the reader.[48] The meter is a distilled triumph of experimental art that brings the words of the short second and fourth lines of each stanza into stark relief. But the collective import of these elliptically emphasized words is ambiguous. On the one hand, the trees have "God" for a neighbor and a "Boy's" attention; on the other hand, they are "Without Design" and their purpose is "Unknown."

"Four Trees," I think, is written in such a way as to make a defini-
tive interpretation impossible. Even within a single poem Dickinson
prefers to keep her perspectives on nature and God experimental and
transient; hence her "doctrines" on such subjects are not to be known.
On the one hand, the speaker makes quickly clear that the trees do not
satisfy the human rage for order. "Without Design . . . or Apparent Ac-
tion," they are as unlike a poem as natural things can be. One finds no
sacraments or intimations of immortality in this still landscape. Yet, as
one starts to realize in the second stanza, "Four Trees . . . " is a charac-
teristic example of what Dickinson chooses to make poetically of an un-
known, inhuman nature. That is, she gives the poem's landscape a de-
sign and an action of her own invention—not too much action, yet
enough to tell a story that complicates the speaker's initial picture. The
story is presented in playfully anthropomorphic terms. The sun and, it
seems, the wind meet the trees. "The Acre *gives* them – Place – " and
they return the favor, bringing "*Him* – Attention of Passerby." Else-
where in Dickinson "Attention" might be preliminary to "Apprehen-
sion," the perception of the divine in nature. Yet here she refrains from
making this transition; her idiom remains quizzically agnostic. Who are
the "Passersby" who attend to the trees? An unidentified "Shadow,"
quasi-immaterial but not necessarily human; a "Squirrel" who comes
upon the trees "haply," either happily or accidentally or both; and a
"Boy," from the tone a boy who innocently enjoys seeing trees but not
one who either worries about their lack of design or creates an imagined
order for them. The astutely whimsical disconnectedness of this list pre-
vents the reader from drawing inferences about it. We can infer neither
that one's happiness depends on Attention, nor that attention here is
tantamount to ignorance. The story, like the syntax employed to tell it,
teases us with possibilities and calls on us to contemplate them without
resolving them.

The most striking speculation in this little story is, "No nearer
Neighbor – have they – / But God – ." Either God is the trees' nearest
neighbor or the next nearest after the sun and the wind. The circum-
stance sounds friendly. We remember that one of Dickinson's speakers
looks forward to meeting "Our Old Neighbor – God" in Heaven (P 623).
Or, as Thoreau puts it with conviction, "*Next* to us is not the workman
whom we have hired . . . but the workman whose work we are."[49] But
what sort of God has been inscribed in this poem, in which trees persist

"Without Design"? He, like his plans and their deeds, is "Unknown." He is not only a God of a story about meeting and neighboring and giving attention in the middle stanzas but also a God suited to the designless space of the first stanza and the message of inscrutability conveyed by the whole poem. Yet should one take fright at such a neighbor? The poem in its evenhandedness leaves it up to the reader. Likewise, the reader can make what he or she will of that last flatly emphasized Unknown. Perhaps, like Dickinson, she or he will make a story out of available shreds of circumstance in an unknowable natural world.

Why, then, does the intellect need the unknown, and why should one thank God for it? Let us first remember that Dickinson's pronouncement on the unknown to the Norcross sisters is a statement of truth voiced fleetingly, a pregnant aphorism but not an encoded doctrine. Moreover, her many attempts to deal with the unknown suggest that it is different things that bring out different responses at different times, and not always something for which one is thankful. Nevertheless, she also wrote, "How invaluable to be ignorant" (*L*, 3:917; *PF*, 36), and necessary too for the body of writing we have surveyed. "Exclusion from comprehension" may well be a key to the human condition as she sees it and a reason for the sense of estrangement she often dramatizes. Yet, while she accepts that any "Plan" promoted or hindered by her "Trees" is "Unknown," her very ignorance makes it possible for her to invent a story about them. An object that is lost becomes a motive for metaphor and the dread of not knowing an occasion for poetic construction. One needs the unknown, in short, to be a poet, not only a poet of inner challenge and crisis, as Salska has finely shown, but also a poet of transient awe in the face of the divine and also, too, an agnostic but reverent nature poet aware of time, a poet who observes the creatures and things of the human and natural world as they go out of sight. In her letter to the Norcrosses, Dickinson says in part that one should thank God for time. Time is the medium of vital life, even if that life includes pain and leads to death. One feels loss in a poem that memorializes time such as "A Light exists in Spring" but also feels grateful for the Light as it exists and passes. Sometimes the ravages of time foster occasions not for gratitude but for confusion or despair or terror in her writing. Nevertheless, the ignorance that time engenders is to her way of thinking the basis for happiness, "Delight without a Cause" (P 774), a delight that can stay with one if it is nurtured intelligently. In a letter of 1876 to Mrs. T. W. Higginson, Dickinson remembers and explains this phrase: "The 'Happiness' without a cause is the best Happiness, for Glee intuitive and lasting is the gift of God" (*L*, 2:560). Such a passage makes clear that for Dickinson the unknown is the ground on which one truly meets God.

Notes

Introduction

1. See esp. Susan Howe, *The Birth-mark: Unsettling the Wilderness in American Literary History* (Hanover, N.H., and London: Wesleyan University Press, 1993), 131–54; Martha Nell Smith, *Rowing in Eden: Rereading Emily Dickinson* (Austin: University of Texas Press, 1992), 51–95; and Ellen Louise Hart, "The Elizabeth Putnam Whitney Manuscripts and New Strategies for Editing Emily Dickinson's Letters," *Emily Dickinson Journal* 4, no. 1 (1995): 44–74. Hart especially makes a persuasive case for attending more closely to the complex interaction of verse and prose in Dickinson's letters. The speculations of these scholars depend partly on the earlier editorial work of Ralph W. Franklin, in *The Editing of Emily Dickinson: A Reconsideration* (Madison: University of Wisconsin Press, 1967); and *The Manuscript Books of Emily Dickinson*, 2 vols. (Cambridge, Mass.: Harvard University Press, 1981).

2. See Marta L. Werner, *Emily Dickinson's Open Folios: Scenes of Reading, Surfaces of Writing* (Ann Arbor: University of Michigan Press, 1995).

3. Howe, *The Birth-Mark;* Paula Bennett, *Emily Dickinson: Woman Poet* (Iowa City: University of Iowa Press, 1990).

4. As Martha Nell Smith has shown, Johnson makes an error in his lineation of "Wild Nights – Wild Nights!" (P 249), but this lapse seems to me occasional rather than representative. Smith, *Rowing in Eden,* 64–67.

Chapter 1

1. For the text of this passage I use Marta L. Werner's careful transcription of Dickinson's accidentals in catalog no. 742a from the Amherst College collection of Dickinson manuscripts in *Emily Dickinson's Open Folios: Scenes of Reading, Surfaces of Writing* (Ann Arbor: University of Michigan Press, 1995), rather than Thomas Johnson's transcription in the *Letters of Emily Dickinson,*

though in contrast to Werner I normalize Dickinson's spacing and do not attend
to her lineation.

2. Henry D. Thoreau, *Walden* (Princeton: Princeton University Press,
1971), 325.

3. *The Collected Works of Ralph Waldo Emerson,* ed. Alfred R. Ferguson,
Robert E. Spiller, Joseph Slater, and Jean Ferguson Carr (Cambridge, Mass., and
London: Harvard University Press, 1971–), 3:29.

4. The draft gets still more Shakespearean in its rhythms (and its thought)
as it continues to where the manuscript breaks off:

> "Oh' had I found it sooner! Yet Tenderness has not a Date – it comes –
> and overwhelms –
> The time before it was – was naught, so why establish it? And all the time
> to come it is, which abrogates the time –. " (*L,* 3:728; accidentals from
> Werner, *Open Folios,* transcription of A 742f)

5. Johnson associates this poem with the death of Charles Wadsworth on
April 1, 1882. See *Poems,* 3:1069. In the "nimble believing" letter, Dickinson
evokes Wadsworth's death along with Lord's visit to her (*L,* 3:727, 729).

Over the course of her life Dickinson is sensitive, as Cynthia Griffin Wolff
argues, to the undermining of religion by nineteenth-century science and to the
creeping liberalism of the Zeitgeist. (See Wolff, *Emily Dickinson* [New York:
Knopf, 1986], 451–54.)

6. For Dickinson's relation to Calvinism, see Richard B. Sewall, *The Life
of Emily Dickinson* (New York: Farrar, Straus and Giroux, 1974), chaps. 1 and
16; Richard Wilbur, "Sumptuous Destitution" in Richard B. Sewall, ed., *Emily
Dickinson: A Collection of Critical Essays* (Englewood Cliffs, N.J.: Prentice-Hall,
1963), 127–36; Karl Keller, *The Only Kangaroo among the Beauty: Emily Dick-
inson and America* (Baltimore: Johns Hopkins University Press, 1979), chaps.
2–4; Barton Levi St. Armand, *Emily Dickinson and Her Culture: The Soul's So-
ciety* (New York: Cambridge University Press, 1984), chaps. 3 and 4; Jane Don-
ahue Eberwein, *Dickinson: Strategies of Limitation* (Amherst: University of
Massachusetts Press, 1985); Cynthia Griffin Wolff, *Emily Dickinson;* and Beth
Maclay Doriani, *Emily Dickinson: Daughter of Prophecy* (Amherst: University
of Massachusetts Press, 1996). In my view St. Armand's and Eberwein's books
are the best balanced critical treatments of Dickinson's use of her religious her-
itage in her writings.

7. The term is from Sewall, *Life of Emily Dickinson,* 24. I draw principally
on Sewall (chap. 16) for my account of Dickinson's education.

8. The Synod of Dort took place in 1618–19 in a town in Holland, but it
was convened partly at the behest of English Calvinists (including King James
I), and its principles were incorporated in later documents such as the West-
minster Confession of Faith, fundamentally influential in British and American
Calvinist denominations. For a clear exposition of the five points of the Synod
of Dort, see Gene Edward Veith, *Reformation Spirituality: The Religion of
George Herbert* (Lewisburg, Penn.: Bucknell University Press, 1985), chap. 1,
esp. 26–27.

9. Westminster Confession of Faith, chap. 6, para. 5; rptd. in *The Confession of Faith and The Larger and Shorter Catechisms* (Inverness: Publications Committee of the Free Presbyterian Church of Scotland, 1970), 40.

10. Westminster Confession, chap. 17, para. 1; rptd. in ibid., 73.

11. The title of a review by Channing, published in *The Christian Disciple* (1820). See *The Works of William E. Channing, D.D.* (Boston: American Unitarian Association, 1880), 459–68.

12. St. Armand, chaps. 1–4.

13. Martha Dickinson Bianchi, *Emily Dickinson Face to Face* (1932); cited in Jay Leyda, *The Years and Hours of Emily Dickinson* (New Haven: Yale University Press, 1960), 2:483. Dickinson made the gesture of turning an imaginary key when she said this.

Joanne Dobson suggests that "a *practical* result" of Dickinson's decision not to publish was to allow her "as a writer, the identity of the literary amateur." She argues that this identity helped keep Dickinson away from the discipline of the marketplace as well as giving her the freedom to experiment. See Joanne Dobson, *Dickinson and the Strategies of Reticence: The Woman Writer in Nineteenth-Century America* (Bloomington and Indianapolis: Indiana University Press, 1989), 51.

14. L, 2:632. From the handwriting Johnson dates this and seven other messages to Susan Gilbert "about 1878" (*L,* 2:630). By then Dickinson had written most of her poems and was settled in her sense of the value of "guessing" for her vocation.

15. The phrase is Martha Nell Smith's, alluding to Dickinson's "I dwell in Possibility – " (P 657). See Martha Nell Smith, *Rowing in Eden: Rereading Emily Dickinson* (Austin: University of Texas Press, 1992), 79–86.

16. See Smith, *Rowing in Eden,* 119–20, for cartooning; Susan Howe, *The Birth-mark: Unsettling the Wilderness in American Literary History* (Hanover N.H., and London: University Press of New England, 1993), 131–53, for experiments with letters and lineation. See Franklin, *Manuscript Books of Emily Dickinson,* xii–xiii, for the history of the composition of the fascicles and sets.

17. Martha Nell Smith suggests that Dickinson cultivates the mode of the letter-poem starting in the 1860s (*Rowing in Eden,* 43). Paula Bennett shows that Dickinson's blurring of genres is especially prevalent in her later "letters." See Bennett, "'By a Mouth That Cannot Speak': Spectral Presence in Emily Dickinson's Letters," *Emily Dickinson Journal* 1, no.2 (1992): 82, 89–90.

18. Paula Bennett, *Emily Dickinson: Woman Poet* (Iowa City: University of Iowa Press, 1990), 19. See this point in the context of Bennett's feminist argument in her introduction (1–23). See also Wendy Martin, *An American Triptych: Anne Bradstreet, Emily Dickinson, Adrienne Rich* (Chapel Hill and London: University of North Carolina Press, 1984), 81.

19. Gary Lee Stonum, *The Dickinson Sublime* (Madison: University of Wisconsin Press, 1990), 79.

20. Another of the gains of current Dickinson criticism is to make us aware of her as a poet who welcomed the erotic in the interstices of her writing. See, among others, Smith, *Rowing in Eden;* Stonum, *Dickinson Sublime;* Bennett,

Emily Dickinson: Woman Poet; Margaret Dickie, *Lyric Contingencies: Emily Dickinson and Wallace Stevens* (Philadelphia: University of Pennsylvania Press, 1991); Suzanne Juhasz, "The Big Tease," in Suzanne Juhasz, Cristanne Miller, and Martha Nell Smith, *Comic Power in Emily Dickinson* (Austin: University of Texas Press, 1993), 26–62; and Robert McClure Smith, *The Seductions of Emily Dickinson* (Tuscaloosa and London: University of Alabama Press, 1996), esp. 5–12. R. M. Smith's discussion of Dickinson's aesthetics suggests a connection between her fascination with the unknown and her interest in reading as a stimulus to (erotic) excitement "contingent on uncertainty" (6).

21. For example, *L,* 2:430, 617. See Martha Nell Smith, *Rowing in Eden,* 29, 143.

22. For Dickinson's preference for lyric fragments to full stories and for her interest in the ear as both receptive and creative, see Dickie, *Lyric Contingencies,* 17ff., 64–67.

23. Dickinson's gift for comedy has been celebrated recently in Suzanne Juhasz, Cristanne Miller, and Martha Nell Smith, *Comic Power in Emily Dickinson.* Their emphasis on Dickinson's comic power, variety, and capacity for distance is salutary in a critical world committed to high seriousness and is relevant also to this study.

24. Following the example of the authors of *Comic Power in Emily Dickinson* (20–21), I use the text from set 13 in *The Manuscript Books of Emily Dickinson,* 2:1351. They point out that in this version "'Stop' is written precisely above 'Spot,' and ends the first verse" (21).

25. This anecdote is from Dickinson's second letter to Higginson, the first letter in which she writes about herself at length to him. Johnson supposes that the two editors were Josiah Holland and Samuel Bowles.

26. See Cheryl Walker, *The Nightingale's Burden: Women Poets and American Culture before 1900* (Bloomington: Indiana University Press, 1982), 87–95; and Bennett, *Emily Dickinson: Woman Poet,* 9–10.

27. See Stacy Lee Spencer, "Women Writers and the Literary Journey, 1832–1844" (Ph.D. diss., University of Michigan, 1991), intro. and chaps. 1 and 4.

28. Dobson, *Dickinson and the Strategies of Reticence,* xii.

29. See Paula Bennett, *Emily Dickinson: Woman Poet,* 84–115. I will discuss these matters in more detail in chapter 4.

30. David Reynolds, *Beneath the American Renaissance: The Subversive Imagination in the Age of Emerson and Melville* (New York: Alfred A. Knopf, 1988), 412–37.

31. See St. Armand, *Emily Dickinson and Her Culture,* chapter 4.

32. Quoted in Charles N. Feidelson Jr., *Symbolism and American Literature* (Chicago: University of Chicago Press, 1953), 119.

33. Stonum, *Dickinson Sublime,* 38.

34. Dickinson is often compared with Emerson, but there is no consensus concerning the meaning of their connection. For thoughtful comparisons and some information, see George Frisbie Whicher, *This Was a Poet: A Critical Biography of Emily Dickinson* (New York: Scribners, 1938), 189–205; Albert Gelpi, *Emily Dickinson: The Mind of the Poet* (Cambridge, Mass.: Harvard University

Press, 1965), 60–62; Roland Hagenbuechle, "Sign and Process: The Concept of Language in Emerson and Dickinson," *ESQ* 25, no.3 (1979), 137–55; Joanne Feit Diehl, *Dickinson and the Romantic Imagination* (Princeton: Princeton University Press, 1981), 161–82; Christopher Benfey, *Emily Dickinson and the Problem of Others* (Amherst: University of Massachusetts Press, 1984); and Dickie, *Lyric Contingencies*, 8–10, 15–18, 31–32.

35. See Leyda, *The Years and Hours of Emily Dickinson*, 1:351; 2:233, 148. Ellipses omitted in the citation from Susan Dickinson.

36. I adopt accidentals from Werner's transcription, *Open Folios*, A 744d–A 744e, though I have normalized Dickinson's spacing and lineation. Johnson prints the Amherst draft cataloged as A 744 as the first part of the "nimble believing" letter, followed by the draft cataloged as A 742. While Werner is generally skeptical of Johnson's efforts to create a narrative of the "Lord letters" and highly critical of the way he attached different drafts to one another without clear justification, she allows that "Letter 750" in Johnson's edition (*L*, 3:727–28) is a "plausible . . . reconstruction," even if it "should be approached cautiously." For details, see *Open Folios*, 288.

37. Emerson, *Collected Works*, 1:88.

38. Emerson's focus on the process of thinking in an unstable world has often been observed in the criticism. See esp. Stephen E. Whicher, ed., *Selections from Ralph Waldo Emerson: An Organic Anthology* (Boston: Houghton Mifflin, 1957), xviii–xix; Leonard Neufeldt, *The House of Emerson* (Lincoln and London: University of Nebraska Press, 1982), chaps. 1 and 2; and Julie Ellison, *Emerson's Romantic Style* (Princeton: Princeton University Press, 1984), 3–14.

An important book that emphasizes Emerson's interest in the flux of the mind is Richard Poirier, *Poetry and Pragmatism* (Cambridge, Mass.: Harvard University Press, 1992), esp. 10–11, 23–24, 27–28, 31, and 112–13. See also Poirier, *The Renewal of Literature: Emersonian Reflections* (New York: Random House, 1987), 74–75, 192, 197, and 221–22, for his discussions of Emersonian "abandonment," "power in transition," and "the self-dissolving or deconstructive tendencies inherent in language."

39. Thoreau, *Walden*, 317.

40. Emerson, *Collected Works*, 2:37.

41. Emerson, *Collected Works*, 2:188.

42. Emerson, *Collected Works*, 1:44.

43. Emerson, *Collected Works*, 2:182.

44. See Poirier, *Poetry and Pragmatism*, 129: "Emersonian pragmatism, like other isms, depends on certain key, repeated terms. But to a wholly unusual degree it never allows any one of these terms to arrive at a precise or static definition." Poirier discusses Frost, Stevens, Stein, and especially William James as Emersonian pragmatists along with Emerson himself.

45. Emerson, *Collected Works*, 1:78.

46. Emerson, *Collected Works*, 2:182.

47. Emerson, *Collected Works*, 3:47, 30, 39, 49.

48. *Walden*, 16, 17, 18, 134, 135.

49. In a letter of April 1881 to the Norcross sisters, Dickinson describes a

fire that almost destroyed the town of Amherst then writes: "The fire-bells are oftener now, almost, than the church-bells. Thoreau would wonder which did the most harm" (*L,* 3:692). Dickinson may have in mind passages from "Sunday" in *A Week,* as when Thoreau writes, "The sound of the sabbath bell far away, now breaking on these shores, does not awaken pleasing associations, but melancholy and sombre ones rather . . . It is as the sound of many catechisms and religious books twanging a canting peal round the earth." Thoreau, *A Week on the Concord and Merrimack Rivers* (Princeton: Princeton University Press, 1980), 77.

50. Nathaniel Hawthorne, *The English Notebooks,* ed. Randall Stewart (New York: Modern Language Association of America, 1941), 433.

51. Quoted in Warner Berthoff, *The Example of Melville* (Princeton: Princeton University Press, 1962), 24.

52. Herman Melville, *Moby-Dick* (Evanston and Chicago: Northwestern University Press and the Newberry Library, 1988), 373, 374.

53. Emerson, *Collected Works,* 3:31.

54. Terence Martin, *The Instructed Vision: Scottish Common Sense Philosophy and the Origins of American Fiction* (Bloomington: Indiana University Press, 1961), 138–39, 145. Martin finds this orthodoxy especially powerful in the first quarter of the century, but other historians suggest that its influence in somewhat altered form extends at least up to the Civil War. See, among others, Rush Welter, *The Mind of America, 1820–1860* (New York: Columbia University Press, 1975); Perry Miller, *The Life of the Mind in America: From the Revolution to the Civil War* (New York: Harcourt Brace and World, 1965), Bks. 1–2; Henry Nash Smith, *Democracy and the Novel* (New York: Oxford University Press, 1978), 12–15; and Lauren Berlant, *The Anatomy of National Fantasy: Hawthorne, Utopia, and Everyday Life* (Chicago and London: University of Chicago Press, 1991), 20–21, 28–34, for what Berlant calls the "National Symbolic."

55. See the opening of "The Flourishing Village," pt. 2, of Timothy Dwight's *Greenfield Village* (1794; rpt., New York: AMS Press, 1970), 31. Often what Leo Marx calls "sentimental pastoralism" is an offshoot of the social orthodoxy, a sentimental expression of orthodox values as justified by guardians of the social order such as Dwight. See Leo Marx, *The Machine in the Garden: Technology and the Pastoral Ideal in America* (New York: Oxford University Press, 1967).

56. For Scottish common sense philosophy, see Martin, *Instructed Vision;* Daniel Walker Howe, *The Unitarian Conscience: Harvard Moral Philosophy, 1805–1861* (Cambridge, Mass.: Harvard University Press, 1970), 27–40; S. A. Grave, *The Scottish Philosophy of Common Sense* (Oxford: Oxford University Press, 1960); William S. Charvat, *The Origins of American Critical Thought, 1810–1836* (Philadelphia: University of Pennsylvania Press, 1936), chap. 1; Garry Wills, *Inventing America: Jefferson's Declaration of Independence* (Garden City, N.Y.: Doubleday, 1978); Henry F. May, *The American Enlightenment* (New York: Oxford University Press, 1976), 341–57.

57. Emerson, *Collected Works,* 1:82.

58. *The Journals and Miscellaneous Notebooks of Ralph Waldo Emerson,* ed. William Gillman et al. (Cambridge, Mass.: Harvard University Press, 1960–), 5:323.

59. Walter Harding and Michael Meyer, *The New Thoreau Handbook* (New York: New York University Press, 1980), 2.

60. T. Walter Herbert, *Moby-Dick and Calvinism: A World Dismantled* (New Brunswick, N.J.: Rutgers University Press, 1977), 26–46.

61. See William Charvat, *The Profession of Authorship in America, 1800–1870* (Columbus: Ohio State University Press, 1968), "Melville," 204–61; Charvat, *Origins of American Critical Thought;* Nina Baym, *Novels, Readers, and Reviewers: Responses to Fiction in Antebellum America* (Ithaca: Cornell University Press, 1984).

62. Perry Miller, *The New England Mind: The Seventeenth Century* (New York: MacMillan, 1939), 10, 21.

63. See Michael Clark's suggestive essay, "The Word of God and the Language of Man: Puritan Semiotics and the Theological and Scientific 'Plain Styles' of the Seventeenth Century," *Semiotic Scene* 2 (1978), 61–90.

64. C. Conrad Cherry, *The Theology of Jonathan Edwards* (Garden City, N.Y.: Doubleday, 1966), 114.

65. Emerson, *Collected Works,* I, 10.

66. See C. Conrad Cherry, *Nature and Religious Imagination from Edwards to Bushnell* (Philadelphia: Fortress Press, 1980), chapter 6, 113–33.

67. Dickinson, P 820; Emerson, *Collected Works,* 2, 37; Thoreau, *Walden,* 135; Melville, *Collected Poems,* ed. Howard P. Vincent (Chicago: Packard & Co., 1947), 254 — from "In the Desert."

68. Emerson's Christ is altogether human and not very mysterious; he concedes only that "Jesus Christ belonged to the true race of prophets." Thoreau writes tenderly but not very piously that Christ possessed a heroic gentleness Carlyle ought to have written about in *Heroes and Hero-Worship.* Emerson, *Collected Works,* I, 81. Henry D. Thoreau, *Early Essays and Miscellanies* (Princeton: Princeton University Press, 1975), 250–51.

69. In fascicle 12 Dickinson first wrote "great," in the last line of the poem then underlined "vast," apparently showing her preference. See Franklin, *Manuscript Books,* 1:232.

70. Melville, *Moby-Dick,* 164, 414, 450.

71. Quoted in Herbert, *Moby-Dick and Calvinism,* 82–83.

72. Eberwein, *Dickinson: Strategies of Limitation,* 227.

73. Lawrence Buell, *New England Literary Culture: From Revolution through Renaissance* (Cambridge: Cambridge University Press, 1986), 134. Buell neatly terms the poem "a finely calibrated disintegration scenario" (133).

74. Melville, *Moby-Dick,* 374.

75. The title of chap. 6 of David Porter, *Dickinson: The Modern Idiom* (Cambridge, Mass., and London: Harvard University Press, 1981).

Chapter 2

1. For example, Jane Donahue Eberwein, *Dickinson: Strategies of Limitation;* Karl Keller, *The Only Kangaroo among the Beauty: Emily Dickinson and America;* Ruth Miller, *The Poetry of Emily Dickinson* (Middletown, Conn.:

Wesleyan University Press, 1968); and Dorothy Huff Oberhaus, *Emily Dickinson's Fascicles: Method and Meaning* (University Park: Pennsylvania State University Press, 1995).

2. For example, Cynthia Griffin Wolff, *Emily Dickinson;* Sandra M. Gilbert and Susan Gubar, *The Madwoman in the Attic: The Woman Writer and the Nineteenth-Century Literary Imagination* (New Haven: Yale University Press, 1979), 581–650; Shira Wolosky, *Emily Dickinson: The Voice of War* (New Haven and London: Yale University Press, 1984), 99–135; and Paula Bennett, *Emily Dickinson: Woman Poet,* 51–83.

3. For example, Vivian R. Pollak, *Dickinson: The Anxiety of Genre* (Ithaca and London: Cornell University Press, 1984), 10, 217–18; and Sharon Cameron, *Lyric Time: Dickinson and the Limitations of Genre* (Baltimore and London: Johns Hopkins University Press, 1979), 155–56.

4. See, for example, Austin Warren, "Emily Dickinson"; rptd. in Sewall, *Emily Dickinson: A Collection of Critical Essays,* 103–4; Robert Weisbuch, *Emily Dickinson's Poetry* (Chicago: University of Chicago Press, 1975), xii; and Porter, *Dickinson: The Modern Idiom,* 37, 184–85.

5. "Behold" is a variant for "achieve" in line 21 and was evidently what she initially wrote, then crossed out (see *Poems,* 3:873). The text of the poem contains a number of variants and was much worked over. In an apparently earlier version of the poem Dickinson used the first-person singular; only later did she make the speaker a "representative we."

6. For an expanded treatment of this point, see Eberwein, *Dickinson: Strategies of Limitations,* 240–45.

7. Porter, *Dickinson: The Modern Idiom,* esp. 1–8, 143–79.

8. Porter, *Dickinson: The Modern Idiom,* 152. "Emily Dickinson is the only major American poet without a project. That vacancy at the heart of her consciousness provided a tragic freedom that constitutes her identity."

9. This particular letter to the Norcross sisters illustrates the danger of designating single ideological tendencies in Dickinson. She kept her options open even when she was being polemically skeptical. Here she goes on to write, "Still, when Professor Fisk died on Mount Zion, Dr. Humphrey prayed, 'to whom shall we turn but thee'? 'I have finished,' said Paul, 'the faith.' We rejoice that he did not say discarded it" (*L,* 3:711). Professor Fisk was Nathan Fiske, Helen Hunt Jackson's father, who died in the Holy Land in 1848, after which Dr. Heman Humphrey, president of Amherst College, published *A Tribute to the Memory of Rev. Nathan W. Fiske.* This is the text Dickinson remembers, seemingly to allow for the possibility that a kind God might really welcome true believers to his heaven. In the next sentence, however, Dickinson recovers her skeptical style with a vengeance. She alludes to Paul's triumphant assertion in 2 Timothy 4.7, "I have fought a good fight, I have finished my course, I have kept the faith," only to sabotage it. Evidently she was ready here to think of Paul as the arch-distorter of Christianity.

10. Melville, *Moby-Dick,* 226.

11. In an illuminating reading Cynthia Griffin Wolff suggests that Dickinson parodies Pope's *Essay on Man* in the poem. See Wolff, *Emily Dickinson,* 344–47.

12. I use the text from packet 24 (fascicle 35), apparently composed in 1863. The earlier version of the poem appears in a letter to Samuel Bowles. The speculation that the poem commemorates the death of Frazar Stearns comes from Johnson's note to the letter to Bowles, *L,* 2:400. I agree with Shira Wolosky that the poem moves from its immediate historical occasion to question God's generosity and kindness in the whole created world. See Wolosky, *Emily Dickinson: A Voice of War,* 61–62.

13. Melville, *Moby-Dick,* 522.

14. See Eberwein, *Dickinson: Strategies of Limitation,* chaps. 1–3, for a thorough treatment that explains and justifies Dickinson's poetic poses of self-restriction. In my view Dickinson assumes a critical distance from these poses even while she is prone to adopt them.

15. The first question and response in the Shorter Catechism, still the basic text for religious instruction in Dickinson's Amherst, is "Quest. 1. *What is the chief end of man? Ans.* Man's chief end is to glorify God, and to enjoy him for ever." *Confession of Faith and the Larger and Shorter Catechisms,* 237.

16. Emerson, *Collected Works,* 3:31.

17. See *L,* 3:799–801.

18. For example, Richard Sewall in *The Life of Emily Dickinson,* esp. chaps. 2 and 16; Karl Keller, *The Only Kangaroo among the Beauty,* esp. chapters 2–4; St. Armand, *Emily Dickinson and Her Culture: The Soul's Society;* Eberwein, *Dickinson: Strategies of Limitation;* Wolff, *Emily Dickinson;* and Doriani, *Emily Dickinson: Daughter of Prophecy.*

19. See Sewall, *Life of Emily Dickinson,* 337–57.

20. See Doriani, *Emily Dickinson,* 173–77.

21. See William G. McLoughlin, *Revivals, Awakenings, and Reform: An Essay on Religion and Social Change in America, 1607–1977* (Chicago and London: University of Chicago Press, 1978), 119–20.

22. In "Herbert and Emily Dickinson: A Reading of Emily Dickinson – " in *Like Season'd Timber: New Essays on George Herbert,* ed. Edmund Miller and Robert DiYanni (New York: Peter Lang, 1987), 354–56, Dorothy Huff Oberhaus argues that in "'Unto me? I do not know you – '" Dickinson imitates poems of George Herbert's like "Love Bade Me Welcome" ("Love" 3) or especially "Dialogue." She also compares Dickinson's poem with Herbert's "Dialogue" in *Emily Dickinson's Fascicles* (16–19). I suspect, indeed, that Dickinson adopts Herbert's thought in Poem 964 as well as his form. A copy of Herbert's *Poetical Works* (1857 ed.) was in the Dickinson library, and she herself copied two stanzas of Herbert's "Mattens" in her own papers; when Millicent Todd Bingham discovered them she first identified and published them as an original poem of Dickinson's. The stanzas are in keeping with Dickinson's personal faith in a God of tenderness and in the mystery of the human heart.

My God – what is a Heart,
Silver – or Gold – or precious Stone,
Or Star – or Rainbow – or a part
Of all these things – or all of them in one?

My God – what is a Heart –
That Thou should'st it so eye, and woo
Pouring upon it all Thy art,
As if that Thou had'st nothing else to do –

(Dickinson's own transcription of the stanzas as reprinted by Oberhaus in "Herbert and Emily Dickinson," 351.)

Diane Gabrielsen Scholl presents a balanced and perceptive treatment of differences and similarities between Herbert's and Dickinson's approaches to the Bible in "From Aaron 'Drest' to Dickinson's 'Queen': Protestant Typology in Herbert and Dickinson," *Emily Dickinson Journal* 3, no.1 (1994); 1–23.

23. John Milton, *Paradise Lost*, ed. Merritt Hughes (New York: Odyssey Press, 1962), 306 (bk. 12, l. 587).

24. Gilbert and Gubar, *Madwoman in the Attic*, 642–50.

25. Compare Ruth Miller's reading: "The knowledge of God remains inaccessible to mortals. Faith in God, belief that Heaven exists, that Immortality awaits us must be felt by intuition." Miller, *Poetry of Emily Dickinson*, 56.

26. Barton Levi St. Armand finds "the Arminian heresy of justification through suffering" in a number of Dickinson's poems. St. Armand, *Emily Dickinson and Her Culture*, 52.

27. I have wondered if in fact this is the poem Dickinson refers to in her explanation to Higginson, "When I state myself, as the Representative of the Verse – it does not mean – me – but a supposed person" (*L*, 2:412). Johnson asserts that she seems to have enclosed "There came a Day at Summer's full" in her second letter to Higginson, dated 25 April 1862 (*L*, 2:405).

28. See Sewall, *Life of Emily Dickinson*, 683–88.

29. See Howe, *Unitarian Conscience*, 6–7, 105–6, for an emphasis on the wide currency of Unitarian ideas in New England in the mid-nineteenth century.

30. Sewall, *Life of Emily Dickinson*, 600. But see also the excerpts from Holland's illiberal criticisms of Whitman cited by Keller, *Only Kangaroo*, 253–58, esp. Holland's assertion that "Spiritualism, whenever it has cut loose from the Bible as the only authoritative revelation from heaven, has gone just as naturally into free love as water runs down hill" (256). Like many of his contemporaries in the establishment, Holland tempered his moralistic conservatism only gradually and grudgingly.

31. As St. Armand points out, Dickinson alludes here to 2 Kings 2.24, in which little children mock the prophet Elisha for his baldness, and he curses them in the name of the Lord, whereupon two she bears come out of the wood and tear apart forty-two of the children. See St. Armand, *Emily Dickinson and Her Culture*, 333, for useful detail concerning the vogue for this grisly biblical text in Dickinson's own Protestant culture.

32. Ann Douglas, *The Feminization of American Culture* (New York: Knopf, 1977). See also the discussion of the "Sentimental Love Religion" in St. Armand, *Emily Dickinson and Her Culture*, esp. 81–97.

33. Thoreau, *Walden*, 78.

34. Dickinson includes this same aphorism in another letter of January 1885, this time to Charles H. Clark (*L*, 3:857). This time, however, her implication is that Clark's deceased brother James and Clark's and Dickinson's friend Charles Wadsworth cannot write them from the afterlife to let them know that "the Years which they behold are also new and happy." In other words, she experiments with a this-worldly affirmation while corresponding with a Calvinist. She promulgates heresy while expressing affection to one more orthodox than she.

35. It may well be that in the spring and summer of 1873 Dickinson had her back up against orthodoxy in her family and community. Her father apparently reconfirmed his conversion then and on 1 May wrote his famous card, later found on his body, "I hereby give myself to God." See Leyda, *Years and Hours of Emily Dickinson,* 2:199–201.

36. The best treatment of Dickinson as a Transcendentalist fellow traveler is St. Armand, *Emily Dickinson and Her Culture,* esp. 188–207, 236–43, 262–71, and 296–97. St. Armand stresses her interest in Higginson and Ruskin as filters for Transcendentalist approaches to nature. Charles R. Anderson's often accepted view, that "the Transcendentalist's easy assumption of merger [between man and nature]" was "the one approach she . . . definitely discarded," is based, I think, on a misreading of Emerson and Thoreau as well as of Dickinson. Anderson, *Emily Dickinson's Poetry: Stairway of Surprise* (New York: Holt, Rinehart and Winston, 1960), 188. For an elaboration of my view that Emerson and Thoreau were aware of the inherent disparity between man and nature and used this disparity artfully and expressively, see my book *Thoreau as Romantic Naturalist: His Shifting Stance toward Nature* (Ithaca: Cornell University Press, 1974), chap. 1.

37. Sewall discusses Dickinson's acquaintance with Mrs. Almira H. Lincoln's *Familiar Lectures on Botany* in *The Life of Emily Dickinson,* 351–52.

38. See the astute speculations on Dickinson's view of time in Charles R. Anderson's fine reading of this poem in *Emily Dickinson's Poetry,* 133–35.

39. Emerson, *Collected Works,* 1:39.

40. *The Poetry and Prose of William Blake,* ed. David V. Erdman (Garden City, N.Y.: Doubleday, 1965), 39.

41. "All liars, shall have their part in the lake which burneth with fire and brimstone" is from Revelation 21.8, not originally from Jonathan Edwards, though he used it as a text in sermons. Dickinson invents a stereotypical Jonathan Edwards whom she can ridicule and make responsible for a saying in the Bible she dislikes. The text was also familiar to her from *The New-England Primer,* in which the item for *L* in "An Alphabet Lesson for Youth" is "Liars shall have their part in the lake which burns with fire and brimstone." *New-England Primer,* rpt. of earliest (1727) extant New England edition, ed. Paul Leicester Ford (New York: Teachers College, 1962), n.p. (For a less ironic view of her play with allusions here, see Keller, *Only Kangaroo,* 69.)

42. I am not persuaded by Cynthia Griffin Wolff's hypothesis that Dickinson experienced a gradual conversion to a Christ-centered Christianity after the mid-1860s and increasingly toward the end of her life. See Wolff, *Emily Dickinson,* 504–19.

43. "Surprise" is one of the Lords of Life in Emerson's "Experience." Rather like Dickinson, he conceives of the all-informing spirit as taking human beings by surprise in its creative and dynamic visitations. See Emerson, *Collected Works,* 3:39–40.

44. I use Ellen Louise Hart's print representation of the original manuscript here, because it is both more accurate and more expressive than Johnson's text in *The Letters of Emily Dickinson* (*L,* 3:830). Hart's text appears in *The Heath Anthology of American Literature,* ed. Paul Lauter (Lexington, Mass: D. C. Heath and Company, 1994), 1:2951–52.

45. For "scenelessness" see Weisbuch, *Emily Dickinson's Poetry,* esp. 15–17, 18–19, 23–24, 25–39.

46. "Vulcanism" is the theory that the surface of the earth is formed by volcanic eruption. Sewall points out that Edward Hitchcock, professor of chemistry and later president of Amherst College during Dickinson's youth, was a distinguished Vulcanist and speculates on her use of Hitchcock's teachings in "Though the Great Waters sleep." Sewall, *Life of Emily Dickinson,* 346n.

47. See *Poems,* 3:1007. I paraphrase Johnson on the dating and attribution.

48. Anderson, *Emily Dickinson's Poetry,* 277. That the sun is meant is suggested also by Poem 1550, in which Dickinson writes "sheen must have a Disk / To be a sun." But while allowing for this meaning we should also be wary of allegory and give full play to "the magic of the signifier," in Roland Barthes's phrase. Roland Barthes, *S/Z,* trans. Richard Miller (New York: Hill and Wang, 1974), 4.

49. On this issue my argument parallels those of Christopher Benfey, *Emily Dickinson and the Problem of Others,* 95 and 108; Shira Wolosky, *Emily Dickinson: The Voice of War,* 169–71; and Wendy Martin, *An American Triptych: Anne Bradstreet, Emily Dickinson, Adrienne Rich,* 136. I disagree with Jerome Loving, *The Poet on the Second Story* (New York: Cambridge University Press, 1986).

50. Ellen Louise Hart has recently discovered that Dickinson included a version of the last six lines of poem 1576, beginning "Adversity if it / shall be / Or Wild Prosperity – ," in a letter to Whitney that recalls "the students singing" after her mother's death. See Hart, "The Elizabeth Putnam Whitney Manuscripts and New Strategies for Editing Emily Dickinson's Letters," in *Emily Dickinson Journal* 4, no.1 (1995); 53–54. For the text of the letter, see *L,* 3:793–94.

Chapter 3

1. The first to focus on Dickinson's habit of challenging "great writers and small . . . even the Scriptures" was Ruth Miller, in *The Poetry of Emily Dickinson,* 222 ff.

Fordyce R. Bennett's *A Reference Guide to the Bible in Emily Dickinson's Poetry* (Lanham, Md.: Scarecrow Press, 1997) appeared too recently for me to use in the development of my ideas and interpretations. I have, however, checked my work against it and made a few necessary revisions.

2. For example, in Genesis 22.11–13:

And the angel of the Lord called unto him out of heaven, and said, Abraham, Abraham: and he said, Here am I.

And he said, Lay not thine hand upon the lad, neither do thou any thing unto him: for now I know that thou fearest God, seeing thou hast not withheld thy son, thine only son from me.

And Abraham lifted up his eyes, and looked, and behold behind him a ram caught in a thicket by his horns . . .

3. Lawrence Buell suggests that she may be "responding to the mawkishness" of nineteenth-century sentimental narratives based on biblical episodes and satirizing sentimental treatments of Abraham and Isaac familiar to her from local sermons and popular poems. Buell, *New England Literary Culture*, 172–73.

4. From a pamphlet of the First Congregational Church, Amherst, containing "The Order for Church Government," "The Order for the Admission of Members," and "Membership," (Amherst; Published by the Church, 1869), 5. The "Articles of Doctrinal Belief," drawn here from the Declaration of Faith adopted at the Council of Congregational churches in Boston, June 1865, is part of "The Order for Church Government." Dickinson no doubt knew that the original source for this particular article of belief was 2 Peter 1.21: "holy men of God spake as they were moved by the Holy Ghost."

It seems to me legitimate to treat Dickinson's pronouncement here, from a letter written late in 1882 to Mrs. Holland, as a gloss on the first lines of the poem she sent to her nephew Ned perhaps in that same year: "The Bible is an antique Volume – / Written by faded Men / At the suggestion of Holy Spectres" (P 1545; see *Poems*, 3:1066–67). If so, Dickinson subverts the doctrinal faith accepted in Amherst in the poem; it, like other writings addressed to Ned, is resolutely antiorthodox. The "Men" who wrote the Bible are now "faded" in memory, and the only ghosts who prompted them were "spectres" conjured by human imagination.

5. Johnson suggests that the text of Parker's that Dickinson refers to is *The Two Christmas Celebrations* (Boston: Rufus Leighton Jr., 1859), a book she may have received in 1859 as a Christmas remembrance from Mary Bowles. If so, she sampled the higher criticism in popular but powerful form. In this sermon-narrative Parker resolutely demystifies the life of Jesus, making him the son of Joseph and Mary and describing him humorously as "a come-outer from the Hebrew church" (8). Parker treats Jesus' doctrine of "piety and benevolence" as similar to his own, even if Jesus made a few "mistakes" (10)—for example, he believed in the devil and in the imminent end of the world. Parker also asserts, "his friends and followers preached his doctrines, but gradually added many more of their own," these new doctrines amounting to "a great mass of fictions" (14, 15). Dickinson seems at times to have agreed with the radical liberal idea that historical Christianity distorted Christ's original message; see *L*, 3:711, for the implication that Saint Paul especially tampered with the faith. See also the discussion of Poem 527 later in this chapter.

Jane Donahue Eberwein discusses Dickinson's use of the higher criticism in *Dickinson: Strategies of Limitation,* 78–79.

6. Dickinson refers to Christ's injunction in the Sermon on the Mount to serve God rather than Mammon and to live one's life rather than worry about material comforts. "And why take ye thought for raiment? Consider the lilies of the field, how they grow; they toil not, neither do they spin. And yet . . . even Solomon in all his glory was not arrayed like one of these." Matthew 6.28–29.

7. In later letters Dickinson twice cites Jesus' words to Nicodemus, "That which is born of the Spirit is spirit," as if to confirm the (Dickinsonian) idea that spiritual renewal has its own unknowable genesis. There is no real contradiction here; for Dickinson one could be renewed on a spring day as easily as while pondering Scripture. See *L,* 2:552, 614; and John 3.6.

8. *Poetry and Prose of William Blake,* 44.

9. See Paula Bennett's fine treatment of this letter and of the more simply optimistic poem ("To the bright east she flies" [P 1573]) the letter includes as part of its dialectical vacillation, in "'By a Mouth That Cannot Speak': Spectral Presence in Emily Dickinson's Letters," *Emily Dickinson Journal* 1, no.2 (1992); 86–87.

10. Sewall, *Life of Emily Dickinson,* 695.

11. Quoted in Richard B. Sewall, *The Lyman Letters: New Light on Emily Dickinson and Her Family* (Amherst: University of Massachusetts Press, 1965), 73.

12. Sewall, *Life of Emily Dickinson,* 696.

13. *The New-England Primer,* rpt. of earliest (1727) extant New England edition, n.p.

14. See Wolff, *Emily Dickinson,* 73, for a useful account of correlative types.

15. Milton, *Paradise Lost,* 10:162. Byron, *Cain,* 3.1.468–85, in George Gordon, Lord Byron, *Selected Works, Revised and Enlarged,* ed. Edward E. Bostetter (New York: Holt, Rinehart and Winston, 1972), 292.

16. In all likelihood Dickinson read the series of excellent, informative articles by Asa Gray on Darwin's *Origin of the Species* and its reception in the *Atlantic* for July, August, and October 1860 (vol. 6:109–, 229–, 406–). She does not perhaps show effects from this reading immediately, but her familiarity with Darwin and her sense of his importance is clear from later letters. She refers specifically to Darwin twice, once very cleverly in a letter of 1871 to Mrs. Holland ("Why the Thief ingredient accompanies all Sweetness Darwin does not tell us" [*L,* 2:485]), the second time in the "nimble believing" letter of 1882 to Judge Lord ("Mrs D. Stearns called to know if we didnt think it very shocking for [Benjamin F.] Butler to 'liken himself to his Redeemer,' but we thought Darwin had thrown 'the Redeemer' away"). Darwin did not create Dickinson's instability of belief concerning Christianity, but he certainly helped to stimulate it.

17. Wolff, *Emily Dickinson,* 144. I am indebted to Wolff's treatment of the meaning of the Jacob story for Dickinson's culture.

18. Weisbuch, *Emily Dickinson's Poetry,* esp. 12–14.

19. Dickinson's transcription of "Let me go for the day breaketh" is beautifully reproduced in Werner, *Open Folios,* 28.

20. I am indebted to Sewall's comments on this letter in *Life of Emily Dickinson*, 698, 725.

21. *Poems*, 1:83.

22. Quoted in Johnson, *Poems*, 1:83. The familiarity of Watts's hymns in Dickinson's local culture, mentioned in all the biographies, is discussed thoughtfully in St. Armand, *Emily Dickinson and Her Culture*, 154–59.

23. My argument concerning the biblical basis of poem 597 follows Wolff, *Emily Dickinson*, 187, 348–49.

For a shrewd reading of Dickinson's ironic treatment of Moses as a type of Christ who is also a victim of the Father, see Mary Loeffelholz, *Dickinson and the Boundaries of Feminist Theory* (Urbana and Chicago: University of Illinois Press, 1991), 62–64.

24. *The Confession of Faith and the Larger and Shorter Catechisms*, 291.

25. See Harold Bloom, *A Map of Misreading* (New York: Oxford University Press, 1975), 69, 77.

26. *King Lear*, 4.1.37–8.

27. *Poetry and Prose of William Blake*, 37.

28. Eberwein, *Dickinson: Strategies of Limitation*, 16.

29. Ibid, 193. See p. 161 for a fine general explanation of "awe."

30. Two lines that are variants of lines 4 and 5 survive, however, in a penciled fragment in the handwriting of the middle or late 1870s.

Has Human Nature gone –
Unknowing of his dread abode –

Such a fragment does not prove conclusively that Poem 1733 can be assigned to Dickinson's last decade, but in the absence of other evidence a late date is probable. I transcribe this fragment from a scrap of paper kept in the Amherst College Special Collections. It belongs with a group of penciled fragments found in Dickinson's possession at the time of her death, all of which Johnson assigns to "the last decade of Emily Dickinson's life" (*L*, 3:914, 921). Johnson prints it as prose fragment 77 (*L*, 3:923) but incorrectly substitutes to for of in Dickinson's text. The handwriting in the two lines seems to be that of 1875 or later. The pencil writing "gives effect of exceptional neatness and careful spacing," and in "Has" and "Human" Dickinson makes her Hs with three separate strokes, a form of H she started to use around 1877. (I quote and paraphrase from Theodora Ward's account of "Characteristics of the Handwriting," included in Johnson's introduction to *Poems* [1955], lvii.)

Perhaps the capitalization and punctuation in the Todd text should be emended on the basis of the fragment. "Human Nature" might replace "human nature" in line 4; a dash might replace the period at the end of line 4 (the period may well be Mrs. Todd's error); and a dash might be added at the end of line 5. Such changes make the syntax clearer and suggest a rhythm of thought more characteristic of Dickinson. The first two stanzas would then read:

No man saw awe, nor to his house
Admitted he a man

Though by his awful residence
Has Human Nature been –

Not deeming of his dread abode –
Till laboring to flee
A grasp on comprehension laid
Detained vitality.

31. In her poems Dickinson uses "awful" generally in the sense of "awe-some" or "dreadful." Yet she was also aware of the colloquial meaning, "ex-tremely bad or unpleasant," as she shows when she writes that "Awe . . . was an awful Mother, but I liked him better than none." This modern meaning was current in the spoken language of New England during her lifetime. In *Our Nig*, for example, Harriet Wilson represents the speech of "professed abolitionists," who have no use for "niggers in their own houses . . . Faugh! to lodge one; to eat with one; admit one through the front door; to sit next one; awful!" Wilson, *Our Nig; or, Sketches from the Life of a Free Black,* ed. Henry Louis Gates (New York: Vintage Books, 1983), 129.

32. Cynthia Griffin Wolff does not discuss "No man saw awe." In my opin-ion the poem calls into question her view that Dickinson thinks of Jacob as the last man to experience the full presence of God. In a note Wolff acknowledges that "the Jewish tradition inclines to the belief that in some sense" Moses saw God's face and that Dickinson was probably aware of a corresponding Protes-tant tradition (Wolff, *Emily Dickinson,* 580). In her reading of Dickinson's po-ems, however, Wolff calls attention only to God's denial of Moses' request to en-ter Canaan. I read "No man saw awe" as, among other things, a reflection of Dickinson's astute reading of the Bible, whatever she knew of exegetical tradi-tion. Given the baffling and dynamic character of her own religious epiphanies, she might have found this contradiction in the Moses story entirely plausible. That is, she could well imagine how Moses both did and did not see God face to face.

33. Cristanne Miller, *Emily Dickinson: A Poet's Grammar* (Cambridge, Mass.: Harvard University Press, 1987), 127–30.

34. Ibid., 127.

35. Ibid., 129; see also 69. Miller suggests that the ecstatic merger in the poem between lover and beloved, worshiper and deity, and reader and poet is "implicitly sexual," as implied in words such as *come* and *consume* (128).

36. Thoreau, *Walden,* 324–25.

37. Dorothy Huff Oberhaus, "'Tender Pioneer': Emily Dickinson's Poems on the Life of Christ," *American Literature* 59, no. 3 (1987); 341–58, is an im-pressive, if one-sided, essay concerned with Dickinson's Christology. Oberhaus argues that "the deep structure of her Gospel poems places them in the poetic tradition of Christian devotion"—in other words, that Dickinson's perspective on Christ was deeply and stably traditional. Oberhaus develops a similar ar-gument at greater length in *Emily Dickinson's Fascicles: Method & Meaning.*

This book contains some striking, intricate readings (I especially like her reading of Poem 906, "The Admirations – and Contempts – of time – "), and it persuades me that some of Dickinson's more obscure poems may well be hermetically concerned with the relation between Christ and Dickinson's persona. As a whole, however, Oberhaus's book seems to me more extreme and less convincing than her separate essays because of its fanciful construction of the fascicles and its drawn-out, single-minded thesis. I am persuaded that Dickinson's imagination was traditionally Christian in some texts but not that it stayed that way permanently or that Dickinson rested uncritically in any orthodox doctrine. Drawing on the Bible (as Oberhaus convincingly shows), Dickinson variously imagined her own Christ.

38. The quoted words are from her meditation on the Bible for Joseph Lyman, discussed earlier in this chapter. In a late (1884?) letter to Martha Gilbert Smith, Dickinson tentatively opposes Jesus the shepherd of human souls to "the Father": "Ineffable Avarice of Jesus, who reminds a perhaps encroaching Father, 'All these are mine'" (*L*, 3:823).

39. These words are of course from Isaiah 53.3, not from the Gospel accounts of Jesus, though they are traditionally associated with the Christian Messiah.

40. The best-nuanced treatment of the place of Christ in Dickinson's belief system is Eberwein, *Dickinson* 247–53. For the view that Dickinson's understanding of the meaning of Christ is chaotic, see Porter, *Dickinson: The Modern Idiom*, 167–69; and Keller, *Only Kangaroo*, 118.

41. Porter, *Dickinson*, 167. I have juxtaposed "personal" from earlier in Porter's sentence. As Porter acknowledges, Dickinson had no interest in America as the Redeemer Nation in which Christ's kingdom might be realized on earth or in the public rhetoric of Puritan typology. Karl Keller even dismisses the idea that Dickinson treated Christ as an antitype, both because her conception of his meaning varied and because for her he usually had no "control over historical events" and hence no political or public significance (Keller, *Only Kangaroo* 116). But "private typology" was a well-established practice in New England writing long before Dickinson. A Puritan like Cotton Mather habitually made Jesus the antitype of his own private sufferings (see Sacvan Bercovitch, "Cotton Mather," in Everett Emerson, ed., *Major Writers of Early American Literature* [Madison: University of Wisconsin Press, 1972], 102–5). Dickinson develops such a way of thinking in the manner of a nineteenth-century creative renegade. (My views on Dickinson's typology resemble Wolosky's in *Emily Dickinson: A Voice of War*, 138–43.)

42. Dickinson sent a copy of the poem full of underlined words to Samuel Bowles. See *Poems*, 2:632.

43. Dickinson was keenly interested in Paul, while she is not known to have had an interest in the redirection of Christianity under Gentiles such as the Emperor Constantine or Saint Augustine. As we have seen, Paul fills various roles for her, including that of the arch-distorter of the faith. Exactly how she came to such an opinion is a mystery. By 1862, the putative date of Poem 527, she would

have read something of Theodore Parker (see n. 5) and might well have known that Unitarians de-emphasized Paul in their reaction against Calvinism. Perhaps she knew of the treatment of Paul in Strauss's *Das Leben Jesu,* though we have no hard evidence for it. She surely knew later in her life that Mary Ann Evans—George Eliot—was Strauss's translator. Evans's translation *The Life of Jesus* appeared in 1846, in good time for its reputation to spread even to Amherst by the 1860s.

44. Dickinson's irony seems to me still more apparent in the variants in the last stanza, according to which the Gentile Drinker "enforced" a sacrament that the saints later "indorsed." The stanza suggests that Christ's mystery has been institutionalized, even "patented," for a market.

45. Dickinson wrote a number of poems in which the protagonist can be read as both Christ and an imagined contemporary man. An example for me is Poem 567, "He gave away his Life – " in which "He" might be both the resurrected Christ (see readings by Eberwein, *Dickinson: Strategies of Limitation,* 250, and Oberhaus, "Tender Pioneer," 354–58) and a Civil War hero such as Frazar Stearns, the son of the president of Amherst College killed in March 1862 (see St. Armand, *Emily Dickinson and Her Culture,* 104–14).

46. For other commentary, see Eberwein, *Dickinson: Strategies of Limitation,* 206; Porter, *Dickinson: The Modern Idiom,* 99, 157–58.

47. As the narrator describes his narrative method in Melville's *Pierre; or, The Ambiguities* (Evanston and Chicago: Northwestern University Press and the Newberry Library, 1971), 54.

Chapter 4

1. See St. Armand, *Emily Dickinson and Her Culture,* 168–73.

2. Greg Johnson, *Emily Dickinson: Perception and the Poet's Quest* (University: University of Alabama Press, 1985), 97.

3. See Benfey, *Emily Dickinson and the Problem of Others,* 14.

4. Given Dickinson's chosen stance of epistemological isolation, it is understandable (however startling) that she sent a version of this stanza to her closest friend, Susan Gilbert Dickinson, beginning, "But Susan is a Stranger yet – ." See *Poems,* 3:971.

5. Sharon Cameron, *Lyric Time: Dickinson and the Limits of Genre,* 26.

6. Cameron, *Lyric Time,* 27.

7. "That 'tis so Heavenly far" is a variant for "That situates so far." See *Poems,* 2:757.

8. See E. Miller Budick's discussion of "Gottfried Wilhelm von Leibnitz," an essay that appeared in the *Atlantic* in 1858, in *Emily Dickinson and the Life of Language: A Study in Symbolic Poetics* (Baton Rouge and London: Louisiana University Press, 1985), 23–27.

9. Emerson, *Collected Works,* 3:29.

10. From John Calvin, *Institutes of the Christian Religion,* bk. 4, sec. 17, 21, trans. John Allen, 5th American ed., 2 vols. (Philadelphia: Presbyterian Board of

Publication, 1844), 2:546–47. See Wolff, *Emily Dickinson,* 212 ff., for an illuminating discussion of Calvin's conception of the sacrament.

11. For a related argument, see Agnieszka Salska, *Walt Whitman and Emily Dickinson: Poetry of the Central Consciousness* (Philadelphia: University of Pennsylvania Press, 1985), chap. 5, esp. 132.

12. For these two variants see *Poems,* 3:1065–66.

13. Also perhaps a variety of personal situations. Ellen Louise Hart points out that Dickinson sent this poem to Susan Dickinson and suggests that it represents implicitly an aspect of her feeling for Susan. The copy to Susan is prefaced with the words, *"Excuse* me – Dollie [Susan] – " and is signed "Emily." See Ellen Louise Hart, "The Encoding of Homoerotic Desire: Emily Dickinson's Letters and Poems to Susan Dickinson, 1850–1886," *Tulsa Studies in Women's Literature* 9 (1990); 261.

14. See John E. Smith, "Editor's Introduction," Jonathan Edwards, *Religious Affections* (New Haven: Yale University Press, 1959), 30–33.

15. See Julie Ellison, *Emerson's Romantic Style,* 7–8, 40–42. See also Stonum, *Dickinson Sublime,* esp. 9–10.

16. Porter, *Dickinson: The Modern Idiom,* 205.

17. Commentators who have dealt with the appeal of the unknown more fully include Roland Hagenbuechle, Robert Weisbuch, E. Miller Budick, Christopher Benfey, Agnieszka Salska, and Cristanne Miller.

18. Cameron, *Lyric Time,* 48.

19. Numerous critics have helped establish these ideas, notably Robert Weisbuch, Sharon Cameron, and David Porter.

20. Porter, *Dickinson: The Modern Idiom,* 149. Porter also treats very fully the connection in Dickinson between her "allegories of ignorance" and her practice of consolation (170–79).

21. Salska, *Walt Whitman and Emily Dickinson,* 132.

22. Salska, *Walt Whitman,* 132.

23. Salska, *Walt Whitman,* 128. See also Cameron, *Lyric Time,* chap. 3, 91–135. Cameron's is the most profound study of the dynamics of these poems, as of many other poems dramatizing psychic disturbance.

24. Salska, *Walt Whitman,* 132. See also 53.

25. Salska, *Walt Whitman,* 146.

26. Salska, *Walt Whitman,* 157.

27. See Cameron, *Lyric Time,* esp. chap. 3; Porter, *Dickinson: The Modern Idiom,* chaps. 1, 5, and 6; Bennett, *Emily Dickinson: Woman Poet,* 32–41.

28. The phrase *sumptuous Destitution* recalls Emerson's "Monadnoc":

Our sumptuous indigence,
O barren mound, thy plenties fill!
We fool and prate;
Thou art silent and sedate.

(Emerson, *Poems,* 69–70)

The echoes of Emerson's poems, which we know were important to Dickinson, seem to me clearer evidence of his presence in her writing than anything from his essays or other prose.

29. Mary Loeffelholz points out how often Dickinson imagines hearing sounds from within a shelter, or music mediated by distance, in *Dickinson and the Boundaries of Feminist Criticism,* 120–21, 135.

30. See, for example, the "gay unknown" of a sunset that then leaves "penury . . . Remedilessly" behind it (P 1675)—another instance of "sumptuous Destitution." See also Richard Wilbur, "Sumptuous Destitution," rptd. in Richard B. Sewall, ed., *Emily Dickinson: A Collection of Critical Essays* (Englewood Cliffs, N.J.: Prentice-Hall, 1963), 132: "To the eye of desire all things seem in profound perspective, either moving or gesturing toward the vanishing point"; and 134: "Her nature poetry when most serious . . . presents us repeatedly with dawn, noon, and sunset, those grand ceremonial moments of the day which argue the splendor of Paradise."

31. Roland Hagenbuechle, "Precision and Indeterminacy in the Poetry of Emily Dickinson," *Emerson Society Quarterly* 20 (1974); 45.

32. My reading of "By my Window have I for Scenery" has been stimulated by E. Miller Budick, *Emily Dickinson and the Life of Language,* 183–86.

33. In fascicle 38, Dickinson first wrote "do" in the first stanza then underlined the variant "serve," indicating her preference. See *Manuscript Books,* 2:927, 929; and *Poems,* 2:603–4.

34. The downgrading of "Sight" in "By my Window" seems to contrast with the affirmation of one's "corporeal person" in Dickinson's letter to the Norcross sisters beginning, "I hear robins a great way off." Here the contradiction may be more apparent than real; the speaker apprehends "in corporeal person" in the poem just as much as Dickinson does in the letter. Nevertheless, the poem looks implicitly toward an incorporeal life in heaven, while the prose passage seems to find "heaven" in life as experienced here. In earlier chapters also we have encountered such uncertainty about the role of the body in the spiritual life. Dickinson did not entirely resolve her dilemmas as a rebellious inheritor of Calvinism.

Whether "the Divine" in "By my Window . . . " approximates a Christian divinity is unclear. When the speaker asserts that she will recover her conviction of the pine's immortality after death, she pays her respects to the Christian story of the soul's transfiguration. But faith in the apprehension of a pine tree is hardly orthodox even when linked to a Christian hope of heaven. (For a different view, see Budick, *Emily Dickinson and the Life of Language,* 185–86.)

35. Thoreau, *Walden,* 312.

36. Joanne Feit Diehl, "Murderous Poetics: Dickinson, the Father, and the Text," in Lynda E. Boose and Betty S. Flowers, eds., *Daughters and Fathers* (Baltimore and London: Johns Hopkins University Press, 1989), 334. In this vigorous essay Diehl restates a view she first expounds in her *Dickinson and the Romantic Imagination,* esp. 163.

37. See Poem 214, "I taste a liquor never brewed – "; and Poem 1575, "The Bat is dun, with wrinkled Wings – ."

38. See Margaret Homans, *Women Writers and Poetic Identity: Dorothy Wordsworth, Emily Brontë, and Emily Dickinson* (Princeton: Princeton University Press, 1980), 12–29, 188–201; and Mary Loeffelholz, *Dickinson and the Boundaries of Feminist Theory,* chap. 4, esp. 134–44.

39. Homans, *Women Writers and Poetic Identity,* 194

40. Bennett, *Emily Dickinson: Woman Poet,* 96. Bennett attributes this activity not only to Dickinson but also to Mrs. Sigourney and other American women poets. See also Martin, *An American Tryptich;* and St. Armand, *Emily Dickinson and Her Culture.*

While I have learned a lot from Bennett's approach to Dickinson's nature poetry, I differ from Bennett in several ways. First, I think that Dickinson's accurate renderings of natural phenomena, observed often for their "intimations of immortality," align her with Thoreau (and perhaps less thoroughly with Emerson, Whitman, and Frederick Goddard Tuckerman) as well as with women poets and artists of her period. Second, Dickinson's post-Kantian awareness of the self-enclosed character of perception sets her apart from other women writers with whom she otherwise has affinities. She is more a poet of intellect, less a poet of sentimental appreciations, than (say) Lydia Sigourney. Third, I am more skeptical than Bennett concerning Dickinson's commitment to a feminine religion of nature. Because "Nature is a stranger" for Dickinson, "Mother Nature" is an ideological fiction in her writing even when she celebrates "her" (e.g., in Poem 790, "Nature - the Gentlest Mother is"). I agree with Bennett, however, that Dickinson casually enjoys imagining a closeness to nature as part of a woman's birthright.

41. See Christopher Benfey's admirable treatment of this issue in *Emily Dickinson and the Problem of Others,* 65ff.

42. See Benfey, *Emily Dickinson and the Problem of Others,* chap. 3, "Nearness and Neighbors."

43. Judith Banzer Farr suggestively compares Dickinson's conception of light with that of Thomas Cole and his "Luminist" successors, a style of painting Dickinson knew well from Austin and Susan's collection as well as from reproductions. See Farr, *The Passion of Emily Dickinson* (Cambridge, Mass.: Harvard University Press, 1992), 245–55.

44. This is Sharon Cameron's emphasis in her "adversarial" reading of nature's light in the poem. See *Lyric Time,* 178–80.

45. Weisbuch, *Emily Dickinson's Poetry,* 61.

46. See John Irwin, *American Hieroglyphics: The Symbol of the Egyptian Hieroglyphics in the American Renaissance* (New Haven: Yale University Press, 1980). See Poems 955, 1100, and 1498 for other relevant uses of "italic" or "italicized."

47. Porter, *Dickinson: The Modern Idiom,* 163. Until recently, "Four Trees – upon a solitary Acre – " lay unnoticed. In the 1980s and 1990s, however, it has generated a flurry of commentary. Wolosky (3–4), Budick (16–18), and Bennett (29–31) follow Porter in stressing human ignorance of nature's purpose in the poem, while, on the other hand, Christopher Benfey makes a strong argument for the poem's essential Romanticism, its affirmation of the conditions of perception. "Dickinson does not so much assert a skeptical view as *accept* such a view, and build on it" (116; see also Loeffelholz, 46). Stonum (16–18) and Farr (295) stress the mystery and "strangely haunting presence" of the scene while also emphasizing "its incompatibility with our epistemological and teleological hopes" (Stonum, *Dickinson Sublime,* 18).

48. Bennett, *Emily Dickinson: Woman Poet*, 30–31; Benfey, *Emily Dickinson and the Problem of Others*, 114. See Cristanne Miller, *Dickinson: A Poet's Grammar*, 37–39, 44–46 for a general discussion of Dickinson's use of "syntactic doubling" and "disjunction."

49. Thoreau, *Walden*, 134.

Bibliography

Anderson, Charles. *Emily Dickinson's Poetry: Stairway of Surprise.* New York: Holt, Rinehart and Winston, 1960.

Benfey, Christopher. *Emily Dickinson and the Problem of Others.* Amherst: University of Massachusetts Press, 1984.

Bennett, Fordyce R. *A Reference Guide to the Bible in Emily Dickinson's Poetry.* Lanham, Md.: Scarecrow Press, 1997.

Bennett, Paula. *Emily Dickinson: Woman Poet.* Iowa City: University of Iowa Press, 1990.

————. "'By a Mouth That Cannot Speak': Spectral Presence in Emily Dickinson's Letters." *Emily Dickinson Journal* 1, no.2 (1992): 76–99.

Berlant, Lauren. *The Anatomy of National Fantasy: Hawthorne, Utopia, and Everyday Life.* Chicago and London: University of Chicago Press, 1991.

Blake, William. *The Poetry and Prose of William Blake.* Edited by David V. Erdman. Garden City, N.Y.: Doubleday and Company, 1965.

Budick, E. Miller. *Emily Dickinson and the Life of Language: A Study in Symbolic Poetics.* Baton Rouge: Louisiana University Press, 1985.

Buell, Lawrence. *New England Literary Culture: From Revolution through Renaissance.* Cambridge: Cambridge University Press, 1986.

Calvin, John. *Institutes of the Christian Religion.* Trans. John Allen. Fifth American ed., 2 vols. Philadelphia: Presbyterian Board of Publication, 1844.

Cameron, Sharon. *Choosing Not Choosing: Dickinson's Fascicles.* Chicago and London: University of Chicago Press, 1992.

————. *Lyric Time: Dickinson and the Limitations of Genre.* Baltimore and London: Johns Hopkins University Press, 1979.

The Works of William E. Channing, D.D. Boston: American Unitarian Association, 1880.

Charvat, William S. *The Origins of American Critical Thought, 1810–1836.* Philadelphia: University of Pennsylvania Press, 1936.

Cherry, C. Conrad. *Nature and Religious Imagination from Edwards to Bushnell.* Philadelphia: Fortress Press, 1980.

―――. *The Theology of Jonathan Edwards.* Garden City, N.Y.: Doubleday, 1966.

Clark, Michael. "The Word of God and the Language of Man: Puritan Semiotics and the Theological and Scientific 'Plain Styles' of the Seventeenth Century." *Semiotic Scene* 2 (1978): 61–90.

The Confession of Faith and the Larger and Shorter Catechisms. Inverness: Publications Committee of the Free Presbyterian Church of Scotland, 1970.

Dickie, Margaret. *Lyric Contingencies: Emily Dickinson and Wallace Stevens.* Philadelphia: University of Pennsylvania Press, 1991.

Dickinson, Emily. *The Letters of Emily Dickinson.* Ed. Thomas H. Johnson and Theodora Ward. 3 vols. Cambridge, Mass.: Harvard University Press, 1958.

―――. *The Manuscript Books of Emily Dickinson.* Ed. Ralph W. Franklin. 2 vols. Cambridge, Mass.: Harvard University Press, 1980.

―――. *The Poems of Emily Dickinson.* Ed. Thomas H. Johnson. 3 vols. Cambridge, Mass.: Harvard University Press, 1955.

Diehl, Joanne Feit. *Dickinson and the Romantic Imagination.* Princeton: Princeton University Press, 1981.

―――. "Murderous Poetics: Dickinson, the Father, and the Text." In *Daughters and Fathers,* ed. Linda E. Boose and Betty S. Flowers. Baltimore and London: Johns Hopkins University Press, 1989.

Dobson, Joanne. *Dickinson and the Strategies of Reticence: The Woman Writer in Nineteenth-Century America.* Bloomington and Indianapolis: Indiana University Press, 1989.

Doriani, Beth Maclay. *Emily Dickinson: Daughter of Prophecy.* Amherst: University of Massachusetts Press, 1996.

Eberwein, Jane Donahue. *Dickinson: Strategies of Limitation.* Amherst: University of Massachusetts Press, 1985.

Ellison, Julie. *Emerson's Romantic Style.* Princeton: Princeton University Press, 1984.

Emerson, Ralph Waldo. *The Collected Works of Ralph Waldo Emerson.* Ed. Alfred R. Ferguson, Robert E. Spiller, Joseph Slater, and Jean Ferguson Carr. Cambridge, Mass.: Harvard University Press, 1971– .

―――. *The Journals and Miscellaneous Notebooks of Ralph Waldo Emerson.* Ed. William Gillman et al. Cambridge, Mass: Harvard University Press, 1960– .

Farr, Judith Banzer. *The Passion of Emily Dickinson.* Cambridge, Mass: Harvard University Press, 1992.

Feidelson, Charles N., Jr. *Symbolism and American Literature.* Chicago and London: University of Chicago Press, 1953.

Franklin, Ralph W. *The Editing of Emily Dickinson: A Reconsideration.* Madison: University of Wisconsin Press, 1967.

Gelpi, Alfred. *Emily Dickinson: The Mind of the Poet.* Cambridge, Mass.: Harvard University Press, 1965.

Gilbert, Sandra M., and Susan Gubar. *The Madwoman in the Attic: The Woman Writer and the Nineteenth-Century Imagination.* New Haven and London: Yale University Press, 1979.

Hagenbuechle, Roland. "Precision and Indeterminacy in the Poetry of Emily Dickinson." *Emerson Society Quarterly* 20 (1974): 33–56.

———. "Sign and Process: The Concept of Language in Emerson and Dickinson." *Emerson Society Quarterly* 25 (1979): 137–55.

Hart, Ellen Louise. "The Elizabeth Putnam Whitney Manuscripts and New Strategies for Editing Emily Dickinson's Letters." *Emily Dickinson Journal* 4, no.1 (1995): 44–74.

———. "The Encoding of Homoerotic Desire: Emily Dickinson's Letters and Poems to Susan Dickinson, 1850–1886." *Tulsa Studies in Women's Literature* 9 (1990): 251–72.

Herbert, George. *The Works of George Herbert.* Ed. F. E. Hutchinson. Oxford: Oxford University Press, 1941.

Herbert, T. Walter. *Moby-Dick and Calvinism: A World Dismantled.* New Brunswick, N.J.: Rutgers University Press, 1977.

Homans, Margaret. *Women Writers and Poetic Identity: Dorothy Wordsworth, Emily Brontë, and Emily Dickinson.* Princeton: Princeton University Press, 1980.

Howe, Daniel Walker. *The Unitarian Conscience: Harvard Moral Philosophy, 1805–1861.* Cambridge, Mass.: Harvard University Press, 1970.

Howe, Susan. *The Birth-Mark: Unsettling the Wilderness in American Literary History.* Hanover N.H.: Wesleyan University Press, 1993.

Irwin, John. *American Hieroglyphics: The Symbol of the Egyptian Heroglyphics in the American Renaissance.* New Haven and London: Yale University Press, 1980.

Johnson, Greg. *Emily Dickinson: Perception and the Poet's Quest.* University: University of Alabama Press, 1985.

Juhasz, Suzanne, Cristanne Miller, and Martha Nell Smith. *Comic Power in Emily Dickinson.* Austin: University of Texas Press, 1993.

Keller, Karl, *The Only Kangaroo among the Beauty: Emily Dickinson and America.* Baltimore and London: Johns Hopkins University Press, 1979.

Leyda, Jay. *The Years and Hours of Emily Dickinson.* 2 vols. New Haven and London: Yale University Press, 1960.

Loeffelholz, Mary. *Dickinson and the Boundaries of Feminist Theory.* Urbana and Chicago: University of Illinois Press, 1991.

Loving, Jerome. *The Poet on the Second Story.* New York: Cambridge University Press, 1986.

Martin, Terence. *The Instructed Vision: Scottish Common Sense Philosophy and the Origins of American Fiction.* Bloomington: Indiana University Press, 1961.

Martin, Wendy. *An American Triptych: Anne Bradstreet, Emily Dickinson, Adrienne Rich.* Chapel Hill: University of North Carolina Press, 1984.

McLoughlin, William G. *Revivals, Awakenings, and Reform: An Essay on Religion and Social Change in America, 1607–1977.* Chicago and London: University of Chicago Press, 1978.

Melville, Herman. *Collected Poems.* Ed. Howard P. Vincent. Chicago: Packard and Co., 1947.

————. *Moby-Dick.* Ed. Harrison Hayford, Hershel Parker, and G. Thomas Tanselle. Evanston and Chicago: Northwestern University Press and the Newberry Library, 1988.

————. *Pierre; or, The Ambiguities.* Evanston and Chicago: Northwestern University Press and the Newberry Library, 1971.

Miller, Cristanne. *Emily Dickinson: A Poet's Grammar.* Cambridge, Mass: Harvard University Press, 1987.

Miller, Perry. *The New England Mind: The Seventeenth Century.* New York: Macmillan, 1939.

Miller, Ruth. *The Poetry of Emily Dickinson.* Middletown, Conn.: Wesleyan University Press, 1968.

Neufeldt, Leonard. *The House of Emerson.* Lincoln: University of Nebraska Press, 1982.

The New England Primer, the earliest extant New England ed., 1727. Reprint, edited, with an introduction, by Paul Leicester Ford. New York: Teachers College, 1962.

Oberhaus, Dorothy Huff. *Emily Dickinson's Fascicles: Method and Meaning.* University Park: Pennsylvania State University Press, 1995.

————. "Herbert and Emily Dickinson: A Reading of Emily Dickinson." In *Like Season'd Timber: New Essays on George Herbert,* ed. Edmund Miller and Robert DiYanni. New York: Peter Lang, 1987.

————. "'Tender Pioneer': Emily Dickinson's Poems on the Life of Christ." *American Literature* 59, no.3 (1987): 341–58.

Parker, Theodore. *The Two Christmas Celebrations.* Boston: Rufus Leighton Jr., 1859.

Poirier, Richard. *Poetry and Pragmatism.* Cambridge, Mass.: Harvard University Press, 1992.

————. *The Renewal of Literature: Emersonian Reflections.* New York: Random House, 1987.

Pollak, Vivian R. *Dickinson: The Anxiety of Genre.* Ithaca and London: Cornell University Press, 1984.

Porter, David. *Dickinson: The Modern Idiom.* Cambridge, Mass.: Harvard University Press, 1981.

Reynolds, David. *Beneath the American Renaissance: The Subversive Imagination in the Age of Emerson and Melville.* New York: Alfred A. Knopf, 1988.

St. Armand, Barton Levi. *Emily Dickinson and Her Culture: The Soul's Society.* New York: Cambridge University Press, 1984.

Salska, Agnieszka. *Walt Whitman and Emily Dickinson: Poetry of the Central Consciousness.* Philadelphia: University of Pennsylvania Press, 1985.

Scholl, Diane Gabrielsen. "From Aaron 'Drest' to Dickinson's 'Queen': Protestant Typology in Herbert and Dickinson." *Emily Dickinson Journal* 3, no.1 (1994): 1–23.

Sewall, Richard B. *The Life of Emily Dickinson.* 2 vols. New York: Farrar, Straus and Giroux, 1974.

————. *The Lyman Letters: New Light on Emily Dickinson and Her Family.* Amherst: University of Massachusetts Press, 1965.

————, ed. *Emily Dickinson: A Collection of Critical Essays.* Englewood Cliffs, N.J.: Prentice-Hall, 1963.

Smith, John E. "Editor's Introduction." to *Religious Affections,* by Jonathan Edwards. New Haven and London: Yale University Press, 1959.

Smith, Martha Nell. *Rowing in Eden: Rereading Emily Dickinson.* Austin: University of Texas Press, 1992.

Smith, Robert McClure. *The Seductions of Emily Dickinson.* Tuscaloosa: University of Alabama Press, 1996.

Stonum, Gary Lee. *The Dickinson Sublime.* Madison: University of Wisconsin Press, 1990.

Thoreau, Henry David. *Early Essays and Miscellanies.* Princeton: Princeton University Press, 1975.

————. *Walden.* Princeton: Princeton University Press, 1971.

————. *A Week on the Concord and Merrimack Rivers.* Princeton: Princeton University Press, 1980.

Veith, Gene Edward. *Reformation Spirituality: The Religion of George Herbert.* Lewisburg, Pa.: Bucknell University Press, 1985.

Walker, Cheryl. *The Nightingale's Burden: Women Poets and American Culture before 1900.* Bloomington: Indiana University Press, 1982.

Weisbuch, Robert. *Emily Dickinson's Poetry.* Chicago and London: University of Chicago Press, 1975.

Werner, Marta L. *Emily Dickinson's Open Folios: Scenes of Reading, Surfaces of Writing.* Ann Arbor and London: University of Michigan Press, 1995.

Whicher, George Frisbie. *This Was a Poet: A Critical Biography of Emily Dickinson.* New York: Scribners, 1938.

Wilbur, Richard. "Sumptuous Destitution." Rptd. in *Emily Dickinson: A Collection of Critical Essays,* ed. Richard B. Sewall, 127–36. Englewood Cliffs, N.J.: Prentice-Hall, 1963.

Wolff, Cynthia Griffin. *Emily Dickinson.* New York: Alfred A. Knopf, 1986.

Wolosky, *Emily Dickinson: The Voice of War.* New Haven and London: Yale University Press, 1979.

Index of First Lines

The Johnson number of the poem is given in parentheses. An asterisk indicates that the poem is quoted in full; other page numbers indicate where the poem is quoted in part or mentioned.

Index

St. Armand, Barton Levi, 7, 162n. 6,
170n. 31, 171n. 36
Salska, Agnieszka, 138–39, 159
Scottish common-sense philosophy,
24–25
Sewall, Richard B., 89
Shakespeare, William, 2, 102–3
Shorter Catechism, the, 24, 25, 101
Smith, Martha Gilbert, 423
Smith, Martha Nell, xi, 163n. 15
Stearns, Frazar, 45
Stonum, Gary Lee, 9
Stoddard, Elizabeth Barstow, 13
Stowe, Harriet Beecher, 12, 13, 24
Synod of Dort, Five Points of, 5–6

Taylor, Edward, 28
Tennyson, Alfred, 145
Thoreau, Henry David, 1, 20–22, 109,
127, 144, 145, 158
Todd, Mabel Loomis, 105, 175n. 30
Tuckerman, Mrs. Edward, 95, 96

Unitarianism, 7, 18, 24, 25–26, 28, 63.
See also Dickinson, Emily, and lib-
eralism
Unknown, the: in death, 112, 121, 124,
135–39, 150; in nature, 1, 54, 130,
139–44, 147–49; in other persons, 2,
120, 135; as preoccupation, 124–25;
in spiritual change, 129, 130–35; in
unknowable subjects, 1–2, 125

Wadsworth, Charles, 15, 64, 77, 86,
112
Ward, Theodora, xii, 175n. 30
Watts, Isaac, 98–99
Weisbuch, Robert, 94, 154
Whitman, Walt, 36, 138, 145
Whitney, Maria, 15, 50, 86
Wilson, Harriet, 176n. 31
Wolff, Cynthia Griffin, 174n. 17, 176n.
32
Wordsworth, William, 54, 145, 147,
149